1984

THE TRANSFORMATION OF EGYPT

The Transformation of Egypt

Mark N. Cooper

THE JOHNS HOPKINS UNIVERSITY PRESS
BALTIMORE, MARYLAND

Published in the United States of America, 1982,
by The Johns Hopkins University Press,
Baltimore, Maryland 21218

Library of Congress Cataloging in Publication Data

Cooper, Mark Neal.
    The Transformation of Egypt.

    Includes bibliographical references and index
    1. Egypt – Politics and government – 1952 –
2. Egypt – Economic policy. I. Title.
DT107.827.C66   1982   962'.053   82-15317
ISBN 0-8018-2836-8   AACR2

Printed and bound in Great Britain

CONTENTS

TABLES

FIGURES

To Carol

ACKNOWLEDGEMENTS

My field research in Egypt was funded by a Fulbright-Hayes Doctoral Research Abroad Fellowship and aided by affiliations with the American Research Center in Egypt and the American University in Cairo. A number of forums have provided comments and stimulation for parts of this work. Parts of Chapters 2 and 3 were presented at the 49th Annual Meeting of the Eastern Sociological Society under the title 'State Capitalism and Class Structure in the Third World: The Case of Egypt'. Parts of Chapters 3 and 4 were published in the *International Journal of Middle East Studies*, Vol. X, under the title 'Egyptian State Capitalism in Crisis: Economic Policy and Political Interests, 1967-1971'. Parts of Chapter 5 were presented as a guest lecture at Smith College under the title 'From Nasser to Sadat: The Transformation of Egyptian Politics'. Parts of Chapter 8 were presented at the 9th World Congress of the International Sociological Association under the title 'The Structure of Semi-legal Revolutions: Between Southern Mediterranean and Western European Patterns', and were published in *Cambio Social en el Sur de Europa*, edited by Jesus M. de Miguel (Papers: Revista de Sociologia, No. 11). Parts of Chapter 9 are soon to be published in the *International Journal of Middle East Studies* under the title 'The Militarization and Demilitarization of the Egyptian Cabinet'. Parts of Chapter 14 were presented at the Yale Political Union under the title 'The Domestic Origins of Sadat's Peace Initiative'. The comments and criticism of the readers and audiences in each of these forums have undoubtedly improved the quality of this work immeasurably.

I owe special thanks to Juan Linz whose guidance over five years has made this project possible.

1 INTRODUCTION

This book spans a period of dramatic change in modern Egypt. The ten years from 1967 to 1977 were punctuated by two massive popular demonstrations. On 9-10 June 1967 several million people poured into the streets to call Nasser back to power after he had resigned in the wake of Egypt's defeat in the June 1967 war. On 19-20 January 1977 several hundred thousand people poured into the streets in an effort to put Sadat out of power after the government had tried to raise the prices of basic consumer goods. In the decade between these two events, Egypt underwent a major transformation. Politically, in June 1967 it was a single party authoritarian state; by January 1977 it was, at least nominally, semi-parliamentarian with a limited number of parties. Economically, in June 1967 it was strongly etatist and essentially closed, dominated by an inefficient public sector; by January 1977 it was partially open, characterized by high-powered private profiteering and international financial difficulties.

The decade is also marked by two dramatic international events: the Middle East War of June 1967 and Sadat's 'Mission of Peace' to Jerusalem of November 1977. Here, too, the transformation is stunning. This book deals with the causes of the internal transformation and the concomitant international transformation. In the Middle East the interaction between the nations of the area and the involvement of the super-powers is so intense that observers tend to look to geo-politics as the predictor of international events.[1] However, this book shows that internal factors are at least as important a cause of international manoeuvres. It is argued that the crisis of the etatist regime in the mid-1960s was a critical factor in causing the 1967 war and a crisis of the semi-liberal regime in the mid-1970s was a critical factor in causing the intensive efforts to achieve peace in 1977. Only by understanding the nature of both regimes, the dynamics of their crises and the links between them can we begin to understand the startling change that occurred in international events.

The period of this study is also marked by two dramatic deaths in Egypt. In late 1970, Nasser died from a heart attack after trying to negotiate peace between the Jordanians and the Palestinians. At his funeral, millions of Egyptians carried his coffin through the streets of Cairo in emotional, anguished mourning. In late 1981, Sadat was assassinated soon after meeting with the President of the United States, a meeting which was part of the process of making peace between Egypt and Israel. At Sadat's funeral, less than a thousand foreign dignitaries marched in silent procession behind his coffin, while all of Egypt remained silent under a state of martial law. Here too the contrast and transformation are striking.

While it is clear that, to a considerable degree, a heart attack and an assassination are random events, one must not discount systematic factors that were associated with each event. It has been said of Nasser that as leader of the Arab world he worked himself to death trying to end the hostilities between two Arab nations. Because this book stresses the importance of domestic Egyptian factors in creating both internal and external crises, it must be recognized that the political economy created the pressures which seem to have undermined his health. In a similar vein, this book argues that the possibility that Sadat would be the target of violence was dramatically increased because he broke with the Arab world and because he failed to improve significantly either the political or economic lot of Egypt by doing so. Both his break with the Arab world and his inability to provide progress were caused by the weakness of the semi-liberal political economy which he had helped to create. In short, even events which depend in large measure on chance have their structural grounding because systemic factors can significantly raise or lower the probability that they will take place. Again, the critical point of origin for understanding such events lies in an understanding of the domestic political economy — in particular an understanding of the strengths and weaknesses of that political economy.

More important than an understanding of any of these spectacular, headline events is a proper understanding of Egypt. Because Egypt is a complex nation at the centre of geopolitics, a quick caricature drawn at a moment of high tension is often used in place of a balanced, in-depth characterization. Such a detailed characterization is the goal of this book and it is formulated on the basis of the belief that the transformation of the political economy was of major importance, not only for the personal fates of the two leaders and for the international situation in the Middle East, but also for the daily lives of the Egyptian people. It may very well be that neither the etatist nor the semi-liberal political economies could have provided a solution to Egypt's complex and formidable problems, but there is a world of difference between the two and traditional explanations have had difficulty accounting for the transformation from one to the other and have underestimated the differences between them.

Marxists have tried to explain the change as simply a minor variation in class relations. However, because their analytic categories are inappropriate, they failed to comprehend the social bases and social limits of the Egyptian political economy.[2] They were forced either to dismiss the changes as insignificant, which denies the obvious, or to seek external explanations. The latter are partially correct, but woefully inadequate.

At the same time, behaviourists have tried to explain the change as simply a minor variation in patron-client relations.[3] They denied the institutional basis of the political economy altogether. For them, politics and policy are the result of the will of a few powerful individuals. In order to make this approach fit the 1967-77 transformation, they were forced both to deny the profound nature of the changes and to date them after the death of Nasser. This approach ties all the changes to the personal alliances and personal preferences of Anwar Sadat. While Sadat's personality and alliances are important, this interpretation is woefully inadequate. It overlooks a consistent pattern of social, political and institutional upheaval that long ante-dated Sadat's rise to power and continued systematically throughout his period in power.

One additional approach, taken by a Weberian, interprets the pre-1967 period as an example of charisma and its routinization, therefore overlooking political economy altogether.[4] The author of that approach, when contemplating the analysis of the Sadat period, readily admitted his oversight and called for an examination of the political economy of Egypt.[5]

This book provides that analysis of the political economy of Egypt between 1967 and 1977. In so doing, it uses concepts of class which the Marxists offer, concepts of politics which the Weberians offer and concepts of institutions, which the behaviourists seem to deny.

It was institutions, embodying basic weaknesses, that created the conditions for change. It was institutions, weak as they were, that sustained the regime through the defeat of June 1967 and the death of Nasser in September 1970. This is remarkable. Few regimes survive a defeat of the magnitude that Egypt suffered in the 1967 war. Few revolutionary regimes in the Third World survive their leader's death. Yet, the regime in Egypt survived both. It is a transformed regime, to be sure, but its roots go back to the very beginning of the July 1952 revolution, which overturned the monarchy of King Faruk and swept a small group of military officers, including Nasser and Sadat, into power.

The fact that the regime was transformed from within is also remarkable. Etatist, Third World economies often liberalize. Authoritarian polities occasionally do. However, few liberalizations occur simultaneously in both the economy and the polity. If the liberalization in Egypt had gone well in either the economy or the polity, not to mention both, the case would have been rare. That neither liberalization was very successful and regardless of the ultimate outcome, the simultaneous liberalization of the polity and the economy is an interesting phenomenon, worthy of attention. The international transformation that followed the internal liberalizations is of such historic import as to demand careful analysis and consideration.

Thus, as I conceive of Egypt and its relationship to war and peace in the Middle East, I believe that we must not only understand why it liberalized, but why it did so in both the polity and the economy and why neither was very successful. Understanding the pressures and crises associated with the transformation leads us to an understanding of Egypt's international behaviour. None of the existing explanations — Marxist, behaviourist, Weberian — is adequate to interpret either the internal transformation or its relationship to the external transformation. This book offers an interpretation that links the nature of the political and economic pressures placed on the regime in the 1967-77 period to the nature and juxtaposition of the institutions through which those pressures played. Armed with this interpretation of the internal political economy, we can begin to explain the external events.

I do not deny that external and personal factors played a part in both the internal and international changes. However, they have received so much attention that I believe it is necessary to go far in the opposite direction to balance the analysis. After a complete and coherent explanation has been built on the basis of the internal political economy of Egypt, the possibility and necessity of integrating other factors can be entertained on a more balanced basis.

The theoretical framework used in this work is straightforward. On the one hand, I believe that we can explain both the internal and external actions of Egypt by utilizing the concepts and categories of political sociology which are routinely applied to other nations at other times. On the other hand, I believe that the usual concepts of political sociology must be construed in a broad sense to include the economic structure, social classes, political institutions and the international situation.[6] Since this work is empirical in nature, theoretical discussions will be kept to a minimum. They will be definitional and only provide an organizing framework for the empirical analysis. I am not testing a theory, I am analysing the specific history of a nation that has played an important role in the post-Second World War era. The empirical explanation is of greater importance than the theoretical precision. As Arthur Stinchcombe has put it: 'What makes explaining a social pheno-menon worthwhile for me is not that it can be reduced to some general logical skeleton, but that the skeleton carries beautiful empirical flesh.'[7]

2 THE NATURE OF EGYPTIAN ARAB SOCIALISM

State Capitalism in the Third World

In order to study the dynamic changes that took place in Egypt in the decade after 1967, it is necessary to have an understanding of the political economy that existed in Egypt prior to that date. Choosing a historical starting-point for describing the pre-1967 political economy can be troublesome. No matter what point is chosen, there is always some earlier event or set of circumstances that seem important enough to warrant at least some mention. One can easily end up in an infinite regression into history.

The history of Egypt, both before the revolution of 1952 which overturned the Faruk monarchy and in the decade and a half after it, has been analysed and discussed frequently.[1] In this book no effort will be made to recount that history in any detail. Rather, the starting-point is a conceptual representation of the political economy in the mid-1960s. It is hoped that this will give the reader a 'feel' for the nature of that political economy as well as creating an adequate basis for studying later changes in it.

The basic conceptualization used here is one that is being applied to nations of the Third World with increasing frequency. One of the most dramatic developments in the social structures of Third World societies in the post-Second World War era has been the expanding role of the state. Although the extent and precise form of the state's involvement in economic, political and social activity has varied from place to place, the trend towards a more important role for the state and the basic pattern in which this role has expanded seem to have been repeated in nation after nation. As a result, a growing number of scholars have begun to speak of a general form of political/economic organization in the Third World — state capitalism.[2]

These scholars seem to agree on a number of characteristics of state capitalism at the descriptive empirical level.[3]

1. The origin of state capitalism lies in weak national economies at the periphery of the international economy with weak national bourgeoisies and disorganized popular classes.

2. State capitalism involves a nationalistic reorientation of economic resources through moderate agrarian reform, nationalization of basic

16

industries, centralization of finance and an expansion of social services.

3. There exists a state-centred interest group which is grounded in this reorientation of economic activity and which attempts to dominate society through essentially bureaucratic means.

4. The societies remain capitalistic, in spite of the expanding role of the state. In fact, the expansion of the state is seen as a buttress to capitalism.

5. State capitalism fails to transform the society in its fundamental structure and is quite unstable.

In this regard, Egypt may be a useful general example of what happens in Third World nations. It reduced the private sector without abolishing it. It nationalized or controlled much economic activity without changing some very basic economic relations. It became a form of semi-populist, state capitalist, developmentalist nationalism — a common form in the Third World. In that form, the state dominates the economy, but is unable to transform it either into a non-capitalist form or into a dynamic capitalist one. The dual failure renders the form of economic organization rather unstable and opens it to a perpetual oscillation between various mixes of state and non-state in the economic structure. This oscillation, too, is quite common in the Third World and it is the central concern of this work. This chapter endeavours to create the basis for an explanation of the oscillation in the economic structure by clarifying the link between the economic and class structures and the nature of political action in state capitalist societies.

Theoretical Framework

The Economy and Class Structure

For purposes of this analysis, the economy is defined as that realm of society in which material resources are produced and distributed. The central focus of my economic analysis is on the way that the state interdicts the free appropriation and flow of resources in the economy. By intervening in the economy, groups and individuals are rendered dependent on the state for the conduct of their economic activity. This dependence creates a vesting of interests in the state which alters the class structure, class interests and political activity in society.[4]

The economy is conceptualized as constituted by two activities — production and consumption. Production has two dimensions, ownership and control. Ownership is the right to appropriate the surplus of economic activity. Control is the ability to have, or determine access to, inputs for the production process and to determine the disposition of the output of the production process. Consumption also has two dimensions, income and access. Income is the degree to which the flow of monetary reward to groups or individuals in society is tied to the state. Access is defined as the extent to which the availability of goods and services for consumption by groups and individuals is determined by the state.[5]

The central argument that I make about the economy is that each of these four major dimensions of the economic structure — ownership, control, income and access — constitutes one major avenue of class definition and interest vesting in the society. This is the key to understanding state capitalism. By altering these four basic economic dimensions in specific ways, state capitalism lodges a vast array of interests in the state.

Table 2.1: Economic Dimensions and the Class Structure of Egyptian State Capitalism

Economic dimensions	Class divisions	Class segments
Ownership	Indispensable capitalists	Private sector capitalists (including various mixed types of production relations)
Control	New upper class	Elite (including bureaucratic and industrial top levels)
		Technocracy (including upper bureaucracy, technical bureaucracy and industrial administration)
Income	State-centred middle classes	Public sector labour
		Bureaucracy (running from lower levels to specialized middle)
Access	Dependent underclass	Small peasants (i.e. field crop farmers)
		Private sector proletariat (including agrarian and industrial/urban)

Table 2.1 describes the class structure of Egyptian state capitalism in terms of these basic economic dimensions.[6] It identifies the major class divisions defined by each dimension and the class segments of which those divisions are composed. This array of classes and class segments is fairly typical of state capitalism.

Overall, I suggest that the process in which interests were vested in the state can be summarized as follows: (1) the state absorbed the interests of the lower classes (dependent underclass) by manipulating access to basic consumer goods; (2) the state attracted the interest of the middle class (state-centred middle classes) by placing it on the pay-roll of the state; (3) the state became the focal point of the interests of the new upper class by giving it direct control over the bulk of econo-mic activity; (4) the state left untouched — and thereby served to support — certain parts of the national bourgeoisie (indispensable capitalists) who were deemed to be crucial to the maintenance of state capitalism. Control for the new upper class and the persistence of the national bourgeoisie have typically been the focal point of the analysis of state capitalism.[7] However, I believe that the wedding of lower-class and middle-class interests to the state is equally important. Moreover, I believe that it is the weakness exhibited by the pre-state capitalist classes — a weakness identified by most theorists as crucial to the deve-lopment of state capitalism — that creates the tendency toward the absorption of the lower classes and expansion of the middle classes by the state. Positions at the top of society can be secured without rapid expansion at the bottom if command of the polity is secure. It is precisely because those who seized the polity lacked a firm political hold that the expansion at the bottom was so rapid. Since this weakness is essentially political, I will introduce the theoretical framework for analysing the polity before I continue with the analysis of the econo-mic and class structures.

The Polity

For basic definitions and concepts to describe the political structure of Egyptian Arab socialism I combine several different theoretical approaches — Theda Skocpol's recent work on the state,[8] David Apter's earlier work on political development,[9] and the work of state capital-ism theorists.[10]

For present purposes, the polity is defined as that realm of society in which societal order and integrity are defined and maintained, usually through a mixture of coercion and consensus. Political activity centres on the power to define societal order and to enforce that definition.

Figure 2.1 describes the polity as well as the overall conception of the political economy as they are conceptualized in this work. The question is, how does one go about defining societal order in practice? Here, I think that Apter's four political functions are instructive.[11] He argues that if a party is to be a useful political vehicle it must be able to (1) recruit membership, (2) allocate resources, (3) gain broader consent from the populace and (4) enforce its decisions (i.e. take disciplinary action). The ability to execute these four activities in the entire society is what political power is about. A decisive ability to do all four would effectively accomplish the goal of defining and maintaining social order. These four functions constitute the essential activities of the polity.

Figure 2.1: The Nature of the Polity and its Link to the Economy

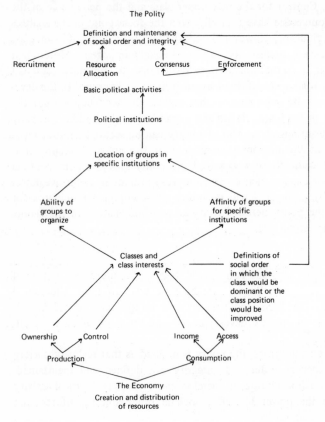

Furthermore, the nature or quality of a political regime can be readily described by the manner in which these four activities are conducted. That is, authoritarian regimes execute these functions in very different ways than liberal democracies, for example, and a convenient

way to describe the difference between regimes is to use the four functions.

When we look at the operation of the polity or describe the functioning of a regime, a series of specific questions arises. (1) Which political institutions have the right and ability to execute these four functions (i.e. which political institutions are vehicles for executing the functions)? (2) Where are political groups located with respect to those institutions? (3) What is the capacity of political groups to actually organize and mobilize to use the institutions (or, in the case of revolution, to create alternatives that execute the functions)?[12]

The link between the polity and the economy arises in a number of ways. (1) Political groups are predominantly class-based or interest-based and the definition of social order that they seek to impose reflects and is intended to solidify the economic and class structure in which they would be dominant or in which their class position would be improved.[13] (2) The nature of classes and their grounding in economic activity affects their ability to organize and mobilize to execute political action.[14] (3) The nature of classes and their grounding in economic activity give them a propensity to conduct their political activity in (i.e. they have an elective affinity for) specific types of political institutions.[15]

As a consequence of these three factors, political conflict typically takes on the quality of upper versus lower class conflict, or conflict between segments of the upper class. The aim of political struggle is to expand the range of political action available to the members of the class, to widen the scope of those institutions in which the members of the class are dominant and to ensure that they are dominant in the most important political institutions (importance being measured by the control over the four activities). The achievement of this objective would give the victors the capacity to reinforce or improve the economic and class position of the class with which they are associated.[16]

This conceptualization of the polity and its relationship to the economy can readily accommodate the approach of state capitalism theory to the polity. State capitalism theorists focus on both lower-class and upper-class political actions. Among the preconditions for state capitalism they note a nationalistic, anti-imperialist turmoil in the lower classes and a dominant class weakened by internal divisions (especially between the agrarian aristocracy, the national comprador bourgeoisie and a more nationalistic bourgeoisie). In the overthrow of the colonial rulers, they place a great deal of emphasis on the emergence of a political movement in the military which capitalizes on the turmoil below and the division above. Ultimately, they see the effort to consolidate the state capitalist polity as centring on a mechanism to incorporate and render quiescent the lower classes, while providing a vehicle through which the dominant classes can exercise their particular political skills.

The nature of the dominant class and the circumstances in which it comes to power places a specific stamp on the political organization of state capitalism. The anti-imperialist tendencies coupled with a goal of societal development are the political and ideological centrepiece around which an alliance of all elements of society is proclaimed. The weakness of the political movement which seizes power makes it tactically necessary to incorporate as many interests as possible into the regime. Consequently, the political structure is typified by a corporatist structure and ideology which seeks a non-class-struggle solution to political and social conflict. The organizational vehicle to achieve this resolution is a bureaucratic alliance of social forces. The bureaucratic form is one which depoliticizes potential opposition and one to which the new military elite is suited and accustomed.

The Development of the State Capitalist Economy and Class Structure

At this point it is helpful to turn to the specifics of Egyptian history. The military coup d'état which toppled the monarchy in September 1952 was staged by a small group of junior officers who were diverse in their social background and political leanings.[17] They lacked a political programme and a political organization. A disgruntled group of officers was swept to the centre of a political vacuum by the total disintegration of political institutions, a genuine nationalist anti-British sentiment among the people, political chaos caused by a broad range of clandestine groups and a humiliating defeat in the 1947 war with Israel.[18] Strong enough to topple an enfeebled monarchy but nowhere near strong enough to decide upon and execute a political agenda, the officers spun a web of *ad hoc* responses to pressing political problems. This web of responses led them to state capitalism.

Coming to power in a political vacuum and without prior political organization, they used the state to create a political base. They used the repressive apparatus of the state, to be sure, but above all, they used the state's expansive and absorptive capacity to create a political constituency. Unable to create a political organization of its own, the regime used the state to claim an extremely broad constituency. By constantly increasing distributive rewards, they co-opted groups that might otherwise have been in opposition.

From this political point of view, the economic history of the regime has two salient features. First, the regime did achieve significant socio-economic gains which should not be underestimated.[19] By any definition of the distribution of welfare in society, and in comparison with other nations at similar levels of economic development, the people made real gains in their living conditions. Second, there was a bias in the distribution of those gains. In agriculture there were equal measures of distribution of land and services to peasants, reinforcement of the position of the agrarian middle class and surplus generated for the state.[20] In industry there were gains for certain workers and even more gains for upper-level bureaucrats who took command of the economic structure.[21]

The economic structure became a halfway house, aiming to distribute gains to all groups except a handful of 'exploitative' capitalists. Investment policy was aggressively developmental, aiming at a rapid and broad-based industrialization. Consumption policy was aggressively populist, guaranteeing rapidly expanding living standards all round.

Thus, a massive state enterprise was created, one which served a number of different functions for different interests. For the elite, it was a fundamental mechanism for gaining command of society.[22] Broad groups in society had come to depend on the massive state enterprise. That enterprise claimed to be complex, technologically advanced and developmental. It had to be run by technicians and experts. These were skills which the new bureaucratic and military elite claimed as its expertise. The groups which were benefiting from the state enterprise became committed to the elite which was running it. In this sense, the elite was creating the basis of its own indispensability.[23] A small enterprise, no matter how technocratic, committed to a moderate development and growth programme would never have been as effective in creating this social indispensability (i.e. the simultaneous proliferation of technocratic roles and the dependence of large groups upon them).

Production Relations

Agriculture. The first goal of the new elite was to dislodge the traditional elite. In the agrarian sector this was relatively easy. Expropriating a few thousand aristocratic landlords revealed the direct producers in a fairly simple, undercapitalized, labour-intensive structure. By cooperativizing agriculture, the state could easily appropriate the functions that the landlord had served vis-à-vis the peasant. At the same time, because cooperativization left private ownership intact, it could release capitalist farmers to pursue their interests.[24]

Cooperativization meant the control of inputs (seed, fertilizer, pesticides) and the forced marketing of the output of field crops (beans, cotton, etc). Aspects of the production process were administratively controlled, but land was individually worked and landowners claimed their profits individually. By controlling the prices of inputs and outputs, the state gained a high degree of control over the farmer's income. It also gained an ability to extract the surplus of economic activity through the manipulation of prices. Nevertheless, private ownership remained important for a number of reasons.[25]

1. Because the product was in the possession of the producer, an impetus to the evasion of state control was created. Where the product is highly divisible and easily marketable, as in agriculture, the ability to evade is high.

2. Fruits, vegetables and animal products were not controlled. The field crop farmer may escape to these 'grocery' crops in order to escape the control of the state. If there is a differential rate of return between field and grocery crops, there will be an impetus to change the nature of output. In Egypt there were at least two sources of differential: prices of grocery crops were not controlled and rose rapidly, and agrarian taxes were on land rather than on the value of output or income. Thus, a premium was placed on the high value-per-acre grocery crops.

3. Grocery crops also require a large initial outlay of capital and generally are much more capital-intensive than field crops. The ability to raise the initial capital and maintain capital intensity was a prerequisite to shifting beyond state control and increasing the rate of return to economic activity. Larger landholders and those already involved in this type of production were much better able to meet these requirements on the basis of their prior capital accumulation.

4. Larger landholders also had better access to inputs and credit to facilitate the shift to grocery crops.[26] These farmers may still have been dependent on the state for inputs (in so far as it monopolized all inputs), but by relinquishing control over output, the state had relinquished control over their income. It had also laid the basis for rapid accumulation of capital by certain farmers who could specialize in grocery crops.

From the point of view of the state, this pattern of production relations meant that, without nationalizing land, the state could gain control over the peasantry. More than 90 per cent of the farmers owned less than five feddans (a feddan is slightly larger than an acre) and produced primarily field crops. By controlling the inputs for production and the output of the major field crops, the state controlled both the production process and the income of the peasantry. At the same time, by not controlling grocery crops, certain groups of larger, more capital-intensive farmers were free to accumulate wealth. Two major class segments are thus defined. The peasants became dependents of the state. The favoured capitalist farmers became its allies.

Industry. In industry the problem of displacing the existing elite and taking control was more complex than in agriculture. Expropriating a few thousand capitalists revealed a complex structure of management, administration and skilled labour, in addition to the broader working class. The pattern of involvement of the state in the non-agrarian sector reflected two basic thrusts. First, there was a very rapid expansion and a strong defence of top-level, state-based positions. Second, the absorption of labour and white-collar workers in public sector industry and the bureaucracy occurred at an extremely rapid rate. The state showed a preference for larger-scale industry, while leaving small-scale industry in private hands. Its accumulation principle seemed to have been in terms of capturing the highly productive enterprises and concentrating technically skilled and educated manpower in the state. By concentrating on a few thousand large-scale enterprises (and leaving several hundred thousand small-scale enterprises untouched) more than half of the industrial labour force and almost 90 per cent of the industrial technicians, foremen, administrators, etc., became employees of the state.[27]

The net effect of this pattern was to give the state-based technocrats significant command of the economy and to expand rapidly the size of groups dependent on the state. Thus, we can identify four class segments here. In addition to creating (1) a new upper class in command of the state and (2) a body of technocrats to run the state's economic enterprise, the impact of the policy on the social structure was to create a good deal of social mobility in the state-centred middle classes — i.e. (3) the public sector industrial labour category and (4) the white collar categories of the bureaucracy.

It is important to recognize that the impact of the state was not uniform across the non-agrarian sector or even branches of industry, for this sheds considerable light on the underlying logic of the expansion of the state. The traditional sectors of the economy, such as the textile industry, basic utilities and the bureaucracy, absorbed huge quantities of labour and increased wages at an extremely rapid rate. Newer, high-technology sectors, such as petroleum and electricity generation, did not. They seemed to be allowed to maintain their efficiency and productivity.

A significant private sector also continued to exist. There were two types of enterprise in the private sector. On the one hand, there was a set of enterprises whose size was too small or activity too unimportant to be of much concern to the state. In these enterprises output, wages, the level of employment and income were stagnant. On the other hand, where a traditional branch of larger-scale industry was defined as indispensable to the execution of growth plans, but appeared to present special difficulties in administration, we find some unique patterns of semi-private ownership. That is, the state found ways of gaining influence while taking partial ownership or partial control.

1. The import/export sector was subject to direct controls because the state monopolized the foreign interface. However, it did not monopolize all production that was oriented toward exports.

2. A counterpart to this on the public side was a group of international middlemen who managed the foreign interface.[28] This sector appears to have become rather independent, with its members maintaining certain privileges in terms of the appropriation of surplus and the disposition of goods.

3. A significant consultancy sector also came into being which can be considered semi-public. It was hardly private in the same sense as private capital. Its basis of accumulation did not exist in the absence of the state.[29]

4. Similarly, there existed a sector of semi-nationalized industry — especially the construction industry. These had been officially nationalized, but were given a special status.[30] They were explicitly left in the hands of their owners in order to 'facilitate their operation'. They were exempted from the typical administrative rules of the public sector and their former owners, now nominally civil servants, appear to have maintained unique rights to appropriate resources and to be exempted from the administrative rules of the state.

These sectors did rather well in their economic activity under state capitalism, especially in contrast to the remainder of the private sector, which stagnated badly. Thus, one major class segment can be identified here. In the capitalists of the private sector and the near-capitalists of the mixed sectors (in addition to the capitalist farmers identified earlier) we find a group whose interest is defined by its continuing ownership and control of capital. It should be stressed that the important role of private ownership, outlined in the agrarian sector, operated in the non-agrarian sector as well. The ability and incentive to accumulate were present and strong. In the non-agrarian sector the issue was not one of escaping state control, as was the case in agriculture. Rather, the objective was to find a configuration which maximized the ability to benefit from the state's developmental efforts while maintaining discretionary independence from the state. The types involving mixed public and private relations did particularly well in this regard.

It is certainly not surprising that there are differences between sectors of the economy and branches of industry in their organization and economic performance. They are different in technical terms. However, just as in agriculture, I suggest that the social organization of production plays a very large part in explaining these differences. The regime used resources in uneconomic ways for non-economic reasons. Accumulating a mass of interests vested in the state, the state used the traditional sectors to absorb labour and create a broader constituency. The traditional avenues of mobility in Egyptian society were thrown wide open by state capitalism. On the other hand, the new highly technical fields were exempted from this policy and the cadre of the revolution was permitted to play out its essentially technocratic role in these sectors. All the while, of course, the elite at the pinnacle of each of the sectors attempted to strengthen its control.

Consumption Relations

Consumption relations are a projection of production relations. That is, the location of groups with respect to production relations determines the general location of groups with respect to consumption relations. However, consumption relations can have an important impact on the lower classes in society — i.e. on those classes which do not enjoy ownership or control. In so far as there is latitude in the manipulation of consumption relations, they can add an important refinement to the understanding of state capitalism.[31]

The starting point for analysing consumption relations is the hierarchy of salaries that exists at the core of the public sector. This defines the income dependence of those whose economic activity is located wholly within the state. Income dependence clearly reinforces the vesting of interest in the state. Those groups which were rapidly added to the payroll of the state, especially the blue-collar and lower white-collar workers, were greatly affected by this dependence.

In addition to directly affecting income, the state manipulated access to consumer goods through subsidies and commodity controls. By subsidizing certain goods — essentially basic subsistence goods — the state reduced their price and made them more readily available to the poorer segments of society. Subsidization became a powerful mechanism for reaching the bottom of the social structure. On the other hand, commodity controls are the way that the state reinforced its impact on middle groups. By controlling the import and production of certain goods (essentially consumer durables) the state affected the consumption patterns of groups with moderate incomes (groups located both inside and outside of the state's economic enterprise).

Thus, the pattern of consumption relations which the state fostered became an important buttress to the production relations that the state had created. On the one hand, having absorbed and created a new lower-middle and middle class, which was directly dependent on the state for its income, the state reinforced the vesting of interest of that class by controlling the production and importation of those goods by which this class defined itself as middle. On the other hand, having gained control over the underclass (the peasantry) on the production side, the state reinforced the vesting of interest of that class by subsidizing basic consumer goods. Here the position of the private sector working class is of particular importance. State capitalism does not affect this class in its production relations or its income relations. It is only when we come to the policy of subsidization of basic consumer goods that the state finally absorbs the interest of this class. Subsidization becomes crucial to the existence of this class. In some senses, it is even more crucial to this class than the peasantry because the private sector proletariat never has in its possession the means of subsistence. Peasants can return to subsistence farming if need be, the private sector proletariat cannot.

Thus, the impact of state capitalism on the lower classes in society is of extreme importance. The expansion of an industrial labour force concentrated in the public sector and lower white-collar workers concentrated in the bureaucracy was unprecedented in Egyptian history. Effectively, labour participated in neither ownership nor control. However, employment policies — the impossibility of firing labour in the public sector and a guaranteed job for graduates of universities and technical schools — was tantamount to a guaranteed income. Consequently, it can be said that these policies did effectively release a significant portion of the labour force from the market. If we add together the public sector industrial workers and the state bureaucracy, we find that roughly 20 per cent of the labour force was removed from the bottom of the market — the lower rung of the ladder of capital accumulation — and placed on the bottom of the ladder of bureaucratic hierarchy. For these classes, this represents a significant form of mobility. Politically, this mobility wedded the new lower-middle and middle classes to the state, thereby freezing the various classes at the lower end of the social structure from which they came.

This is one of the main lines of non-upper-class interest in society. These classes have a strong interest vested in the state. Their mobility is insecure in the absence of state capitalism and the defence of state capitalism becomes the defence of their interests. This can be called the etatist interest and it is defined by income dependence.

A second line of non-upper-class interest arises out of the subsidy policy. This can be considered a form of populism. What had been the sub-proletariat and proletariat of capitalism (landless or small peasants, low-skilled urban workers) becomes the dependent underclass of state capitalism. The state depends on these classes for its political mass appeal, they are dependent on the state for their subsistence. The interest of these classes is also vested in the state, but in a fundamentally different way than that of the labour elite and state bureaucracy. They have not achieved mobility through the state, therefore they have no mobility to defend. They must defend their subsistence, but whoever offers mobility in exchange for the subsidization of subsistence can attract their interests. This can be called the populist line of interest and it is defined by subsidy dependence.

The Development of State Capitalist Political Institutions

The expansion and absorption of lower- and middle-class interests in the state stemmed from the basic political weakness of the officers who staged the coup in 1952. Their behaviour in the polity consistently reflected this weakness. Because of their initial weakness, the Free Officers were constantly forced to make alliance with their political competitors. However, because of their internal divisions, they were unable to make durable alliances or to take forceful measures. The slow yet insistent 'radicalization' of the regime — a slow yet insistent march toward state capitalism — took on a clear pattern. There was a skirmish with one political competitor which was ultimately decided by repression and followed by a half-hearted attempt to fill the void in some fashion, usually through an alliance with another competitor. The new alliance would ultimately degenerate and another skirmish would ensue.

In each encounter with a competing elite, the regime's action betrayed its basic political weakness. Each skirmish called forth an attempt to create a political organization *after the fact*.[32] The banning of parties in 1953 called forth the Liberation Rally. The Sinai war of 1956 called forth the National Union. The socialization of the economy in 1961 called forth the Arab Socialist Union. The officers knew that a demonstrably popular base was important and that a political organization to channel and utilize it was indispensable. They had grown up in the battles in the streets against the British and they knew which groups were available as constituencies. It was by paying careful attention to these constituencies in the early days that they built support. They knew that the immensely popular foreign policy that Nasser had chosen and his personal popularity and charisma were not enough to organize the polity effectively. They had to translate this mass appeal into a routinized organized basis of political support.

However, their efforts to create a political organization were halting and ineffective. Most of the officers seemed to lack the necessary skills. The continuing divisions within the core of officers resulted in an inability to eliminate competition completely. Division at the top would not permit strong measures in any particular direction. The absence of middle-level cadre to execute whatever decisions were made reduced their effectiveness. Without strong leadership from above, traditional power structures remained in place and the newly created political organizations remained unwieldy mass organizations that were divorced from the root of power. Familiar political institutions could not be abandoned. Instead, a formula was sought that would permit the regime to routinize the mass appeal it was creating without permitting the structure formed for routinization to provide a vehicle for counter-interests in society.

Thus, the regime's hold on power was limited by the stormy unity at the core of the officers' movement and the weak political organizations it was shackled with. Individuals were promoted and demoted, but the interests they represented could never be effectively eliminated. The regime was never absolutely sure that if it broke the core, finally and decisively, it could maintain its hold in power. Rather than narrow itself and set upon a particular course, it constantly expanded, incorporating more political, economic and social functions and more interests. It eliminated only what was absolutely necessary to eliminate, only when it was extremely hard pressed to do so. First it eliminated the agrarian elite, then its primary political competition on the streets (the Muslim Brotherhood). Later it eliminated the foreign bourgeoisie and, later still, it expropriated parts of the national bourgeoisie. At each stage, it rushed in with state functionaries to try to fill the void. Still, it left much of the underlying structure undisturbed and it attempted to ensure its control of that structure by escalating the promises to each of the constituencies that it had appropriated.

The political structure to effectuate this co-optation was a corporatist alliance of all social forces.[33] Each sector of society would have its proper representation within one overarching political organization. The Arab Socialist Union (ASU), the vehicle for operationalizing the alliance, was the third attempt by the regime to build a political organization and it was taken more seriously than the previous two. With the move into etatist economics and the nationalization of a great deal of industrial activity (roughly between 1958 and 1961), the state had become responsible for almost all aspects of social life. The need for an effective political organization was even stronger than it had been.

However, the elite remained ambiguous about how to create such an organization. It needed control, but it feared the creation of a powerful, autonomous organization — at least those segments of the elite which would not be in control of the organization feared it. Thus, even though the ASU was given greater attention than the earlier political organizations, its ability to execute the basic political activities was still not very great.

As far as recruitment is concerned, the party was inclusive. That is, it embraced a large part of the adult population as members — perhaps 70 per cent of the electorate. Its structure was pyramidal with each lower level selecting representatives to the next highest level of organization. However, there never was any real tie between the top and bottom. Advancement through the party counted for little. Rather, members of the existing elite were parachuted into the party and thoroughly monopolized upper-level positions. At the same time, the party had certain vanguard elements — intended to be activist and a source of recruitment for leadership — but the cadre schools to train them were never developed and they proved to be mere cliques that fought for control of the party.

As a resource allocation mechanism, the party did not effectively monopolize resources, nor dictate their allocations through law, nor allocate them as a political machine. Formally, the party played the second role.[34] Through its national conferences it was supposed to set down general policy. However, few of the participants at those national conferences doubted that policy was actually set elsewhere and few believed that the party could actually call anyone to account for bad decisions or poor execution. In practice, the party may have had some capacity to act as a political machine, but the resources available for such purposes were only at the local level and of small consequence compared to the resources that the regime disposed of through the executive branch of government.

As an enforcement mechanism, the party was never fully developed. It could not call decision-makers to account for bad decisions. It could not police the execution of any decisions. It did not even effectively exercise the function of political discipline. Since membership in the party was a requisite for all political activity and much social activity, being purged from the party formally constituted strong political punishment. However, in practice, discipline at the elite level never originated in the party and discipline at the mass level never flowed through the party. The elite was disciplined by Presidential appointment and dismissal; the masses were disciplined by the police.

In a sense, the regime could get away with an overbureaucratization of these functions. Members of the elite alternately (frequently simultaneously) held parallel positions at the top of the political and governmental structures. They rarely needed the weight of the party to sustain their actions. The weight of the state — through either its repressive or absorptive capacities — was adequate. In the short period between the creation of the ASU (in 1962) and the June 1967 war, the cost of this structure — lack of personnel, loss of expertise, immobility in decision-making, poor execution of decisions — could be glossed over so long as centralized control was adequate.

Popular consent was a different matter. Nasser's personal charisma and the foreign policy that he pursued provided overarching support for the regime, but a more effective and operational means of generating and tapping support would have been extremely useful. Here the costs of failing to have such a mechanism — constant repression — were high. The regime devoted significant resources to executing this function, but the results were mixed.

The party's ability to generate consent was hampered by a major division between the national and subnational levels. Its structure was never completed. In particular, a full set of elections never took place and numerous appointees dominated the structure. It was also constantly faced with competing institutions, institutions which cut into its ability to execute its functions.

One of the most vital assets with respect to generating consent is the

control of information. Formally, the party had control over this
function because it had control over the press. Effectively, this was not
the case. The President repeatedly went over the head of the party and
communicated to the people through the press. The dominant figure in
the press, Muhammed Haykal (editor of *al-Ahram*), was quite independent of the party and became a powerful figure. As a source of information, Haykal, in particular, was more reliable, freer to criticize,
concerned with a broader range of issues and generally better informed
than the party's own information apparatus.[35]

Similarly, the National Assembly competed with the party as the
primary vehicle for expressing the will of the people.[36] It was independ-
ently elected and was representative of the corporate groups in society.
It had powers of decision-making, powers of publicity and powers of
administration.

There were other organizations as well — trade unions, cooperatives,
local government councils — which cut across these functions. All of
these were centred in and manipulated by the executive branch. The
net result was a thick layering of institutions, none of which had firm
control over specific functions, which the regime maintained on the
basis of an all-embracing, ambiguous ideology.

The working alliance of these forces, representing the working
population, is the legitimate successor to the alliance between
feudalism and exploiting capital; this new alliance is tantamount to
having substituted a healthy democracy for the reactionary democracy.

National unity, the result of the alliance between these forces
representing the people, has the capacity to bolster the Arab Socialist Union . . . (a) the peasants and workers should hold the majority
of seats in all political and popular bodies at all levels . . . (b) the
authority of the elected popular councils should prevail over that
of the state's executive bodies . . . (c) there is an urgent need to
create a new political body within the Arab Socialist Union which
will recruit suitable candidates for leadership . . . (d) the collective
character of leadership must be guaranteed during the phase of
revolutionary momentum . . .

Popular organizations — more specifically, the cooperative and
trade union organizations — can play an influential and effective part
in strengthening a healthy democracy . . . it is time to set up unions
of farm workers . . .

Criticism and self-criticism represent two of the most important safeguards of freedom . . . the press, having become the property of the Arab Socialist Union, has been freed of the influence of the single ruling class . . .

The New Revolutionary concept of healthy democracy should govern everything that can influence the training of the citizen, priority being given to education, legislation, and administrative regulation.[37]

While recognizing the ambivalence and weakness of this structure, we should not lose sight of the role that the various political institutions played for the diverse interests in society. The elite was intent on maintaining control, but it could not cut itself off from the other interests in society. It had to channel them through some set of institutions in order to let demands be expressed. One of the elite's problems may have been that it created too many channels for the expression of demands. It tended to hear a din of contradictory voices, rather than a message which it could interpret and respond to. For the politically active members of society, the institutions represented an opportunity to engage in a continual debate over the structure of the economy, polity and society. While the active core of politicians was involved in the debate, the broader constituencies which they represented paid attention. They expressed their demands, engaged in debate and registered their opinions when they could. They said as much in their self-interest and self-defence as they could. There was cynicism, to be sure, but enough small victories were ceded to keep the interest of the various groups. Moreover, one never knew when some major victory would be won. This was particularly true when politics and political conflict became intense. At those moments, one wanted as many political avenues and instruments as possible to mobilize in one's interests. The tense periods before and after the 1967 war were just such moments.

3 THE CAUSES AND CONSEQUENCES OF THE JUNE 1967 WAR

The Economic Crisis of State Capitalism

The analysis of the economic and class structure of what I have called semi-populist, state capitalist, developmental nationalism can lead us directly to an understanding of the tendency for an oscillation in the economic structure. The diverse interests which the state attracts render the economic structure extremely vulnerable to a resource crisis. In order to create the necessary social mobility and to generate the resources to sustain the constant absorption of interests, the state becomes committed to an aggressive expansion policy that is far beyond its means. The state's economic enterprise is hard pressed to meet the demands of both populism — pursued in the name of the masses — and developmentalism — pursued in the interests of the technocrats and capitalists. The mass subsidization of subsistence, coupled with the constant expansion of employment in the state and an aggressive investment policy, place the regime in an extremely precarious resource position. A commitment to maintaining the availability of middle-class goods adds to the problem, as does the inability to maintain the productivity of labour.

The aggressively expansionist structure consumed resources at an avaricious rate. So quickly did it consume resources that in a mere six years it created the conditions for an internal and international explosion. As the rate of investment was pushed up, the rate of public consumption rose even more dramatically and the foreign debt skyrocketed in an effort to fill the gap between limited domestic resources and expanding domestic consumption.[1] By the end of the first five year plan, 'the share of net imports in GDP (Gross Domestic Product) rose to 7 percent. Egypt could not sustain such a deficit.'[2]

One may argue that these are the growing pains of an economy aggressively trying to develop. With a little bit of patience, a little bit of fence-mending, a bit of belt-tightening, the difficulties can be weathered and the economy will be much better off in the long run. However, it was precisely those qualities which the structure of developmentalist populism lacked. The regime could not extract resources from the broad constituencies it was wooing. Retrenchment for such a regime is difficult, if not impossible, for retrenchment forces the regime

35

to extract a price from its own constituencies.[3]

We should not underestimate the achievements of the regime in redistributing income. In terms of the vertical distribution of income, there was considerable levelling. In terms of the horizontal distribution between rural and urban areas, there was considerable equalization. However, the achievement was made by pumping the bottom up with resources that the regime did not really have. The result was a permanent inability to tamper with the policies — wages, prices, subsidies, employment — which had created the achievement.

The inability to restrain consumption for political reasons was coupled with another weakness, the inability to make the available resources produce at optimum levels. Projects could not be brought on line, capacity was underutilized, 'unsaleable rubbish' piled up. Of utmost importance, the productivity of labour seems to have collapsed. The problems were partly administrative — the economy was just poorly run — and partly political — labour was continually added with little concern about what it might actually produce. This labour insisted on its new rights, though it did not actually participate in management. The achievement of workers' rights, as far as it went, was an accomplishment that should not be belittled. However, it was purchased at the cost of leaving no one to shoulder the responsibility for maintaining productivity, not management, not the state, least of all the workers themselves.

A comprehensive understanding of the magnitude of the economic tasks which had been undertaken may have been lacking. Different groups were pushing for different goals, for different reasons. The regime did not have the ability or the desire to choose among these groups and all their demands were taken on.

It is by no means clear whether target setting during these years was performed with any consideration of the problem of consistency. The men who pushed the first five-year plan and its investment targets (El Boghdady and El Kaisouni, among others) were not the same individuals as those who pushed for Arab Socialism, with its consumption effects (Ali Sabri and his entourage). The President, upon whom the ultimate decisions about these matters rested both formally and de facto, may not have been correctly informed about the targets, however, the 'system' had no choice but to increase the payments deficit and do its best to finance it.[4]

There are several observations that are vital to an understanding of the breakdown of the populist, developmentalist state capitalism. First, it was the internal demands that the 'system' generated that forced it to increase its demands on the international actors with which it was associated. The timing and direction of these demands must be underlined. The vulnerability of Egypt to the whims of international actors had become acute precisely because of these internally generated demands.

> The dangers of this policy were comprehended at the lower levels of government at an early stage, and the Treasury as well as the Central Bank tried to get messages through to the President in this connection. Whether these did not reach him, he did not take notice of them, or whether he thought that he would be able to continue playing off the United States and the Soviet Union against each other and thus obtain financing beyond what the Treasury and the Central Bank thought realistic or justified is not known. As long as the two powers agreed to play the game, the payments problems were overcome. But when first the Soviet Union, in 1964 (when Krushev refused to postpone the High Dam loan payments) and one year afterwards the United States (abrogating PL 480 sales) [the delivery of wheat to Egypt and other nations under The Food for Peace Program was authorized by Public Law 480 which is referred to as PL 480] backed out, the potential inconsistency immediately became an established fact and targets had to be sacrificed.[5]

Second, when the international actors refused to meet the demands, either explicitly or implicitly, surgery in the form of retrenchment became necessary. This put immense pressure on the all-embracing alliance that state capitalism had tried to create.

Third, the developmental and populist aspects of state capitalism represented distinct and separate legs of the alliance upon which the regime was founded. They could be separated. First a 'reform' government under Ali Sabri on the left was formulated to try its hand at putting the economic house in order. Then a 'reform' government under Zakariyya Muhyi-al-Din on the right was formulated to try its hand. The Muyhi-al-Din government was not a 'liberalizing' government, but it stood for a strong dose of 'economic' rationalization — increase in prices and taxes, the encouragement of private foreign investment and accommodation with the United States. While Dekmejian assures us that 'in no sense were the new policies to be understood as the end of the socialist ideology and concomitant etatist practices in Egyptian society',[6] it was a clear indication of very deep-seated problems.

The Breakdown of Political Order

The inclusionary alliance of state capitalism had begun to break up and the primary manifestation of this is observed in the polity. The intensity of political struggle moved in close coordination with the performance of the economy. As the economic pressures associated with the exhaustion of resources increased, they created increasing pressures on the political structure. Efforts to contract the economy meant that someone had to pay the price. However, the constituencies of the state capitalist regime resisted. Among the broader population, efforts to raise prices for consumer goods met 'with widespread popular unrest'. A conspiracy known as the Last Muslim Brotherhood Conspiracy, combining both political and economic causes, was uncovered. 'Many of the key conspirators were relatively young members of the new middle class – engineers, scientists, pilots and students.'[7] At the elite level there was the 'sharpening of factional rivalries between the pragmatic moderates under Muhyi-al-Din and the doctrinaire socialists led by the ASU Secretary General, Ali Sabri'.[8]

In response to the Last Muslim Brotherhood Conspiracy, we can see the strengths and weaknesses of the political structure. The plot was large enough – 'as many as 27,000 arrests took place on a single day in August, 1965'[9] – to suggest that there was a serious problem with the political support for the regime. In the response, the party could not be relied upon to shore up that support. The religious establishment, the press and, of course, the police played parts that were as large, if not larger.

The situation began to oscillate furiously. Growing out of the assassination of a rather well connected ASU official, which seems to have been motivated by both personal and political factors, a period of radicalization was embarked upon. The army was brought in to conduct a programme of defeudalization, while the party was left to debate and discuss the radicalization. The party could not be relied upon to carry the task out itself. However, the army, under a rather well known member of the upper class, Field-Marshal Amer, was hardly the best institution to radicalize the society. The Committee to Liquidate Feudalism seemed to move more for personal than political reasons and little of political value was accomplished.

It is against this background that we must understand the hostile diplomatic moves that led to the 1967 war. It may well be that Nasser began to gamble in international affairs in order to relieve the pressures that were building on his regime. It was an attempt to pull off a foreign policy move as a solution to domestic problems and weaknesses. This was a tactic that had worked in the 1950s when institutional pressures from the military and an impatience to make significant progress had led Nasser into the sequence of events (purchase of arms from the Eastern bloc, aggressive negotiations over the financing of the Aswan dam, nationalization of the Suez Canal) that led to the Sinai war. The ability to erase the defeat in the Sinai war and to hold on to the canal in its aftermath were major political accomplishments upon which a great deal of Nasser's popularity rested. The world has become accustomed to and cynical about nationalization of foreign holdings and the purchase of arms from whoever is offering them, but in 1956, at the height of the cold war, these were bold moves. Coupled with the fortuitous circumstances that enabled Egypt to win the diplomatic struggle in spite of having lost the military battle, they captured the imagination of the Egyptian and Arab peoples.

In 1967, however, the increase of diplomatic tensions in the Middle East, which Egypt clearly instigated, led to the June 1967 war, for which she was just as clearly unprepared.

Dating the domestic crisis before the war is a vital insight into the breakdown of populist developmental state capitalism. It gives us a different view of the relationship between internal and international factors. There is no doubt that Nasser was under international pressures prior to the war. He had been negotiating a middle course, but as the economy went bad and the polity became chaotic, this became difficult. Five years of close association with the Soviets had not solved his problems and the Soviets were not giving anything away. The West demanded major concessions to help him set his economy right. Their demands would have undermined the populist alliance. The demands of the Soviets would have hurt a number of groups as well. Nasser hesitated to do either. The problem was the internal political economy. He could not make the economy work and his political alliance was not malleable.

At the same time, dating the economic crisis before the war blocks us from using the war as an easy excuse for the economic failure of Egyptian Arab Socialism. There is no doubt that the war was a blow, but it fed into existing difficulties. The economy had run out of resources well before the war. The public sector had ceased to expand in a meaningful sense. It is difficult to say whether an effective reform would have been worked out in the absence of war, but the two such efforts which had been undertaken prior to the war failed completely. The interpretation given here is that the political muscle necessary to carry out such a reform was lacking. Again, the problem was the political basis upon which the economic structure had been laid, and the economic basis upon which the political structure had been laid.

The Consequences of Defeat

Needless to say, the defeat in the war only made matters a great deal worse. The war sealed the fate of the etatist economic structure in a number of ways. (1) Before the war, problems and inefficiencies could be cushioned, glossed over, or argued away. After the war, the weakness and inefficiency appeared glaring as resources dried up. (2) The impact of war costs did not fall randomly. Physical destruction, the diversion of public funds to war costs, the ability of the government to extract resources more easily from the public sector than the private sector, all placed the public sector under severe resource pressures and gave it the air of a sinking ship. All those who had any flexibility found it in their interests to abandon it. (3) Under the pressures of defeat, old, conservative, Arab enemies had to be embraced and they were not going to fund the deepening of socialism in Egypt.

Politically, the war increased the pressures on the regime immensely. The structure had been forcibly deflated and the costs of contraction had to be borne by the various interests that had been catered to in the past. Moreover, the regime had failed in the most basic of political activities, the maintenance of international integrity. Some members of the regime would have to pay the price for that failure. Indeed, in most such circumstances the regime as a whole pays the price.

As we examine the furious political activity that followed the war, we observe a near total breakdown of political order, one that carried the political chaos of the pre-war period to new heights. Yet, the regime survived. Four basic changes in the polity are easily identifiable. (1) There was an escalation of conflict within the elite. (2) There was a semi-autonomous mobilization of mass, anti-regime violence. (3) Middle groups came forward to state their demands and apply pressure to the political institutions and leadership. (4) There was a shift and expansion of the institutions, the arenas of politics.[10]

The manifestation of pressures on the regime that has attracted the attention of students of Egyptian politics is the debate in the press over the liberalization of Egyptian society. On one side was Haykal at *al-Ahram*; on the other side there were a number of leftist intellectuals in the daily, weekly and monthly press at *al-Jumhurriyya, al-Akhbar, Ruz al-Yusif* and *al-Tali'ah*. The debate represented a split in the intelligentsia between a moderate core and a more extreme left. It also represented a division in the ruling elite and between political institutions. The moderate core was centred in the executive and legislature; the left was centred in the party.

While the starting point for the debate was foreign policy, with Haykal calling for a more balanced approach, it immediately went beyond that.[11] The party had been trying to politicize the military and Haykal talked as though he were defending against a coup by the party. At just that moment, the military seems to have become involved in a coup attempt of its own. Certainly the pressure from the party could have goaded the severely demoralized military into action. There was clearly a very strong desire on the part of the military to forestall any deep penetration into it by the party.[12]

This was an old line of personal and institutional division and the evidence suggests that it had become more rigid and intense in the wake of the defeat.[13] The army, personified in Field-Marshal Amer, had consistently blocked the party, personified in Ali Sabri, from achieving a firm political hold. Whether or not there were coup attempts and coup plans in the party and the military, these two sectors of the elite were certainly jockeying for position in a more explicit and desperate manner than had been their custom. The 'suicide' of Field-Marshal Amer,[14] one month after Haykal's attack on the ASU and two weeks after the alleged military coup, is an indication of this. The subsequent promotion for Ali Sabri[15] reaffirms it, as does a quick succession of other plots.[16] There had been plots before, but these had always been on the fringes, coming from excluded groups. The regime had always been plagued by squabbling and bickering at its core before, but now the coups and plots moved into the core. Elite members had risen and fallen before, but they had not reached so high nor fallen so far.

The escalation of the struggle was thoroughgoing in another sense. In defence of the party, Haykal was attacked by the left as a representative of particular bourgois class interests.[17] This attack against Haykal could only be multiplied against Amer. A number of actions by the regime — desequestration of land, release of certain prisoners — suggested a turn to the right. This may have goaded the party into escalating its rhetoric.[18] There had always been class differences within the elite, with various members having ties to specific classes, but now these class differences were used as weapons in the escalating public debate. It can safely be said that there was a rather intense period of move and counter-move on the left and the right and few punches were pulled in the scramble to establish a strong political position.[19]

This was the elite probing and jockeying in a very new fashion. While the threat at this level seems to have been reduced by the end of September 1967, it appears that the elite seriously misjudged its ability to do business as usual — both within its core and vis-à-vis the masses. It produced an effort at the old balancing act — plans for further nationalizations,[20] a trip to Moscow by leftist leaders,[21] some more releases of political prisoners,[22] informal encouragement of the private sector[23] — but things had changed.

In June 1967, when millions poured into the streets to call Nasser back to power, the masses had acted autonomously, although Ali Sabri had apparently arranged for a small-scale demonstration. In February 1968 the masses came into the streets again, this time to express their anger at the military. In November 1968, there was another set of riots. In fact, mass anti-regime violence became a permanent feature of the polity after the June defeat. This violence had a number of clearly identifiable characteristics.

1. The violence was a communications process. It appears that the ASU was involved in stimulating it, but it could not control it. Initial contacts through the ASU to the administration were insufficient. The next step was for the rioters to take their grievances to the National Assembly. In most cases, the Assembly seems to have been able to quiet matters a bit. In this regard, it is important to note that at this moment Anwar Sadat was President of the Assembly and he seems to have served an intermediary role between the mob and the regime.

2. Both sets of riots in 1968 were aimed at the state repressive apparatus. In February it was the military and in November it was the police.

3. While there was always a specific spark that had set the demonstrations off, there was always a broad set of demands and grievances expressed. Particularly in February, a flood of demands from various groups in society came forth. Students and workers were always involved, but in a number of instances middle-class groups — doctors, lawyers, journalists — also expressed their demands.

4. The government responded to the demonstrations at a very broad level. While playing down their significance and extent, the February

demonstrations brought forth the *March 30 Program*, the basic blue-print for the reform of the political economy. The November demonstrations brought forth an emergency session of the ASU National Congress.

Thus, to the change in elite politics, we should add a change in mass politics and middle-class politics. This change from below forced the regime to try to restructure the political economy. Not only were there conscious efforts to restructure the polity, but there seems to have been an unplanned, natural shift in the array of political institutions. The army had weakened and the security forces were under pressure. The ASU had shown its aggressiveness and its inadequacies. The National Assembly showed real signs of coming to life, as the press had already done.

These factors interacted forcefully. Division at the top made it difficult either to effectively suppress or satisfy the demands coming from the bottom. Demands in the middle drove the segments at the top farther apart. In the process the arenas of politics (the institutions) expanded as groups sought a forum to state and press their demands. The combination of escalating elite divisions and escalating mass inputs made the balancing act which Nasser had performed before the war increasingly difficult. The margin for error was dramatically reduced. Elites could not tolerate minor defeats and masses could not be as easily rendered quiescent.

Given the intense pressure on resources in the economy and the turbulent situation in the polity, more extensive reforms were necessary. Those efforts at reform began the decade of the transformation of Egypt.

4 THE POLITICAL ECONOMY OF REFORM

The *March 30 Program* was to serve as a blueprint for reorganizing the political economy.[1] It was announced and defended by the President in a series of speeches and then submitted to the electorate in a plebiscite. Thereby, it was raised to the status of a 'Document of the Revolution'. Its intention was to moderate the escalating political conflict. There was something in it for just about every group, but the overall tone of the document was decidedly liberal. Political rights were to be guaranteed and political activity was to be regulated through a routinized process of election. The economy would be liberalized. A broader scope for private activity was envisioned. Incentives and reward by merit would be the primary motivator of economic activity and a depoliticization of the public sector would take place.

The Economy

The prescription for economic recovery was a blend of continuity and change, with a strong dose of liberalization. Science and technology were extolled (an old slogan) and the three forms of property (public, cooperative and private) were brought forward from the National Charter. The commitment to development was reaffirmed, with the petroleum sector singled out for mention. Economic opportunities were to be expanded and economic rewards were to be distributed by merit. The administration of economic activity was to be conducted on the basis of efficiency and science, not politics.

The reform of the economy had two basic thrusts — freeing the private sector and reforming the public sector. Each of these basic thrusts was constituted by a number of policies and elements.

The Private Sector

One element of the effort to free the private sector was a decision to free the flow of commodities and currency in the hands of individuals. Those who were likely to be in possession of foreign exchange or to desire to import commodities with their 'own exchange' were a very special group in society. As the Minister of Economics put it in 1968, these were 'physicians, lawyers, artists, engineers, publishers, agents of foreign firms and investment offices and the like'.[2] The intention was to capture their foreign currency holdings from abroad and, presumably, to have them put those holdings to productive work in Egypt. Whatever the intention, the impact was clearly to the advantage of very specific groups in society.

A second element in freeing the private sector was to expand the areas of economic activity that were open to it.

> In order to open wider scope for expanding exports to various markets and to raise our exports, especially of non-traditional goods through small scale operations in which the private sector is interested and to achieve the flexibility which characterizes this sector, the old system of confining some markets to certain companies of the public sector was abolished.[3]

A third element was to re-establish the rights of private property. For example, a new law regulating landlord-tenant relations was specifically aimed at 'encouraging the private sector to play its proper role'.[4] Although private interests were not given a totally free hand by the law, it did return certain rights to the landlord. In a similar vein, the discussion of the desequestration of property was a sign that things had changed.

The tendency to open up opportunities to upper-class individuals was also present in agriculture. For example, a decision to permit large landholders to keep private stocks of cotton enabled them to realize higher returns by 'playing the market'.[5] Similarly, the decision to permit a sale of orchards by the Agrarian Reform Authority in plots of up to twenty feddans (instead of ten) served the interests of larger, wealthier farmers.[6] This was also the impact of the policy encouraging the production of fruits and vegetables. The exportation of these crops, which were capital intensive and very middle class, was made almost a national duty.[7]

The Public Sector

The second thrust of the economic policy was the reform of the public sector. This was carried in the Hegazi scheme for financial and administrative reform. Administrative rationalization had the centre stage, but the scheme also came to grips with the core of the problem: productivity and efficiency in the public sector. Ultimately, this implied the imposition of 'economic' criteria on the sector. In the case of companies operating at a 'loss', this meant contraction.

> *It is imperative that such units be eliminated, or at least shrunk, in*
> *case of need, after it is proved that their maintenance is no longer*
> *possible from an economic point of view,* and a decision should be
> taken for their liquidation.[8]

It is safe to say that the policy was permeated by the ideology of
efficiency and the scientific administration approach of the *March 30
Program*. On the one hand, scientific administration meant the removal
of political inputs from economic decisions.

> There is a true feeling among the workers that they are the posses-
> sors of the true interests in the production units and they are respon-
> sible for them. Also, the political organizations feel, themselves, the
> responsibility.
> But how to organize these relations?
> There is no doubt that the fundamental responsibility lies with
> the administration, but in order to guarantee that this administrative
> responsibility leads to a correct path, the workers and the political
> organization must participate to know that what happens is correct.
> I saw the experiment [in Kafr al-Dawar] in which a production
> committee was created; represented in it was the Administrative
> Council, the Union Council, the ASU Council. The president of the
> Administrative Council did not head it, the president of the factory
> did. The Council debated everything in the company and the Coun-
> cil reached all announcements and its opinion was advisory, not
> obligatory and [decisions] went to the Administrative Council to
> see if they were possible to implement or not. When the specialized
> technical apparatus advised the Administrative Council of the non-
> executability in the opinion of the council, they would be informed
> of the reasons which led to that.[9]

This policy, which would clearly place the political and non-economic
below the technical, was generalized in Presidential Decree 280/3,
March 1969.

On the other hand, scientific administration, even if it meant the
reduction of the intervention of the state in certain ways, also meant
the fundamental liberation of the technocrat.

> Such a sector cannot be ruled by the restrictions which rule govern-
> ment departments and the system of work in it cannot be developed
> in a manner which brings it within the scope of government control

and thus loses its basic element of success. Consequently, this sector has to be managed on scientific and practical principles.[10]

The largest part of the administrators believe faithfully that if they obtained more power or freedom in work they could achieve the ideal means in work. This issue is, in my opinion, the base of the subject . . . My opinion as the minister responsible for some of the units of the public sector, or a large part of them, is that we prac- tised an excessive control and an excessive intervention, for the results which we expected did not occur as a result of increased intervention, which led to an increase in difficulties rather than goals. Also, it did not lead to an increase in the delimitation of responsibility, but the opposite; it led to an increase in avoiding responsibility.[11]

The number of specific examples of decisions about economy policy could be multiplied indefinitely. Table 4.1 summarizes a large number of decisions that were made with respect to the economy in order to stress the fact that a basic policy change had occurred. The frequency of decisions in 1968 and 1969 reflects the push to free the production and consumption of goods. Decisions affecting goods (part 'a' of the table) are primarily decisions which release imported materials that are intended for later re-export. This is the production side of the equation. That a number of decisions such as these had been made prior to 1967 may reflect the severe problems of an administered economy, but the flood of decisions after September 1967 is not likely to have been a response to administrative problems. This was part of the conscious effort to liberalize the economy. More releases were issued in the two months after the passage of the *March 30 Program* than in the previous three years.

The consumption side of the equation is currency and import/export activity (section 'b' of the table). Here it is important to note the inter- play of easing decisions (which made the flow of goods freer) and blocking decisions (which made the flow of goods more difficult). There was a concentration of blocking decisions in 1964-6, the period of the crisis of state capitalism and the unsuccessful efforts at belt- tightening. In 1968-9 we observe the easing decisions. However, the release of currency and import/export activity immediately led to abuses. In essence, an illegal import/export business came into existence and efforts were made to block it after 1969. Thus, we observe an increase in the number of blocking decisions in 1970-2.

Table 4.1: Decisions Affecting the Flow of Goods

	1964			1965			1966			1967			1968			1969			1970			1971			1972		
	SOURCE	NUMBER	DATE	SOURCE	NUMBER	DATE	SOURCE	NUMBER	DATE	SOURCE	NUMBER	DATE	SOURCE	NUMBER	DATE	SOURCE	NUMBER	DATE	SOURCE	NUMBER	DATE	SOURCE	NUMBER	DATE	SOURCE	NUMBER	DATE
(a) Goods	T	40	12/5	T	24	22/4	T	58	28/3	T	7	10/1	T	6	28/2	L	68	19/8	D	162	25/7	D	23	25/2	D	157	3/2
Easing decisions				T	35	29/4	T	60	28/3	T	17	*	C	1	4/4	L	76	12/12	D	449	26/5				D	240	9/3
				T	57	12/7	T	64	23/6	C	1	28/9	C	2	4/4	D	133	6/2	D	842	21/4				D	605	3/6
				T	96	15/11	T	66	23/6	C	2	28/9	C	3	4/4	T	101	28/10	D	844	21/4				D	607	3/6
				T	98	29/11	C	4	25/7	C	3	28/9	C	4	23/6	T	113	14/6	D	1171	16/7				T	126	25/4
				C	101	6/12	C	24	11/7	C	4	1/10	C	5	23/6	T	140	28/10	D	1360	20/9						
				C	105	6/12				C	5	1/10	C	6	23/6	C	1	15/7	T	47	13/4						
										C	.6	1/10	C	7	23/6	C	2	15/7	C	68	25/6						
										C	10	1/10	C	8	23/6	C	3	15/7	C	69	2/7						
										C	11	1/10	C	9	23/6	C	4	15/7									
										C	12	1/10	C	10	23/6	C	5	15/7									
										C	13	1/10	C	11	23/6	C	8	15/11									
										C	14	2/11	C	12	23/6	C	9	15/11									
										C	15	23/11	C	13	23/6	C	10	15/11									
										C	16	23/11	C	14	23/6	C	11	15/11									
													C	15	23/6	C	12	15/11									
													C	16	26/10	C	13	15/11									
													C	17	26/10	C	14	15/11									
													C	18	26/10												
													C	19	22/9												
													C	20	22/9												
													C	21	22/9												
													C	22	18/11												
													C	23	18/11												
													C	24	18/11												
													D	29	12/12												

(b) Currency and Import/Export (easing)							
E 550 12/7	E 826 17/1		L 19 16/9	E 143 23/4	E 290 30/4	E 403 1/5	E 83 3/2
E 870 9/12			E 364 12/6	E 167 6/5	E 291 30/4	E 744 30/6	E 334 20/4
			E 543 13/8	E 1009 10/6	E 413 20/4	T 348 25/7	E 365 5/4
			E 601 19/9	E 1010 10/9	E 500 7/5	E 2234 ***	E 486 30/5
			E 792 18/3		E 544 7/5	E 2286 ****	E 491 30/5
					E 554 27/7		E 546 17/6
					E 800 14/10		E 602 29/6
					E 858 6/8		E 650 11/7
					E 1423 29/10		E 661 12/7
					E 1508 8/11		
					E 1793 **		
					E 346 22/11		

(blocking)							
E 206 30/3	L 24 26/5	E 78 10/5	E 292 6/5	S 138 24/5	S 288 8/10	S 148 21/4	E 82 3/2
E 737 14/10	E 245 2/6	E 79 10/5		E 154 23/4	S 292 8/10	S 150 21/4	E 83 3/2
E 776 9/11	E 431 29/8	E		E 156 8/5	S 295 8/10	S 215 6/6	E 128 30/1
E 789 9/11					S 325 8/11	S 324 1/12	
E 808 16/11					S 366 *****		

L = Law, E = Economics Ministry, T = Treasury, S = Supply Ministry, C = Commerce Ministry, D = Presidential Decree
*4 April 1968, **13 January 1971, ***1 January 1972, ****18 January 1972, *****4 January 1971

Source: Federation of Egyptian Industries, *Yearbook*, various issues.

Conflict Over Economic Reform

There was resistance to these policies at every turn. For example, the policy of expanding the consumption of upper-middle-class goods that would be certain to result from the liberalization of currency and import regulations came at a time when the ASU was calling for a redoubling of the war effort. Consequently, the ASU wanted a restriction of luxury consumption. The Minister who had announced the policy (Aziz Sidqi) was forced to give a rather tortured defence of it at the ASU conference in September 1968.[12]

When the policy of reforming the public sector came up, it too was resisted. The first sparks were struck in the summer of 1968 when some relatively minor desequestrations took place. These steps occasioned an open debate in the press.[13] By September, the regime was defending the socialist character of the reform of the public sector and its intentions not to abandon the sector.

> In speaking today about financial and economic reform in the public sector, we must re-affirm the principles of efficiency and justice; efficiency in production and performance, and justice in distribution. We are not going back on our socialist line. We affirm that socialism is efficiency and justice.[14]

Again the forum was the ASU and the regime was being called to account for what appeared to be anti-socialist behaviour. This was the basic pattern and tone of the rhetoric that would run throughout the late 1960s and the 1970s. Hegazi would be forced to repeat the speech time and again as the criticism was voiced over and over.

The debate was not limited to the ASU and the press. It could break out in other places as well. For example, at a Conference of Administrative Leaders at which the Minister of Economics had first suggested the scheme for removing political input from economic decision-making and freeing the technocrats, there were those who rejected the underlying principle.

> In relation to the manpower surplus, and I have been on the Council of Distribution of Workers for many years, it does not happen that one surplus graduate is forced on the public sector as a public sector, but the distribution of graduates is left to the public sector as a whole and the internal distribution is left to the whole sector.
> If errors in application have occurred in putting a person outside his speciality, this is not the error of the state, as a state, but th

error of the organizational units within the sectors.[15]

Of course, hordes of graduates had been forced on the public sector as part of the expansion of state capitalism. However, what was at stake here was the very basic question of the relationship of the state to units of economic production and the role of individuals or enterprises within that relationship. In the pre-1967 ideology, the state had been supreme. The reformers took the opposite view, blaming the state and seeking to free the individual to rectify the problem.

It is important to recognize the significance of a conference such as this and the debate that occurred there. Reform was aimed at and had to be sold to these people. That the regime placed a great deal of importance on this conference can be ascertained from the composition of the speakers (see Table 4.2). Over the years, the conference had been addressed by a blend of technical people and lower-level politicians. Suddenly, at the first conference following the issuance of the *March 30 Program*, three full Ministers appeared, constituting one-quarter of the speakers. Minor politicians were eliminated almost entirely.

Table 4.2: Speakers at Administrative Leadership Conferences

Conference	Ministers	Under-Ministers	Governate officials	ASU Sec.	National Assembly	Total number
2 May-19 May 1966	0	5	0	1	1	32
29 October-1 December 1966	0	5	1	0	0	27
3 February - 2 March 1967	0	5	1	1	0	10
9 September - 5 October 1967	0	5	0	2	0	33
4 November - 30 November 1967	0	3	2	1	0	23
9 September - 3 October 1968	3	1	0	0	0	12
4 October - 31 October 1969	1	3	0	0	0	21

Source: *Conference Reports*, various issues.

The use of all the available vehicles to support or oppose the policy was frequent on both sides. For example, when the law to regulate landlord-tenant relations came up in the National Assembly, there was a heated exchange over the Committee to Set Rents.[16] As originally proposed, the law required the attendance of a member of the ASU at meetings in order for the meeting to be considered valid. The legislative committee to which the law had been referred removed this condition, thereby permitting the Committee to make decisions without any political input – i.e. with only technical inputs. A host of charges against the ASU veto power on committees such as these was made by the members of the legislature. In particular, charges were made against the role of the ASU members on the Agrarian Reform Committees. Those who insisted on the stipulation that an ASU member be present at committee meetings were major leftists, who were extremely well placed in the National Assembly and, in this instance, they carried the day.

At the root of this debate was the issue of political power over economic action, with the ASU defined as the organization which would resist the liberalization. This issue kept popping up in a variety of forums. An interesting incident with a similar theme – one that shows the layering of political institutions and the interconnectedness of these issues – involved a specialized company for foreign exchange operations. This company had been set up in 1968 after the decision to free the flow of foreign exchange and currency. The workers in an existing public sector company complained that it hurt the profits of their company. The argument passed through the ASU Secretary General to the Minister involved. Unsatisfied with the answer given by the Minister, the issue was turned over to a member of the National Assembly. That member then pursued the matter in the form of a question posed to the Minister. Underlying the issue was the relationship of the ASU to the company and the need to maintain efficiency.

We in the ASU felt that the answer did not supply anything new to enable us to respond to the workers in this unit. And the minister put forth these three considerations in his answer:
(1) This decision protected the public wealth.
(2) This decision dealt with a point of the internal operation of the company, and the *ASU had no right to enter into the internal organization of the company.*
(3) The company was completely successful before the expansion (into free market activities) and the minister would study the means to support the company if there was a need for that.[17]

In sum, the economic policy of the *March 30 Program* took on a tangible form. It stimulated a great deal of debate, debate which swirled through the political institutions. That debate took on a clear and specific pattern. It is a pattern that frequently emerges in the process of liberalizing a 'closed' economy. That pattern can be described as follows:

1. Economic reform on this scale is not simply a battle of individual personalities, or even small cliques. It tends to: 'represent wider social groupings whose material situation is likely to be affected by the outcome of the debate'.[18]

2. The underlying structure of the reform is biased toward certain professional groupings: 'Professional qualified personnel such as doctors, lawyers, academics, engineers, scientists and the like'.[19]

3. Individuals based in the party apparatus are directly threatened by the reform because: 'An emphasis on economic rationality and profit criteria is not readily compatible with an industrial role based primarily on the exercise of political skills.'[20]

4. The impetus to reform stems from those technocratic groups 'who felt relatively disprivileged in an egalitarian system'.[21]

5. The justification for the reform is proper incentive to achieve greater efficiency:

The economists and their white collar supporters argued that the reforms would be to the worker's benefit, since the introduction of wider pay differentials would provide incentives for greater effort and efficiency; this would increase productivity and so improve living standards all around.[22]

6. The political operatives defend their position in terms of a populist orientation:

by claiming to support the interests of the manual workers against the claims of the white-collar professionals for a larger slice of the national cake . . . from their angle, socialism was being threatened at its very base by the advocates of 'capitalist economics'.[23]

7. The defence has a genuine social base since: 'Workers feel a certain anxiety at the possibility of unemployment and the erosion of egalitarianism.'[24]

This is the logic of the *March 30 Program* and the pattern of the ensuing debate. The quotes cited above are the ways in which one author described the debate that took place in Czechoslovakia in 1968. Without claiming that Egypt in 1968 and Czechoslovakia in 1968 are very much alike, it would seem that the political logic of liberalizing closed economies has a certain underlying structure to it. This conflict of interests becomes one major element in the political struggle over reform. It establishes a basic left-right division which permeates both the economic and political reforms. From 1968 onward, this juxtaposition of interests was not only visible, but also a major dividing force in the political economy.

The Polity

The Logic of Political Reform

The political reforms contained in the *March 30 Program* reinforced this conflict of interests and institutions.[25] The steps that the *Program* declared necessary in order to rebuild the society included the reconstruction of the armed forces, repair of the economy, criticism of past mistakes and the building of foreign alliances to liberate the occupied territories. Of special note was the criticism of past mistakes. The document identified 'centers of power, who had stopped on the path of corrective action for fear of losing their influence', as the central culprit. Public trials were to be held which would 'place before the masses a complete picture of the deviations and errors of the previous stage'. At least symbolically, the masses were promised an explanation for the failure of the regime to execute its political functions.

The antidote to the underlying political problem that the centres of power posed was declared to be a rebuilding of the ASU on the 'basis of elections from top to bottom'. The potential virtues of the ASU were extolled at great length, while the actual practice that had occurred in it — especially the policy of appointing individuals to leadership positions — was criticized. After elections had rectified the ASU, the National Conference was to meet and take over the task of writing a constitution which would set out guarantees for personal freedom as well as freedom of thought, publication, opinion, scientific research and the press. Further, the constitution would define the role of institutions, guarantee the sanctity of the judiciary, ensure the right of judicial recourse for citizens and the right of review of the constitutionality of legislation by the court. Finally, the constitution would set a specific time limit during which individuals could serve at the highest executive levels. With respect to the immediate exigencies of politics, the Central Committee of the ASU would come into permanent session to guide the formulation and implementation of policy.

The political question is, for which constituency is such a policy intended, and why? A small, essentially middle-class group in society utilizes freedom of the press, judicial recourse and electoral rights; a small group advocates efficiency through science; a small group benefits from incentives and promotion by merit. The educated citizen was to be raised to the dominant political position. He was to be free to execute his rights, to practise his role and to benefit from that practice by promotion and incentives. At the time the *Program* was issued, only about twenty per cent of all Egyptians were literate.

Why, then, is this small group singled out? There are clear historical reasons in the political economy of the regime. The officer corps was centred there. It was the origin and bedrock of the regime. The severely demoralized military was targeted twice by the policy — once directly in the call to rebuild the army, once indirectly in the political and economic goals of the *Program*. The technocracy was also singled out. The scientific tone of the document, its technical efficiency implications and depoliticization of the economy, as well as the opening up of opportunities and rewards that it promised, were all in the interest of the technocracy. Practically, the revolution had reinforced the agrarian middle class and tied it to the educated middle class by expanding educational opportunities.

In choosing this particular policy, a routinized, dependable basis of support was being sought. Claims to generalized populism were subjugated to the interest of this core group of middle classes. The *Program* initiates a re-orientation of the regime and a narrowing of its constituency. This consisted of a shedding of constituencies on the left and a gaining of constituencies on the right. The political arithmetic of the shift was a loss in mass appeal, but a gain in dependable support. Needless to say, such a shift did not go without opposition.

Conflict Over Political Reform

As Haykal expanded the concept of an 'open society', a concept that was clearly within — in fact, at the core of — the *March 30 Program*, the left responded by escalating its charges of class bias and counter-revolution.[26] While there were points of agreement between Haykal and his opponents — criticism of military rule and the centres of power — there was no real agreement on solutions.[27]

The electoral strategy chosen by the *Program* was no boon to the leftists and they made a point of doubting the elections beforehand.[28]

The election results gave substance to the doubts. Irregularities in the conduct of the election were widespread. As the left had feared, elections were the vehicle for the existing social forces to express themselves, rather than for the radicalization of the masses.

Beyond the elections, a technocratization of the cabinet and the invigoration of the National Assembly could not serve the party's aims to politicize the society.[29] In fact, the efforts to politicize society were undertaken outside of the party. Thus, when Popular Forces Groups, a sort of people's militia, were set up, they were outside the party and competition with it.[30] When Councils of Experts were created to scientifically study and advise on solutions to problems, it was not clear that they were under party control.[31] At the same time, the party was loosing whatever grip it had on the Assembly.[32] The elections to the Assembly revealed a good deal more turnover than the ASU elections. For a number of reasons only 27 per cent of the incumbents were returned (78 per cent of those incumbents who ran) and 7 per cent were 'independents'. The Assembly would prove to be a heated and productive body.

If the institutions and masses continued to boil, the elite did not cool down either. Taken as a whole, the changes that occurred after March 1968 ran in favour of the centre and the right. Notably, Haykal saw his opposition in the press reduced and he moved into the cabinet as Minister of Information.[33] Similarly, Sadat gained a prominence he had not previously enjoyed and moved into the Vice-Presidency.[34]

The Impact of Economic Reform

In the above discussion, policy choices and policy changes have been presented in a straightforward political analysis. That is, policy is examined to ascertain its likely impact and the political reasons underlying it are then constructed. This approach rests on the fundamental assumption that policy and politics are coherent — that they are structured and predictable. At a minimum, the political actors must believe that they are. If the actors do not at least believe that their decisions matter and that there is a cause and effect relationship between decisions and outcomes, then there can be no rational basis for decision-making or for political/economic analysis. In the debates over economic policy that have been reviewed, the actors certainly behaved as though the decisions mattered. In this section I demonstrate that, indeed, they did have an effect, one which was entirely predictable.[35]

Macro-Economic Indicators

The pattern of imports and production of consumer goods (see Table 4.3) indicates that the decisions to free this type of activity and consumption did have an impact. The great bulk of liberalizing decisions for imports came in 1969 and 1970, as was noted above. As a result, the imports of consumer goods increased sharply in 1970. Every major consumer durable had recovered and surpassed the totals from the early 1960s by 1970. By and large, production had recovered as well.

Given the specific social groups which the ministerial speech had noted, the importation and production of automobiles is of particular importance. It can be said that locally produced cars are upper-middle-class commodities, while imported cars are upper-class commodities. There was a veritable explosion of automobile imports in 1969, 1970 and 1971. The number of cars imported in 1970 alone was greater than the total imported in 1963-7. The total for the three years after the war was two and one half times greater than the five years before the war.

The economic activity of the private sector exhibits a similar pattern (see Table 4.4). Starting from a low in 1966/7 all of the indicators of private sector economic activity made a sharp upturn in the immediate post-war period. Of particular note are the investment and export figures. Private sector investments were comparatively small in relation to the public sector, but they steadily increased in their average size. There appears to have been a bit of a recession in 1970-2, but, by and large, the private sector investments shifted from being quite small 8,500 LE (Egyptian pounds) per investment in 1965/6 to being quite respectable, 47,900 LE in 1969/70. If we exclude the major public monopolies, which consumed large parts of the public investment, private investment was accounting for a healthy share of total investment after the war.

Of equal, if not more, significance, is the series on exports. In the post-war atmosphere foreign currency was at a premium. The private sector, responding to the opportunities underlined by the minister in 1968, proved increasingly adept at providing that currency. Industrial exports from the private sector showed a steady and rapid growth, increasing from less than 3 per cent of the total before the war to 15 per cent in the early 1970s.

Those aspects of agrarian production which were most decidedly private and middle/upper class — fruits, vegetables and animal products — did extremely well in the post-1967 period. The share of this output in total agricultural income increased from an average of 43.1 per cent in the three year period prior to the war to 45.2 per cent in the first

Table 4.3: Consumption of Consumer Durables

	1963	1964	1965	1966	1967	1968	1969	1970	1971	1972	1973
Imports											
Total											
Consumer goods (000,000 LE)					38.6	23.8	26.7	59.0	60.0	55.8	62.0
Passenger cars											
Number (ton/piece)	1,088	1,125	2,158	1,811	1,023	3,545	5,944	9,489	15,196	3,998	7,448
Value (000 LE)	748	783	1,471	1,192	629	1,666	2,511	5,174	8,260	3,312	6,185
Televisions											
Number (ton piece)	423	14	21	378	36	84	249	13,867	23,309	18,352	18,745
Value (000 LE)	716	26	30	451	47	106	312	476	822	689	720
Television parts											
Number (ton)	1,102	2,965	2,553	1,759	196	112	884	1,166	1,654	701	528
Value (000 LE)	1,713	3,425	3,387	2,218	273	187	1,245	1,305	2,241	1,546	1,310
Refrigerators											
Number (ton/no.)				164	106	121	132	1,546	1,835	1,285	2,095
Value (000 LE)				109	77	88	95	119	136	100	156
Sound equipment											
Number				2,802	2,245	2,912	3,557	4,760	8,764	9,393	18,677
Value (000 LE)				111	83	74	85	111	164	188	373
Sewing machines											
Number (ton/no.)				29	45	58	107	7,217	7,927	10,616	15,230
Value (000 LE)				26	38	56	102	125	168	179	292
Domestic Production											
Automobiles (no.)	5,507	4,696	3,327	552	494	1,891	2,325	3,590	5,750	5,380	5,591
Televisions (000)	39.5	81.7	56.2	50.4	48.6	29.9	43.2	64.2	66.9	75.6	49.1
Refrigerators (000)	26	37	45	62	9	30	75	54	62	55	39

Table 4.4: (a) Indicators of Economic Activity

Year	Investment[a] Private Total	Investment[a] Private Avg./Proj.	Investment[a] Public Total	Investment[a] Public Excl Pet. and Iron	Use of Credit[b] Private	Use of Credit[b] Public	Industrial Activity Production Private	Industrial Activity Total	Industrial Activity Industrial Exports[a] Private	Industrial Activity Industrial Exports[a] Total
1964	3.4	.0085	95.2	76.6	390.8	722.8				93.4
1965[b]	2.6	.0041	79.0	56.6	396.8	880.8			2.1	87.6
1966	3.7	.0114	58.5	41.7	374.9	948.1	275	1,024.5	1.9	87.1
1967	9.8	.0287	71.9	41.4	404.6	990.8	285	1,073.0	4.3	117.8
1968	12.5	.0479	70.7	40.5	434.6	1,041.8	294	1,198.0	11.3	146.6
1969	7.8	.0299	84.4	32.5	455.6	1,146.9	324	1,327.7	13.2	146.6
1970	6.9	.0246	101.4	39.6	490.5	1,248.7	349	1,425.5	16.7	139.9
1971					505.1	1,350.0	372	1,577.5	17.7	149.8
1972								1,625.0		
1973	16.7	.0519	87.0	50.0	559.6	1,636.3	441	1,731.2	30.2	162.4
1974	19.1	.0534	111.3	56.5	788.2	2,059.7	523		54.1	224.8
1975[c]	19.0	.0671								

a Federation of Egyptian Industries, Yearbook, various issues.
b Middle East News Agency, Economic Weekly, 2 October 1976.
c First three-quarters only.

Table 4.4 (Cont'd)

(b) Capital Crops (1963-73)

| Year | Percentage of total agricultural income[a] | | | | Exports[b] (000,000 LE) | |
	Animal products	Fruit	Veg.	Total	Total[b] veg.	Oranges[c]
1963	31.7	3.1	8.3	43.1	44.8	.3
1964	32.2	4.0	7.1	43.3	37.8	.5
1965	29.9	3.7	9.1	42.7	35.5	.3
1966	28.0	4.2	11.2	43.4	45.7	.5
1967	26.0	4.1	10.9	41.0	53.0	.8
1968	30.2	4.5	11.4	46.1	74.5	2.0
1969	28.8	4.7	10.4	43.9	61.3	6.4
1970	30.8	4.4	10.4	45.6	51.8	6.8
1971	26.7	4.7	10.0	41.4	48.7	9.0
1972	31.4	4.9	11.1	47.4		
1973	30.3	4.6	10.6	45.5	na	15.8

a *Evaluation of National Income from the Agrarian Sector*, CAPMS, various issues.
b *Statistical Yearbook*, CAPMS, various issues.
c Federation of Egyptian Industries, *Yearbook*, various issues.

three years after the war. After a decline in 1971, which coincides with the recession we have seen in private industrial activity, grocery crops rose again to an average of 46.5 per cent of total income in 1972/3. The exportation of oranges, another activity encouraged by the new economic policy, clearly shows how responsive economic activity could be. It accounted for barely 1 per cent of total vegetable exports prior to the war. After the war it rose steadily, reaching 18 per cent by 1971-2.

A number of patterns in the public sector are relevant to the present discussion. First, investment activity dropped sharply prior to the war. This reflected the resource crisis that state capitalism had generated on its own. The war marked another sharp drop in this activity, though the immediate pre-war level was rapidly recovered. However, investment in non-petroleum and non-iron projects did not recover the pre-war level until 1974 and, in fact, it never did reach the 1965/6 level. In this sense, a major shift in the focus of the public sector seems to have occurred. Prior to the war, iron and petroleum accounted for roughly 25 per cent of total public sector investment; after the war they accounted for about 50 per cent. At least implicitly, the state had begun to restrict the scope of its activities by altering its investment patterns. Second, in the post-war period, the use of credit in the public sector grew rapidly in relation to investment, production and exports. The basis for an inflationary and fiscal crisis was being created in this reliance on credit.

The Distributive Effects of the Policy

In the debate over economic policy, we identify class positions with equity issues — the distribution of resources between groups in society. It is the potential shift in economic resources that stimulates political action. The macro-economic shift in economic activity leads one to suspect that a shift in the distribution of wealth was taking place. Although the direct evidence here is sketchy, it does suggest that such a shift occurred.

If we examine the labour share in income or the movement of real wages we find evidence of such a shift (see Table 4.5). In agriculture, labour's share had increased following the socialist measures of 1960-2 but it had reached a peak in 1966. It then turned downwards and continued a steady decline throughout the post-war period. In industry, labour's share in income peaked in 1964-5 and turned downwards before the war. After hovering at a level somewhat below that of 1962 through the late 1960s, it turned down again in 1970. Data on real wages are more suspect because of the difficulty of choosing a cost-of-living deflator, but regardless of which deflator we choose, the pattern is repeated. Industrial real wages peaked somewhat earlier than agrarian wages and both exhibited a steady decline after the war. These changes in wages represent a redistribution of wealth from the working classes towards the state and the private sector capitalists.

The agricultural terms of trade (i.e. the value of agricultural commodities compared to other goods) suggest that specific rural classes were being favoured by the new economic policy. Between 1966 and 1972 large farmers (more than 20 feddans), who accounted for most of the output of fruits, vegetables and animal products, found that their terms of trade with respect to manufactured inputs improved by 40 per cent (i.e. the same quantity of output bought 40 per cent more manufactured inputs). In that period, their terms of trade with respect to manufactured consumer goods improved by 18 per cent. The terms of trade for small farmers (less than 5 feddans) improved only half as much. Thus, not only was there a shift of wealth from the urban to the rural areas, but middle- and upper-class farmers did extremely well.

Table 4.5: Indices of the Share of Wages in Income and Real Wages

Year	Share of wages in income Agriculture[a]	Industry 1[b]	Industry 2[c]	Average annual real wages Agriculture 1[d]	Agriculture 2[e]	Agriculture 3[f]	Industry 1[d]	Industry 2[e]
1959				100	100		100	100
1960	25	27.5		91	87	123	84	81
1961	31	29.1		108	100	113	91	83
1962	30	35.7		118	104	122	119	107
1963	29	35.2		126	104	127	119	107
1964	29	35.3		134	102	138	112	101
1965	32	33.4		137	114	135	101	86
1966	33	32.5	32.9	136	125	170	96	88
1967	31	34.8	28.9	134	117	162	98	86
1968	31	33.0	25.9	135	114	156	97	82
1969	28	32.4	25.5	132	108	151	96	78
1970	29	30.6	24.7	129	107	138	91	78
1971	27		23.4			140		
1972	25		23.9			143		
1973	24					140		
1974	22					125		

a Federation of Egyptian Industries, *Yearbook*, various issues.
b Robert Mabro and Samir Radwan, *The Industrialization of Egypt 1939-1973*, p. 179.
c Central Bank of Egypt *Economic Review*, various issues, based on values added.
d Wages per capita deflated by official cost-of-living index. Federation of Egyptian Industries, *Yearbook*.
e Wages per capita from Ibid., deflated by cost-of-living index in Samir Radwan, *The Impact of Agrarian Reform on Rural Egypt* (Geneva International Labor Office Working Paper, 1977).
f Ibid., p. 29.

Direct measures of the distribution of wealth are available for the agrarian sector and they all point in the direction of a worsening of that distribution. Indices of landlessness, families below the poverty line and the GINI index of inequality, though subject to doubt because of the incompleteness of the data base, point to a dramatic worsening of the distribution of wealth.[36]

Conclusion: The Indecisiveness of Reform

Thus, the policy decisions made by the regime and the political debate, even political struggle, that was being carried out in the press, the ASU, the executive branch, the legislature and the military had a firm grounding in reality. In the polity, a defeat could mean the loss of power, or as in the case of Field-Marshal Amer much more. In the economy, a defeat could mean a large and rapid shift in the economic resources and activity.

With the *March 30 Program* the regime had tried to quiet the domestic scene by taking a turn away from the 'dogmatic socialism' of the previous half decade. In the economy it was successful in shifting the emphasis away from the public sector toward the private sector. However, it did not produce any real economic improvements. At this crucial juncture, the revitalization of the public sector was indispensable to the revitalization of the economy because the public sector was so large. While such a reform of the public sector might have been economically feasible, it cut across too many political and bureaucratic interests to permit a thorough and effective execution. Perhaps a radicalization of the regime could have cut through these interests, but the regime had always lacked the necessary power and organization. In the shaky days after the June defeat, the regime took the exact opposite direction.

On the other hand, the policies which were easiest to execute were also the least likely to achieve the goals that the regime had chosen. The expansion of private and individual economic activity, the encouragement of capital crops, etc., were easily achieved. The interests were there, waiting to be released. However, the pursuit of these interests did not necessarily drive towards the economic goals. The private sector was small. The forms of profit available in all parts of the private sector were not necessarily productive. The luxury consumption policy was marginal at best. The net result of the policy was that the public sector became bogged down in a morass of conflicting interests while the private sector became a magnet for quick and counter-productive profits.

Nor had the regime managed to quiet the political situation a great deal. Anti-regime violence was reduced, but the bickering and jockeying for political position went on. The regime lurched chaotically along with bitter debates occurring repeatedly in all arenas of politics. Moreover, international tensions continued. In late 1970 a dramatic change in this tumultuous scene took place. On 30 September Nasser died. The one figure who had the capacity to maintain a modicum of harmony and order was removed from the midst of an extremely volatile scene.

5 THE GHOST OF NASSER AND THE RISE OF SADAT

The Transition in Leadership

When Nasser died, the polity lost its most stable and stabilizing element. Nasser's personal charisma had provided a major support for the regime. His skills in political juggling had enabled him to balance the divergent elements of the coalition of interests that state capitalism had created. His death left a turbulent political scene and an uncertain political future. Two interpretations of Nasser's legacy have been offered by traditional political scientists — the societal and the charismatic. Both lead to essentially the same conclusion — Nasser's legacy was a guarantee of instability.[1] The societal argument can be summarized as follows: 'Unincorporated society creates the conditions of personal power. Personal power demands constant juggling. Constant juggling blocks the formation of durable political groups and consistent policy. Power is dissipated and the "unincorporated" nature of society is reinforced.'[2] The charismatic argument can be summarized as follows: 'The charismatic relationship is a direct relationship between leader and followers. The direct relationship renders intermediaries (organizations or individuals) unnecessary. The failure to institutionalize power returns politics to the pre-charismatic pattern once the leader is removed.'[3]

Both arguments point to two critical problems that the death of the leader presents. First, those who are second in command — the lieutenants, who have been barely tolerated and often despised — must guarantee that they can continue to rule. This is the upper-class problem of maintaining command and control. Second, for the masses, Nasser's popularity and his death created a symbolic and emotional void.[4] The masses had lost the most significant symbol of their nationalistic, collective solidarity. The two problems are intermingled. The elite will mobilize all of its political resources to maintain its hold and one of those resources, an extremely powerful one, is the manipulation of available symbols.

All of this would have been true whenever the leader disappeared, but the leader had disappeared at a moment when the elite and the masses were under immense pressures. It is at this point that the above two interpretations leave a great deal to be desired. They do not readily lead to an understanding of how the issue of succession is resolved. They state the problem, but they do not provide the basis for a systematic analysis of the solution that follows. Here we must turn to an analysis of the political economy – class interests and political institutions.

On the one hand, the distribution of personal alliances was not random at the moment of Nasser's death, nor was it very flexible (see Figure 5.1). One group with major influence was centred on the party (i.e. Ali Sabri). Another group was centred on the state security apparatus. The moderates were scattered in the executive branch (i.e. Sadat), the press (Haykal) and the legislature. Another more liberal group was out of power but still had some influence (i.e. Zakariyya Muhyi-al-Din). The differences that existed between the individuals, the institutions and the interests that they represented had been legitimated in three years of open political debate. On the other hand, the aspirants to power were essentially indistinguishable in their claim to succession. All claimed to represent basic policies – anti-Israel, Pan Arabism, Egyptian nationalism – which had run throughout the post-revolutionary period. All had strong ties to Nasser. All had long records of service to the revolution.

Figure 5.1:   The Structure of the Egyptian Elite at the Death of Nasser

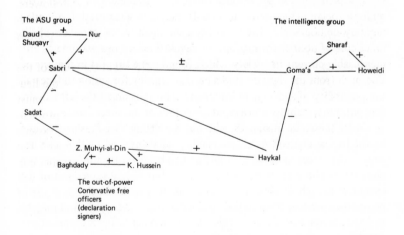

If anyone was isolated in this configuration of interests and institutions, it was Sadat. However, he was also the beneficiary of the juxtaposition of interests and institutions that existed at the moment. As Vice-President, the legal rational authority of the constitution moved him

into power. The constitution leans towards consensus. The party proposes the candidate and the Assembly nominates him. Then, the people express their will in a plebiscite (yes or no vote). It is possible that a candidate would muster only small majorities at each stage and possible that he would be rejected, but that is far from likely. At the moment, the leadership intended to maximize the margins all around. By so doing, it would demonstrate its ability to lead. Even the full sixty days allowed by the constitution was not utilized. That would have appeared too hesitant. In this case, speed meant stability and the ability to remain in power. From this point of view, Sadat made sense because he was the Vice-President.

There were other factors that pushed in this direction. First, the Soviets were counselling speed and continuity. Their investment in Egypt was huge and they were not inclined to upset things at this moment, even though they had clear preferences. They had made their desires for a stronger party known in the mid-1960s. Though they seem to have had some success in getting leftists out of jail and into the ASU in 1964-5, that move had not rendered the party dominant. At this moment, with matters in such delicate balance, a strong thrust by the party could not be contemplated.[5]

Second, a group of liberals who were out of power approached Sadat with 'a plan for the provisional ruling of a collegium of Nasser's old senior associates (themselves included) leading to a restoration of parliamentary democracy'.[6] They had been the most liberal members of the inner core of politics throughout the revolution and this was one clearly identifiable current in society which found some support in the press.[7] The push from the right created a certain urgency for action to forestall the possibility of a change in leadership. This reinforced the left's desire for continuity, stability and a rapid resolution of the succession question.

Under these circumstances, who but the sitting Vice-President would be the logical choice? As a personality, Sadat inspired neither awe nor envy.[8] His career under the revolution had been among the less spectacular. He had been more rightist than most, but he had stayed out of the executive branch of government and out of trouble. In the post-1967-war period, he had been in the Presidency of the Assembly and seemed to have played a moderating role. At this moment of great tension and stress, he provided the least threat.

Moreover, Sadat seems to have agreed to some form of joint rulership. Ali Sabri (on the left) would be Vice-President and sit in on the cabinet meetings. Sadat (well known for his rightist leanings) as President, would not. Thus, the balance of political forces and social interests would be maintained. The left and the right would sit together. However, with the overarching figure of Nasser gone, the left and the right would have to try to balance each other directly. It proved to be a short-lived arrangement.

Once the successor had been agreed upon, the regime set about making that choice stick. An ideological and policy barrage ensued. At a meeting of the ASU on 5 October 1970 Sadat set the tone of unity and continuity. On 6 October the ASU issued a broad policy declaration calling for unity, liberation of territory and praising the Soviets. At that meeting, Mahmoud Riyadh (the Foreign Minister) issued a strong anti-United States statement. On 7 October Sadat went before the National Assembly. In his speech accepting its unanimous endorsement for the Presidency, he struck what was to be the keynote of the entire campaign: 'I have come to you along the path of Gamal Abdul Nasser and I believe that your nomination of me to assume the responsibility of the presidency is a nomination for me to continue on the path of Nasser.'[9]

The entire period, before and after the plebiscite, was permeated with the ghost of Nasser. However, the ghost of Nasser was not the man and the path was not exactly what it had been. A furious period of popular consumption was embarked upon.[10] Prices were reduced on a wide range of consumer goods. Promotions were announced, custom duties lowered, public utilities improved. If the Nasserist policy in the early days of the revolution had been to appeal to the unrepresented sections of pre-revolutionary society, the successors of Nasser, eighteen years later, aimed their policy at the beleaguered sections of revolutionary society. Price reductions, the lifting of import restrictions, the talk of democracy, freedom, all were most appreciated by the middle class. All had started with the end of hostilities in June 1967 and the regime knew the direction that it had to follow. In form, it was early Nasser; in substance it was late Nasser, the Nasser of the *March 30 Program*; in impact, it was effective, for the crisis of succession was successfully and peacefully negotiated.

Sadat in Power

There is a slow, but steady, progression from Sadat as the passive President in whose hands the political structure places power and to whom it dictates action, to Sadat as the active President taking the initiative, building political support, gaining popularity and power. The greater the initiative he took, the more the coholders of power complained. The more they complained, the more Sadat found allies.

For example, on 28 December 1970, less than two months after he had been elected, Sadat ordered a sweeping reform of sequestration and confiscation policy. *Al-Ahram* applauded. 'The decree insures guarantees of personal freedom and security for all individuals in all circumstances and guarantees the right of litigation.'[11] This was, after all, a tangible step toward the 'open society'. It could not endear Sadat to the left. However, Sadat was in search of a constituency, the constituency of the *March 30 Program*, because the major power bases in Egyptian society were not available to him. The security services, the party, even the cabinet were blocked to him. Nevertheless, a popular, non-institutionalized constituency was available, and he had the one type of legitimacy that was really acceptable to this constituency, the electoral mandate.

Collective leadership or not, it was Sadat who had received seven million yes votes on 15 October 1970. Collective leadership or not, it was Sadat who announced the reduction of prices. It was Sadat who personally extended the cease-fire with Israel. It was Sadat who reaffirmed the *March 30 Program*; Sadat who took the decision to alter sequestrations; Sadat who took steps to balance Egypt's foreign policy vis-à-vis the United States.[12]

By March the aura of unity was dispelled. *Al-Ahram* and *al-Jumhur riyya* repeated their earlier round of foreign policy debates after Sadat suggested that a phased withdrawal of Israeli troops from the occupied territories could lead to an opening of the Canal.[13] Buoyed by the defence of his position at home and mildly encouraging reactions from the United States, Sadat took a bold step on the path of Abdul Nasser.

At a series of meetings between 14 April and 17 April 1971, the details of a new Arab Union were worked out. The Federal Arab Republic including Syria, Egypt and Libya, with an open invitation to the Sudan, was created on paper. It was at these meetings that Ali Sabri became convinced of the impossibility of communal leadership. Sabri was against the union, to be sure, but what was more apparent was the fact that Sadat was becoming the sole leader of Egypt. Sabri complained bitterly throughout the conference that Sadat was exceeding his powers in agreeing to enter the union, but Sadat paid no attention, nor was there any real reason why he should have. Not only had Sadat taken the decision over objection, which explicitly broke the illusion of unity and consensus, but he would reap a tremendous personal political gain from the union.

Sabri took up the challenge. At a meeting of the executive committee of the ASU, the proposal to join the FAR was defeated. Sadat insisted that the issue be taken up before the entire Central Committee of the ASU. When he tried to address the meeting of the Central Committee, he was hooted down. The President was mortified and angered. Ali Sabri had rebuked the President and precipitated a crisis. Exactly what the crisis meant, however, was unclear. It was not certain that Sadat was responsible to the ASU for any particular piece of policy. It was not clear what the loss of a vote in the ASU meant.

Shifting the forum to the National Assembly a week later, regardless of who engineered this step, did not resolve matters. If the intention was to let tempers cool, Sadat's did not and the interim produced some real benefit for his position. He tested his support in the army and found that it was strong. Historically, the army had resisted the party and it seemed that it would continue to do so. The interim also produced an absolute majority in the parliament in support of his position. Historically, the legislature had resisted the party and it seemed that it would continue to do so. A proposal offering full support for Sadat was presented to the Assembly with 185 signatures (an absolute majority) before the session began. This absolute majority would prove useful in the days to come. The Union was overwhelmingly approved by the National Assembly on 29 April. Sadat had moved to the forefront.

Before we enter into an analysis of the furious political activity that filled the ensuing six months, some comment on this rather remarkable sequence of events is in order. The virulence of the political institutions and the political individuals who peopled them is notable. The Executive Committee and the Central Committee of the ASU (about 150 of the most important political individuals in society) had voted against the President. A week later, an overwhelming majority of the National Assembly (300 or so of the most important political individuals in society) had voted for him. Such sequences of events do not occur in 'closed' societies. In established open societies, they take on a specific meaning (usually a vote of confidence or no confidence). Egypt was in a limbo between the two — sufficiently open to generate genuine expressions of disagreement, but not open enough to have a regularized mechanism for resolving those differences.

In this ambiguous context, Sadat seems to have risen to the occasion. At the annual May Day Rally, two days after he had received the vote of support in the National Assembly, he snubbed Ali Sabri and attacked him outright.

Thus, no individual or group may be entitled to claim any authority separate from that of the people or to claim a position from which to impose opinions on the people or to adopt a disguise under slogans or to maneuver to create a position of influence from which to dictate to the people.[14]

The following day, Sabri was relieved of his post of Vice-President.

On 17 May Sadat announced that a coup attempt, led by Sabri and joined by a number of other cabinet ministers, had been foiled. From the events which followed we can extract a few important insights, while maintaining a healthy scepticism of the actual details.

Whether or not a coup attempt occurred (and there appears to have been one), it was necessary as an excuse to finish the matter decisively. The heads of the army, the police, the party, the intelligence apparatus and the information apparatus rolled with remarkable ease, once they had been charged with plotting against the regime. Sadat moved forcefully and he appeared to be moving in the direction in which social forces had been moving. The central themes of the post-war period were the central themes of Sadat's moves against the 'conspirators'.

> Finally, the heads of conspiracy and rebellion have come into the open. Centers of power had wanted to impose their domination over the people, using means of suppression and deceit.
>
> If ever anyone raised his voice calling for reforms in the revolution or demanded that a blemish on socialism be removed, or dared to criticize the petty Czars, he would be thrown to the lions or to the dungeons — accused of conspiring against socialism and the revolution.[15]

Sadat moved with more speed, dexterity and firmness than many had thought him capable of. By the end of May he was firmly seated alone in power. He had re-organized the cabinet (14-16 May); appointed key governors (14-16 May); had parliamentary immunity lifted and eighteen members expelled from the National Assembly (14 May); had street demonstrations in his support (15 May); purged the police, intelligence and information apparatuses (16-17 May); appointed a provisional secretariat of the Arab Socialist Union (17 May); disbanded the ASU Central Committee and replaced it with the National Assembly (20 May); set up a committee to carry out elections to the ASU (20 May) and a committee to write a new constitution (27 May); and had come to terms with the Soviets (25-27 May), whose domestic fellow-travellers were taking the political heat.

It was both a 'masterly lesson of how to proceed from quasi-impotence toward supreme power', and a lesson in how 'to head off a coup'.[16] It was much more than that. The conspirators seemed to have control over the intelligence apparatus, the information system, the ASU and its secret organization and the top of the military. 'All that was in their hands and they were unable to do a thing.'[17] Sadat had a great deal more than that going for him. Beyond the power of the Presidency, which he could and did use to dispose of his inferiors, the legitimacy of having been duly elected President was his. He was not only the Commander-in-Chief of the Army, but he had also opened a frank dialogue with the military and he was sensitive to its needs and vulnerabilities. He claimed to stand for democracy and there was a strong sentiment for democracy and against the clandestine activities of the intelligence apparatus. He stood for openness and unity, as opposed to the clandestine manoeuvring of small cliques. Finally, he was just as legitimately the heir of Nasser, even more so, as any of the conspirators.

In a real sense, it was four years of political struggle come to fruition. Sadat had come on the path of Abdul Nasser and that path led back to the *March 30 Program*. Haykal, who had carried much of the burden of liberalization in the 'Open Society Debates' of 1968, could only continue to do the same:

> We were gambling on the future of freedom in Egypt. We accepted censorship only on the question of national security, but otherwise, we refused the censor many times. We said to the censor, 'if you insist on deleting this story or that one, we will print it anyway and you'll have to confiscate the newspaper'. The censor never dared.[18]

Haykal's observation is worth reflecting on, for the role of Sadat will loom large in the 'Corrective Revolution', as 14-17 May 1971 came to be called, but we should not overlook the role of others. Political struggle had been intense for several years and outcomes had begun to take on a finality that they had not in the past. This made active politics and an aggressive political stand more of a gamble than they had been. One such as Haykal had become accustomed to the heat of political struggle.[19] The fact that the juxtaposition of interests and actors dictated that he throw in with Sadat at this moment was important, for Haykal carried considerable weight in the political structure. There were others — some who had come to the fore since 1968, some who would come to the fore in 1971 — who were also willing to take a gamble. Perhaps they did not have Haykal's experience with political struggle or his importance, but they played a part. Taken together, they played an important part.

One can point to the statement of full support for Sadat that surfaced in the 29 April 1971 session of the National Assembly to discover those who were willing to gamble.[20] So far as I can tell, it was the only motion in the decade between 1967 and 1977 presented with a majority of signatures beforehand. It was a *fait accompli* and a definite commitment. Sides were being drawn up and the members of the legislature knew it well.[21]

It took some effort two weeks later, on 14 May, to engineer the special session at which eighteen members of the Assembly would be expelled. In fact, the Speaker of the Assembly refused to call a session at which he would be purged. Though it is not clear exactly where the initiative came from (on 14 May Sadat took credit for it;[22] on 20 May he gave credit to the Assembly[23]) there was a body of members (an absolute majority) who had gambled on Sadat before and on whom he could count. The message he received was full support.

> After the definitive decisions which the Assembly took in this session, the members unanimously came to a frank and clear statement for the President to read to all the Arab People. The Assembly unanimously announces its absolute support for the President of the Republic in all the steps he takes and in the decisions he announces to achieve democracy and to overcome the centers of power and terror and to elevate the words of right and law so that all the people may feel that they live in a land of freedom, honor, tranquillity and security.
>
> The Assembly promises the President that it will always be behind him on the path of freedom, tranquillity, the rule of law, complete national unity and socialism.[24]

As with Haykal's stance, it is difficult to conceive of the members of the Assembly taking any other position. They had become committed to Sadat earlier. They had fought a running battle with the party — whose heads had fallen in the abortive coup. The institutions and the style of rule that the conspirators represented were contrary to their own institution and style. The nature of their claim to authority was different. It is certain that if things had worked out differently and the conspirators had been victorious, both the members of the Assembly and the Assembly as an institution would have suffered.

It is always difficult to say exactly when the outcome is no longer in doubt and, thereby, to distinguish between the discrete acts which created the outcome, those which reinforced it and those which merely followed along. However, it is worth noting that this strong message of support came very early in the final confrontation, before the people knew the whole story. Furthermore, Sadat pointed to the statement of support as one of the key elements in the justness of his actions.[25] I think there is no doubt that the Assembly, just as Haykal, contributed to the outcome. Many others did as well.

It appeared, as Fuad Matar put it, that 'nothing happened'. The conspirators issued their call for a coup but the military refused to break ranks, the state apparatus would not support the conspirators, the Assembly exercised its constitutional functions and the President exercised his legal powers swiftly and definitively. In fact, a great deal had happened. As Haykal suggests, the issue of democracy had been joined. The institutions which played their proper parts would demand their just rewards — a structure in which they could exercise their powers. By mobilizing, by having to mobilize, each one of these institutions in its particular way, Sadat had committed himself to democracy. He had promised, just as the Assembly had promised him, freedom, honour, tranquillity, the rule of law, national unity and socialism.

The New Political Economy

On the domestic front, the path to redeeming the promise was clear, the *March 30 Program*. By July, the people were on the way to the polls, for that was the central solution offered by the *Program*. In the last six months of 1971, some Egyptians would vote eight times — for representatives in syndicates, the ASU and the National Assembly (now called the People's Assembly); for an international federation and a permanent constitution.

On the international front, Sadat was no less aggressive. He declared 1971 the year of decision, in which he promised to deal with the Israelis one way or another. He made an offer through US Secretary of State William Rogers to open a dialogue with the Israelis. He reiterated it and stuck to it through intense international manoeuvrings, but nothing came of it. He signed a 'Friendship Treaty' with the Russians, a treaty which played a highly symbolic part in weathering the events of May. For the moment, at least, Sadat showed he had the capacity to talk to both super-powers at the same time.

However, he also knew where his domestic interests were and he would not permit his relations with the super-powers to interfere with his handling of those interests. Thus, the treaty with the Soviets did not stop him from launching an anti-communist campaign both at home and abroad. In mid-July, he reacted swiftly to a leftist coup in the Sudan and helped to restore Gaafir Numeri to power by flying Sudanese troops stationed in Egypt back to Khartoum. In the middle of the summer, when workers at Helwan protested against the anti-communist campaign in the Sudan and the anti-communist rhetoric in Egypt, their strike was forcefully put down. The illusion of national unity was destroyed. Sadat, who had appointed the first fully-fledged Marxist to the cabinet, had shown that he would do battle with the left, if the situation dictated it. The situation would do so repeatedly. Although those who claimed to represent the left had been toppled in May, the interests on the left were still present and someone would try to represent them. Sadat knew that his own constituency was in the centre, even on the right — the constituency of the *March 30 Program*.

> If he is ever to achieve this vision of an Egypt founded on faith and technology, he will more than ever need the skills of his growing managerial class and the last pill those bourgeois technocrats will swallow is Soviet style Socialism.[26]

By September, Sadat was ready to sum up the prior period. It was an apt moment to sum up, for a new stage was about to begin. The highly symbolic acts — purges, elections, ratification of constitutions — were about to be operationalized. At least, that was the aspiration of the President, for, as he put it, 'we worked out the plan for the reorganization of the state'.[27]

The President's summary of the plan for the reorganization of the state is pure *March 30 Program* and it thoroughly dominated the ensuing six years. It was composed of a number of points that are familiar by now.

First, 'we have to respect the State's authority', which 'should be the authority of the alliance of the working forces . . . Let everything be by democratic dialogue, but for anybody to imagine that he can take the authority of the state in his hands, No!'

Second is the 'sovereignty of law. Everything in the new state should be subject to the law and everything should have its particular jury. If our legislation is incomplete, our legislature will provide the necessary laws.'

The authority of the state and the rule of law rest on political institutions. Each institution would play its proper role and the President would oversee all political activity:

> We are building the state on the basis of institutions . . . there are
> political institutions, executive institutions and legislative institutions.
> We have already laid the basis. But the application will take time.
> We all, as a people, should be guards, protecting the application of
> all this . . . As a nation of institutions, not at all of individuals . . .
> institutions which have powers and clear relations among them.
>
>   Then, as the Constitution states, the President is the arbiter among
> the whole. His is not a party either with or against anybody . . . If he
> feels unable, he resorts to the people, in a direct plebiscite. This is
> the philosophy on which our constitution is based.

This overwhelming emphasis on the authority of the state and the
paternalistic view of power would prove to be extremely difficult political principles around which to organize a more liberal polity.

The remaining points that the President made were pure *March 30
Program* in the economy:

> The third point is the upsurge of government. The routine, the
> regulations which are the public sector, the regulations which are in
> agriculture . . . all the things which we inherited and which tie our
> hands, all these must go.
>
>   I shall set up a free currency bank, that is a free zone or rather
> free zones associated with it . . .
>
>   Moreover, there is the law concerning Arab and Foreign Capital.
> There is already foreign capital invested in the petroleum industry
> and in some of the pharmaceutical companies and we can hope to
> have foreign capital invested also in the fields of petroleum, tourism
> and luxury housing.
>
>   The final point involves the re-organization of the government
> machinery, for there is a muddle and confusion in government organ-
> ization.

Every change that the President said he would introduce, he already
had in his pocket. Between 15 August and 10 November Sadat issued
sixty laws by decree (see Table 5.1). Within the nation of institutions,
decree laws hold a special place. They can be issued by the President in
the absence of the Assembly and they have the force of law until the
Assembly returns to session. When the Assembly returns, the law must
be considered *in toto*, without amendment. Given the importance of
the President in the Egyptian system, this 'preempts' the legislative
process.

Table 5.1: Presidential Decree Laws

By date of issuance	
Date	Number of laws signed
15-30 August	1
1-15 September	6
16-30 September	12
1-15 October	14
15-30 October	6
1-10 November	15
Unknown	6

By content	
Topic	Number of laws signed
Schools	4
Employment	6
Social Services	6
Retirement	4
Religious	11
Courts	4
Military	6
Police	1
Political Rights	4
Sequestrations	1
Legislature	3
Local Government	1
Public Sector	2
Foreign Commerce	5
Finance	3

Source: *Official Gazette*, various issues.

If we examine the temporal distribution of these laws, it becomes immediately apparent that the President's speech was very pointed. He had held back on issuing these laws until after the constitution had been ratified, after the Assembly had been dissolved and after the people had been told what to expect. He had used the structure of the polity very carefully to have his way. The laws cut across every sector of the polity and economy which Sadat had mentioned in his speech. In effect, the restructuring would be by decree.

The legislative prerogative of the President had been exercised. Other prerogatives would also be exercised in late 1971. The events of May had reorganized the top of the elite, but the remainder of the elite had to be renovated as well. If we examine the distribution of Presidential appointments in the year between November 1970 and November 1971, we can appreciate the importance of late 1971 (see Table 5.2). In the months of September, October and November 1971, the President made 1,237 appointments; in the previous ten months he had made only 562. The concentration of appointments in late 1971 can be said to be directly connected to the restructuring laws of 1971. They gave the President the opportunity to renovate the secondary elite. We need not assume that these appointments represent changes in leadership to appreciate their importance. They could all be reappointments (which they are not) and they would still make the point. A new President is in office and it is at his pleasure that the appointed elite serves. The President had definitely exercised his prerogative as Head of State.

The President exercised his prerogative as head of the ASU at the end of October. Technically, the election for the new People's Assembly was controlled by the party because the party had the duty of certifying candidates as eligible for office. When the period for filing for candidacy closed, 15 per cent of those who had applied had not been certified.[28] The ASU officials said that there had been administrative problems. Some believed that the action, or inaction, was politically motivated. The President simply extended the deadline and made sure that all candidates were certified. He had preempted the role of the ASU.

The exchange over certification was pointed enough. The President intended to block the ASU from influencing the outcome of the elections. He meant to have his way, but by strictly legal means. In the week before the election he again acted forcefully — as head of the party, as Head of State, as head of the executive. New Governors (25), Secretaries and Under-Secretaries of the ASU in the districts (125) and members of the 'Popular Local Governments' (625) were appointed. On the day before the elections, the Local Government Executive Councils were named. In the six days before the elections, eight hundred purely political appointments were made. These must be added to the nine hundred plus administrative appointments that were noted above. The timing is of utmost importance. At a crucial moment, local alliances were scrambled, informal influence was short circuited, Presidential patronage was asserted and loyalties were re-affirmed. If the President had acted to ensure impartiality, he had also used his great power to ensure a favourable outcome.

Thus, in the latter part of 1971 the basic elements for restructuring the political economy were laid down. The top of the elite had been successfully purged of 'anti-liberal' elements. The legal structure had been set through a new Constitution and Presidential decree laws. The intermediate elite had been renovated. A highly favourable People's

Table 5.2: Presidential Appointments at the Middle Level (November 1970–November 1971)

Month	Sub-Minister	Governate Sub-Governor	High Court	Public Sector Director	Public Sector Technical director	University High	University Low	Religious	Other	Retired	By re-organization	Total	Total excluding public sector
November	28		7	9	13			1	16			74	52
December	2			6	6							14	2
January	14			4	19				7		36	81	58
February	8			26	13			4				51	12
March	16		2	8	6		4	1				37	23
April				1	3		1					5	1
1-14 May	5	3	7	6	4		1					26	16
15-31 May	13	1	7	4	2							27	21
June	36		11	11	8	2	1	12	32	2	48	160	141
July	10		3	26	17			6		1	23	89	46
August	17										5	22	22
September	11		5	48	25		7	24	24	9	16	145	72
October	47	13		807	15	2	3	1	21	19		928	106
November	25		1	3	11			1			126	167	153

Assembly had been voted in. It had been a period of furious political activity that matched in energy, if not drama, the early part of the year. The President had been precise in his legality, aggressive in his action and meticulous in his attention to detail.

Conclusion: The Survival of the Regime and its Leadership

At this point, some reflection on the ability of the regime to survive two such massive shocks as the defeat in June 1967 and the death of Nasser in September 1970 are in order. Very few regimes have such staying power. In fact, in Egypt, it was not so much a case of the forcefulness of the regime, as the weakness of alternatives.

Whether we call it a political vacuum or a political balance, the fifteen years of Nasser's rule had not produced any political forces strong enough to alter the polity radically at the moment of defeat in 1967. There were no powerful political alternatives available either in terms of leadership or in terms of institutions. In a certain sense, a deadlock existed in which inertia played a very large part. If anyone was going to dislodge the regime, he had to marshal a good deal of force. That was no easy task. At the very top, leadership positions had been effectively monopolized and the state's repressive powers had been used to undercut clandestine organizations. In a broader segment of the population, it would seem that the regime had created enough institutions and maintained enough interest in them to ensure that it would not be toppled from without.

Here we should also recall the great mass of interests which the etatist enterprise had created in the regime. If one was going to replace the regime, one had to have some idea of the political economy which would be constructed after the political change. Such a vision was necessary both to attract support and to motivate the individuals who would execute the coup d'etat. A society of forty million people had been structured around a set of economic and political institutions; it was not so easy to restructure it. Given Egypt's massive economic problems, such a vision was not easy to come by.

The riots of February and November 1968 had shown that changes were necessary, but they had not been sufficient, nor were they necessarily intended to topple the regime. If the regime was going to be toppled, it would have to come from within the core. It would take the form of a sharp turn in one direction executed by one of the constituent elements of the core, at the expense of the others. It would seem that the two political institutions with the capacity to do so – the army in 1967 and the ASU in 1977 – mounted some challenge, though it is not entirely clear that these were full-fledged coup attempts. We can attribute their failure to a number of factors.

A necessary condition for seizing the state is command of the military. In both 1967 and 1971 the military just would not mobilize in support of those who wanted to topple the regime. Perhaps in 1967 there was some possibility of this – that would explain why Amer, who was popular in the military, was eliminated – but the threat seemed feeble. The chances of the military mobilizing in 1971 were probably much less. The bourgeois officers had little love for the ASU and the secret services which were so heavily represented in the group of 'conspirators'. Also, if they were bourgeois, it would seem that the *March 30 Program* and the direction that Sadat promised to follow represented their interests far better than the alternative which the ASU promised. In both cases, we must not overlook the fact that the military, having suffered the defeat of 1967, was not a reservoir of legitimacy. Coups, it would seem, are not made by one or two generals, but by a broader sense in the officer corps that the military can, should, and has the right to intervene in politics. Egypt does not have a long tradition of such intervention, nor was this the moment when the military would make great claims to such a course of action.

Two other points arise along these lines. To overturn Nasser or Sadat was to overturn a representative of the original intervention of the military in politics. Nasser and Sadat were among the very first non-aristocratic Egyptian army officers. They had participated in and engineered the overthrow of the king and the expulsion of the British. The military had been back in the barracks for more than a decade. No matter who led the coup, at best his claim to represent the tradition of intervention would be equal to theirs. Similarly, we should not overlook the fact that Nasser and Sadat had the weight of legal rational authority on their side. Each was the President, duly elected and constitutionally sanctified. Those weaned on the justness of duly constituted authority, as the military, are prone to lending some credence to such constitutional, legal rational authority.

At a minimum, the military was neutral. It would not rush into the streets to overthrow the regime. The obverse may also have been true. It was entirely possible that if the military had been called on for a sustained action in the streets to support the regime, it would have refused. That was a question of the pressures that civilian politicians could generate. Those who wished to overthrow the regime seemed to be unable to bring matters to such a point. The failure of civilians, especially the ASU, to mount such a threat successfully can be attributed to a number of factors.

First, as was the case with the military, the party certainly was no great reservoir of legitimacy whose call to overthrow the regime would excite the masses.

Second, as was the case with the military, the party's claim to leadership of the revolution was not necessarily stronger than the claim of the other institutions.

Third, power was fragmented. Whether it was the military threatening civilians or one set of civilians threatening another, none commanded the necessary resources to push the threat to a decisive conclusion. Each had a narrow type of political resource concentrated in a particular institution. There were competing institutions with overlapping functions and opposing interests. The constant checking and balancing that Nasser had built up made a coup a complex matter. There was a variety of constituencies and sources of political power available and each challenge seems to have driven political institutions, forces and individuals into a temporary alliance to resist the threat. If the ASU instigated unrest in 1968, the police and security forces put it down. When the ASU and the secret services challenged the President in 1971, he turned to the National Assembly and the press for support. The alliances were temporary and shifting, but they kept the regime from being overturned.

Fourth, if the President is intent on resisting, he has the resources to do so. He has the power of appointment and dismissal. He can quickly remove his opposition while garnering support. In both cases of a serious threat to the President, he quickly formed the centre of an alliance which resisted the challenge. Nasser coupled great personal popularity with executive power. For Sadat, who lacked that popularity, executive power, coupled with a capacity for decisive action, a genuine flair for the dramatic and a remarkable sense of timing, proved to be adequate.

Under these circumstances, it would seem that those who wished to overturn the regime could neither execute a quick and decisive show of force to remove the President, nor marshal sustained disturbances, either in institutions or on the streets, to pressure him out of office. Thus, one can say that the political institutions served the regime well. By no means a model of stability, they did absorb the political pressures and avoid a coup.

At the same time, it should be recognized that the situation of deadlock creates constant pressures on the regime to pull something off, lest the opposition slowly build enough strength to threaten again. Thus, to say that the regime survived is not to say that it thrived. If balance and fragmentation lay at the core of survival, they also lay at the core of its inability to make far-reaching changes and to accomplish a great deal. Plagued by this weakness, its search for domestic solutions was halting and not very effective and its tendency to turn to external manoeuvres to relieve the pressure was reinforced. The next chapter examines just such a turn.

6 THE CAUSES AND CONSEQUENCES OF THE OCTOBER 1973 WAR

The Year of Turmoil

When 1971 ended without the decision on the international front that Sadat had promised, a protracted set of student demonstrations began.[1] When Sadat gave a rather lame excuse for his failure to deal with the Israelis, the protest seems to have grown nastier. By and large, these were leftist students protesting passivity on the international front, but other factors seem to have contributed to the hostile atmosphere. On 17 January Aziz Sidqi was appointed Prime Minister and Sayyid Marei became First Secretary of the ASU. While both men had long been associated with the socialist revolution — the former with the public sector and the latter with agrarian reform — they both had rather conservative reputations. This was the first cabinet that Sadat had formed since the events of May and it seemed to antagonize the students.

By 23 January, the tone of the debate had escalated considerably. The government's plans to impose austerity and to open enlistments among the students met with derision. A decision to carry the demonstrations outside the University was made and a march to the People's Assembly was planned. The meeting came off, but, in the words of the President, 'upon the return to the University, they renewed the strike, without any intervention on our part'.[2] The government moved to clear the University and the demonstrations spilled over into the streets.[3] The disturbances which spread over downtown Cairo lasted from 24 until 27 January.

The point to be underlined in the riots and the response to them is that the regime was being pushed to live up to its claims.[4] Sadat had promised two things — action on the international front and democracy on the domestic front — and he was being called to account. Constant pressure to deliver on those promises would come from a number of sources. The students led the way, but other groups followed willingly. In early February it seems that the student movement received some support from a variety of other groups — workers, engineers, journalists, doctors — to the effect that 'the student movement is only an expression of the general malaise in the face of the current situation and on that point the students are not alone'.[5]

83

If the students seemed to be pushing on the left, by demanding an end to the talk of negotiations, there were also those who were pushing on the right. On 4 April Sadat was given a memorandum signed by a group of liberals made up of many of those who had come forward at the time of Nasser's death with their proposal for joint leadership. It struck several major themes.

It is now time, five years after the defeat, to draw the policy for the national liberation on the basis of Egypt's vital forces alone — spiritual and material. What we want is for Egyptian-Soviet relations to revert to the natural and safe framework which should character-ize the relationship between a small country, jealous of its inde-pendence, and a great power, which naturally seeks to extend its influence.

Mr. President, the recent student unrest has expressed the prevailing anxiety in Egypt about its fate. This anxiety had been compounded by the formation of the recent government. The Egyptian people's doubts increase regarding the ability of the present set-up to liberate the homeland.[6]

Apparently responding to these pressures on the right and discontent in the military, Sadat expelled the Soviets two months later. This 'move was initially popular in both the army and the civilian population [i.e. Sadat knew his constituency was on the right not the left] '.[7] However, when he failed to produce anything tangible from the Americans, even supporters of the move began to wonder. Sadat was responding to domestic imperatives, not manipulating international actors. A process had begun, similar to the one which typified the mid-1960s, in which domestic pressures dictated international actions.

All of 1972 and the beginning of 1973 were pressure-filled, indeed. After the student demonstrations of January 1972, there were reports of other student demonstrations in April and December of that year and January and February of 1973. There were reports of disturbances among the workers in February, March and April of 1972. There were also repeated incidents of inter-religious strife from August to November 1972. In addition, there were reports of disturbances in the army in February, July, October and November 1972 and February 1973.

Things did not go well in parliament either. The President had used his powers to pre-empt the legislature freely and when the decree laws came up for debate in early 1972, there were members who objected vigorously.[8] Towards the end of 1972, the Assembly locked horns with the government over a number of policies.

> The deputies attacked with irony an announcement by the government on the preparation of Egypt for battle which did not appease their uncertainties, a budget whose figures had any significance had not been presented in the general plan, a foreign policy which gave no details on the relations of Cairo with the Arabs or foreigners, and total silence on the latest developments of the Egypt-Soviet relations.
>
> The deputies reproached the government for having violated the Constitution on many occasions in making changes in the budget without consulting the Assembly, of permitting the public debt to mount in silence, of having an incoherent commercial policy; some even went so far as to put the conception of the budget, itself, in doubt.[9]

Just as the students and others were willing to call the regime to account, so too, was the legislature. Simply put, the government's policy was going nowhere. Economic reform and moderate liberalization produced no tangible improvements and the people were becoming restless. War costs continued without war. The private sector fell into a recession. Reform of the public sector did not even appear to be implemented. The students were back out on the streets. The government was lambasted in the press and the Assembly.

The Year of the War

In March 1973 President Sadat responded by taking the Prime Minister's portfolio for the first time. He formed a cabinet which was, in fact, a war cabinet. After more than a year of turmoil, it was time to take action. Whatever the costs, the internal front had to be quieted. It could not stand this level of agitation for long, certainly not if preparations for war were to be carried out. In his initial response to the student demonstrations of January 1972 Sadat had said: 'it was incumbent upon us to put our house in order'. A year had shown that the initial response had not been effective. Now he took a different and harsher tack by taking the Prime Ministry and deciding to quiet the domestic situation.

His measures seemed to work for a number of reasons. To begin with, one does not so easily attack the President in Egypt. As Prime Minister, the press would be unable to constantly ridicule governmental authority, for it could not attack the President. To ensure that this would be the case, about ninety journalists of leftist persuasion were expelled from the ASU, which blocked them from writing. Furthermore, at the time that Sadat took the Prime Ministry, Sidqi was removed from the cabinet and Marei was removed from the First Secretary's role in the ASU. For the moment, two figures who had been focal points of dispute for over a year were removed. Sadat also seems to have made some judicious choices in renovating the military command. The cabinet of March 1973 was a signal to the military that war was the order of the day. Finally, arms began to flow in from the Soviets. In sum, domestic actors had dictated that the moment for action had better be at hand and international actors had provided an opportune moment. Once again, Sadat responded effectively to the pressures of the situation.

An account of the war lies beyond the scope of this work. Numerous studies which focus on the military and international causes and consequences of the war already exist. Having argued that internal political factors were at least as important as military and international factors in bringing the war about, I concentrate on internal factors in the conduct and the consequences of the war.

Beginning in March, perhaps January, Sadat concentrated his efforts on the war. He carefully worked out international conditions and gave his military the necessary time and resources to plan, train, and execute the action. He guarded the domestic front carefully, keeping the lid on, taking no new initiatives, and so on. There is no better indication of this than the fact that less than a week before the war he reinstated the journalists who had been expelled from the ASU six months earlier. He expected that they would sing his praises after the war was carried out and, indeed, they did. However, the praise turned sour when Egypt later accepted the terms of a cease-fire.

Disagreements will persist as to the necessity of the cease-fire. Was Sadat 'duped' by the Americans? Did the Russians impose it on him? Could the Israeli counter-attack have been crushed irrespective of the attitude of the super-powers?

Haykal's assessment seems quite fair. The Egyptians had planned the initiative. They had dictated the start of the war and planned a political war with limited objectives.

The President argued strongly in favor of a limited war, making his favorite point that if he could win only ten millimeters of ground on the east bank of the Suez Canal this would immeasurably strengthen his position in subsequent political and diplomatic negotiations.[10]

Having planned such a war, Haykal argues that Egypt erred in its plan, for it had not planned on how to end it.

Moreover, having gained a significant measure of success, the Egyptians were predisposed to conserving it, rather than boldly attempting to try for a larger success. With the crossing of the canal they had 'rid themselves of the acute sense of inferiority which had burdened them since the defeat of 1967',[11] and they could not risk losing that. It is important to stress that this thinking existed very early in the war:

> It may be that the spectre of previous defeats inhibited those in command from taking anything that could possibly be construed as a risk. The security of the army may have weighed more with them than the exploitation of an unlooked for degree of success.[12]

Once the Third Army was threatened, these fears became critical:

> After the meeting was over Ismail had a few words alone with President Sadat in another room. He said that he was now speaking for history as a patriot, and if the President saw a way open for a ceasefire on acceptable terms he would support his decision. 'I'm not pessimistic,' he said. 'Our army is still intact. But in no circumstances should we get involved in any military development which will again face our armed forces with the threat of destruction . . .'[13]

That Haykal sees the conservative attitude both before and after the Israeli breakthrough is important. Sadat claims that after 16 October Egypt was fighting both the Israelis and the Americans who were flying supplies almost directly into battle. This changed the terms of the war. By Haykal's account, there was a crucial period prior to 16 October when the primary constraint was internal, rather than external. My argument has been that the crucial constraints are always internal. Be that as it may, the cease-fire guaranteed that the praise of Sadat would be mixed, at best, and the regime would be faced with the problem of translating a psychological, emotional, partial military victory that had ended on a decidedly sour note into a political victory.

To make matters worse, things did not go well on either the international or the domestic fronts. Even before the fighting ended Egypt lost its initiative. The Egyptians seemed to 'lose' the cease-fire. They had a falling out with the Syrians that was difficult to patch up. Once fighting ceased, circumstances deteriorated. The Israelis were not in a conciliatory mood. Relations with the Soviets did not hold up. The Arab front continued to fragment. Once Egypt got into the diplomatic process things seemed to bog down. As they bogged down, the inevitable pull of the domestic situation began to take over. Military expenditures continued while the military sat out in the desert with its material and morale deteriorating. Economic liberalization floundered as Arab enthusiasm remained in words rather than deeds.

The October war had opened long-term prospects in terms of a potential reduction of the military burden, expanding trade, investment opportunities vis-à-vis the West and increased Arab petro-dollars flowing into Egypt. However, it had also created short-term economic problems, in terms of raw material shortages, consumer goods shortages, and an increasing foreign debt. As negotiations wore on, the short-term problems extended and seemed to swallow up the prospects of the long term.

A Mandate for Change: The *October Working Paper*

In the spring of 1974 the regime circulated the *October Working Paper*. Without having produced the bulk of the necessary international conditions — least of all peace — the regime invoked the October victory to declare its bold new programme for change. In typical style, this document was submitted to a plebiscite and raised to the level of a 'document of the revolution', along with the National Charter of 1962, the *March 30 Program* of 1968, and the *Permanent Constitution and National Action Program* of 1971.

The *October Working Paper* is 'moderate in tone and studiously ambiguous',[14] yet it does push the changes in the political economy to their logical conclusion. First, it glorifies the October victory, thus affirming that a new stage had begun. Such glory provides the basis for chastizing the opponents of the regime.

The October war was the answer of the great people of Egypt through and by their glorious Arab nation. It was an answer on the level of Egypt whose effects went beyond our immediate cause in order to alter the position of the whole area and reflect on the position of the entire world . . .

Before the war we heard so many campaigns of defeat and despair. We will not pay heed to the tunes of doubt which cannot come up to the levels of our achievement and the tasks which we are still tackling: tunes which have evaporated under the sun of Great October.

Such voices are not yet capable of assimilating the outcome of our victory or of perceiving the wide horizons opened by October before the potentialities of the nation, so that they can affect events and reach the limits of wresting all their legitimate rights.[15]

In substance, the *Paper* deals exclusively with economics. The public sector is praised as the backbone of the economy and criticized for being inefficient and avaricious. This was an old tune, but a new note was added. The public sector is now defined as essentially a supporting actor for two other sectors, the foreign and the private sectors. In fact, the *Paper* devotes almost as much attention to the private sector as the public sector.

The private sector has an important role in development, and we should admit that we have not always met its requirements nor created conditions to promote its productive activity.

Successive contradictory decisions and acts have neutralized the private sector as a productive agency, led it into parasitic investments, and induced its owners to adopt patterns of extravagant consumption when they did not find a way of investing in stable production.

It is time for these conditions to disappear altogether and for the private sector to find real stability and encouragement towards maximum production to meet the needs of the society.[16]

The shift in ideology is sharp. The failure of the national bourgeoisie to come forward and make an alliance with the revolutionary regime in the mid-1950s was one of the major justifications for the move into Arab socialism. Now the fault is located in the regime. Symbolically, the national bourgeoisie is rehabilitated by this one statement alone.

The foreign sector now was expected to play a very large role. It was to provide both finance and technology. The equation was: Egyptian potential plus Arab capital plus Western technology equals development and progress.

In politics, the *Paper* offers little new. The 'alliance of the working forces' is embraced and parties are rejected.

> The people have accepted the system of the alliance of the working powers of the people as the outline of their political life. In the battle of construction and progress we are in dire need of this to grow. Therefore, I reject the call for breaking up national unity in an artificial way through the creation of parties. But I also do not accept the theory of the one party which imposes its tutelage on the people and takes away freedom of opinion, depriving the people of actually exercising their political freedom.[17]

Submitting this paper to a plebiscite was a very typical action. It is too long and involved to be properly debated and there was never any chance that it would be rejected. However, these plebiscites play a role. They establish a claim to legitimacy and they structure all ensuing debate. They are also an indication of what the regime intends to do. With the weight of many millions of votes behind it, the regime can push ahead, chastise its opposition and execute its policies.

The next part of this work examines in detail the policies that the regime chose to pursue.

7 THE POLICY OF ECONOMIC LIBERALIZATION

The Approach to the Analysis

The *October Working Paper* has stipulated a new economic policy symbolized in the equation: Arab capital + Western technology + abundant Egyptian resources = development and progress. This new policy, which carried the liberalization of the economy farther than anything since the movement into etatist economics in the late 1950s, became known as *al-infitah al-iqtisadi* (literally, the economic opening). It proved to be one of the most hotly debated and explosive issues of the entire post-1967 period.

In order to describe and assess the policy of economic liberalization, I define two basic policy positions – the one presented by the government and the other presented by the parliamentary left. These two positions represent the fully developed alternatives that faced the regime at this moment. At points I describe the direction in which the more extreme right or left would have pushed the policy. At all points, I catalogue the various pros and cons of the policy (see Table 7.1).

This approach is taken for a number of reasons. First, the left/right division has been shown to be the fundamental political dividing line in Egypt. It adequately and correctly describes the conflict in the political economy. Second, utilizing the publicly-stated hopes and fears of these two sets of recognized political actors makes it abundantly clear that choices were actually being made. Hansen had suggested that, in the early days, the message about the dire implications of the Arab socialist economic policy might not have got through to the leadership. There can be no doubt about whether the message was available to the decision-makers a decade later as they created the policy of economic liberalization. All of the debate was part of the public record for any and all to see and analyse. Third, juxtaposing two very different views of the policy also serves to establish criteria by which to judge the policy. In essence, each side made a set of predictions about how the policy would operate and what effect it would have. Comparing the results of the policy to the predictions gives us an understanding of what happened and why.

For purposes of the discussion, the policy is divided into two parts – basic principles and specific economic activities. The former are derived from the debate over the Law for Arab and Foreign Investment.[1] The

Table 7.1: The Costs and Benefits of Government Policy Choices in the Economic Liberalization

Policy area and choice	Benefits (Government claims for the policy)		Costs (Leftist critique of the policy)	
	Domestic	Foreign	Domestic	Foreign
Technology				
Permit less than the most advanced technology	More investment stimulated; More employment created	High profits based on wage differential; Egypt's labour and infrastructure are suited to less than advanced technology projects	Failure of long term industrialization; Dumping of used and dated equipment on the local market	
Extend incentives to Egyptians	Stimulates more investment; repatriates Egyptian capital from abroad		Undermines social equity of state capitalist regime; loss of state revenues	Egyptians will flood the market, blocking out foreign projects
Finance				
Open local banking	Spillovers from a financial centre	Integrated banking attracts capital	Foreign banks tax local infrastructure and squeeze out local institutions	
Revived stock market; eased repatriation of profits; freed currency	Stimulates economic activity	Attracts capital	Loss of control over capital and currency	
Tax incentives; reduced tax burden; exemptions extended to Egyptians	Stimulates economic activity; induces local investment; maintains equity between Egyptians and foreigners	High profits	Loss of state revenue; loss of social equity	
Labour				
Free the movement of labour	Rationalize the distribution of labour; Repatriation of wages earned abroad	Appropriate labour attracted to projects will increase productivity	Internal migration of labour to foreign projects saps the public sector; External migration creates a shortage of skilled labour; state loses resources invested in training; repatriated wages will not lead to productive investment	

Policy				
Free wages	Restore incentives	Foreigners will pay going rate	Undermines social equity; permits foreigners to bid labour from the public sector	Foreigners may squeeze out domestic
Industrial activity and the public sector				
Broad opening to foreign and private activity	Stimulates economic activity	Stimulates economic activity	Inadequate planning and control	
Sale of public sector	Improved capitalization	Attracts foreign expertise for joint ventures	Loss of control over capital	
Decentralization of the public sector	Rationalizes production; increases flexibility		Loss of resources and expertise; inability to plan and coordinate	
Agrarian policy				
Entry of foreigners	Industrialize agriculture; export earnings	Incentive to invest	Squeeze out food production	Foreigners bid up land prices
Freeing the land market	Restoring market balance; encourage private investment		Expulsion of small owners; decline in short-term production; food insufficiency	
Import policy				
Stimulate commerce through incentives and elimination of restrictions on trade	Attract funds; reduce import obstacles	Supporting services provided for industrial projects	Luxury imports will consume resources; state revenues will be reduced; pressure on infrastructure	Foreign industrial projects squeezed out by commercial projects
Construction and housing policy				
Encourage Arabs to invest in luxury housing	Encourage tourism; attract hard currency	Arabs prefer this type of investment	Shortage of resources; shift of resources to foreigners; construction blockages will be an obstacle to industrial projects	Foreigners will monopolize the best land

latter are derived from the series of laws legislated in the two years after the Law for Arab and Foreign Investment was enacted.

Basic Principles of Economic Liberalization
Technology
The fundamental argument offered in favour of liberalization was the need to import technology and attract capital to sustain economic development. Egypt simply could not do it alone:

> [Egypt] must raise the rate of investment of national income to a rate above twenty percent. If we acknowledge that in recent years, in spite of great efforts which we have put forward to mobilize savings, in addition to what we were able to obtain in foreign loans, we were not able to raise the level of investment above eleven or twelve percent; then it becomes incumbent upon us to search for other sources, in addition to our own efforts, to fill the gap.[2]

Moreover, the old approach in attempting to carry out these transfers — government to government arrangements and multilateral agreements — just would not work:

> At the same time, the transfer of technology from one country to another cannot be organized simply by government agreement, nor by international agreement . . . but the only path for technology to enter the country is with its own capital. Therefore, in order for us to march with the times and in order for us to benefit from advanced technology, which, in fact, develops from one day to the next, it is inevitable that we make use of the existing relations between capital and technology by attracting it here in investment projects.[3]

Finally, it was necessary to move quickly to attract Arab capital:

> Some of the countries gain interest on their savings that reaches a million dollars a minute and these countries face a real problem in relation to their economies — they face the problem of how and where to employ the funds. Until now, the existing capital markets in Europe, America and elsewhere were able to attract these funds because of the absence of obstacles, and because there is no control on currency and because there is complete freedom of operations . . . The train can pass us by because capital never waits. If capital

begins to be directed toward other markets, it will be very difficult to divert it from those markets. Thus, we must commence our efforts now.[4]

However, when it came to specifying the types of projects which actually would be permitted to enter the country, the lofty goals were sacrificed. The right argued that Egypt would have difficulty attracting advanced technology projects and that it might not benefit from such projects.

Technical development, as we see it in Europe and America, creates industry dependent on less manpower capacity and increased machine capacity. That is because labor's wages in these countries are very high. Here in Egypt, we have a large surplus of labor and we want to put it to work and that could be less expensive than depending on machines which use less labor.[5]

Thus, the right pushed for a very open approach to liberalization[6] — an approach in which the level of technology, the condition of equipment and the nature of the projects were ignored. It simply wanted to stimulate economic activity, without concern for the nature of that activity.

The left had a rather different perspective. It insisted that all technology imported into Egypt be the most advanced and that all equipment be new. As a matter of principle, it argued that advanced technology was the key to long-term growth.[7] Anything less than the most advanced projects could be provided by domestic resources and was not the type of project that Egypt needed to have foreigners undertake. As a practical matter, the left went on to assert that, if the door were left open to low technology in any form, there would be a flood of projects which would be essentially useless. Moreover, it doubted that the state had the capacity to oversee, manage and weed out these useless projects if the possibility of undertaking this type of activity were left to the discretion of the authorities.

It is interesting to note that the left and right agreed on the types of projects that would come to Egypt if the door was simply thrown open. It was not high technology, but low technology that would be attracted. For the left, these projects made no sense, certainly not if foreigners undertook them. For the right, they made all the sense in the world because they created employment and stimulated economic activity. In effect, the government followed a course that was close to the right — permitting all types of projects and making decisions on a case-by-case basis.[8]

Finance

The question of finance was tied to the issue of technology. Not only was there a logical link between the two, as we have seen, but in order to attract capital, the government believed that it was necessary to provide a number of financial incentives to foreign investors. The government committed itself to opening the financial structure to foreign activities. Banks were invited to Egypt and given the right to engage in a full range of activities, including banking transactions that were wholly internal to Egypt. Tax exemptions were offered and the terms for the repatriation of profits were eased considerably. Incentive rates were established for the conversion of currency and the government committed itself to floating the currency at some future date.

For the right, freedom and security for financial transactions were the key elements to economic liberalization.

> We want Egypt to be a financial market, as London was in the past, especially since there are billions of surplus pounds in the Arab nation.
> We must overcome the closure in which we were and open truly. I guarantee you that if we limit the operation of banks to investment without internal banking transactions, no banks will come to Egypt.[9]

It argued that, in addition to directly attracting projects, there were many externalities, or indirect benefits, that would accrue to Egypt if she became a financial centre.[10] These included the creation of a pool of expertise for other activities to draw on, the development of secondary services for other activities to benefit from, leakage of resources into the domestic economy from the financial transactions, improvement in the credit rating and an added impetus to industry through spillovers and necessary supporting projects for the financial industry. The goal of becoming a financial centre became one of the major aspirations of the liberalization policy.

Of course, the left objected. From its point of view, financial transactions were not the objective of liberalization; advanced technology projects were.

but in regard to the operation of pure bank transactions, I believe that there is great peril to the existing institutions. I do not believe that one of the guarantees of the aims of the liberalization policy is to put an end to the existence of our present institutions.[11]

The left argued that financial activities would become the focal point of the entire policy, since they were high-profit operations that were easy to undertake. They argued that foreign financial institutions would tax the Egyptian infrastructure, rather than enhance it. They were also concerned about the loss of control over capital markets and the loss of state revenues that financial operations coupled with foreign projects would lead to. As each and every concession which was offered to foreigners was extended to Egyptians, the left's fears in this regard were reinforced.

For its part, the government responded to these assertions by insisting that it was impermissible to place Egyptians at a disadvantage vis-à-vis foreigners; that indirect revenues generated by increasing economic activity would offset any direct losses; and that the administrative supervision of the policy would ensure against abuses.[12]

Labour

The third ingredient in the liberalization recipe was the abundance of Egyptian labour. Theoretically, this labour was available at a relatively low wage and therefore would attract foreign investors. However, in order for this abundant labour to be an attraction, it had to be freed from certain constraints — constraints which the Arab Socialist laws of the 1960s had established to protect the labour force.[13] The government proposed to ease the physical movement of labour, both internally and externally, to free the setting of wages and to liberalize the movement of currency and funds from abroad.[14] The argument presented in support of these steps was a classic free-market argument — removing these constraints would reallocate resources in the most efficient manner:

First, I want to make it clear that if we do not hold to the complete freedom of the individual in the shadow of competition, we cannot realize any progress. He who wants to travel, let him travel. Today we are a nation of thirty-seven million people. If we were not concerned with training centers to create skilled labor in the past, today we are concerned and our need for this kind of labor will compel us to train manpower in these specialties. We must not believe that the lack of labor hinders the battle for development. This is not true, freedom and competition create abundance.

The carpenter who goes abroad transfers a hundred pounds a month in hard currency to Egypt, i.e. in excess of a thousand pounds a year in hard currency. We do not achieve such income from the export of the yield of ten feddans of cotton, on which we spend much for fertilizer and seed.[15]

The left responded, arguing that if labour and the wage rate were freed, foreign projects would attract the most productive labour, sapping the public sector and the domestic economy.[16] Permitting skilled labour to migrate abroad, when such labour was in short supply at home and when the state had expended considerable resources in training it, seemed like an expensive way to help some other country industrialize. The left was not convinced that the savings which this labour would repatriate would find their way into productive uses. Moreover, freeing the wage rate would undermine the equity principles that had been established by the Arab Socialist regime.

The government responded to the latter charge by arguing that tax policy, not wage policy, should be the instrument for achieving equity.[17] However, when the government immediately tried to lower taxes, arguing that the extremely progressive income tax was a disincentive to investment and production, the objections on the left were reinforced.[18]

Spheres of Economic Activity

Industrial Activity and the Public Sector

Because most large-scale industrial activity had been taken over by the state in the 1950s and 1960s, it was necessary to make specific decisions about which fields to open up to foreigners and private sector Egyptians and what relationship they would have to state-run enterprises. Existing legal stipulations on these points were subject to many interpretations.[19]

The government took an open approach. It considered just about every field open to foreigners and decided to make decisions on a case-by-case basis.[20] Further, it would permit foreigners to have total ownership of specific projects (except banks) and to own up to 49 per cent of public sector companies.

In recognition of the fact that competition would soon be coming from foreigners and private sector Egyptians and that the public sector was in no condition to meet the challenge, the government also produced another 'reform' of the public sector. In addition to allowing sale of shares up to 49 per cent of the public sector companies, which was deemed necessary to improve their capitalization, the highest level of organization in the entire sector, the *mu'assassat*, was dismantled. The *mu'assassat* were the overarching bodies that ran entire industries and it was argued that their elimination would create greater flexibility:

> In the past the public sector received complete protection so it could stand on its own feet. The time has come to give it freedom to burst forth and face the challenge, for foreign investment companies and private sector companies will be formed and the power of the public sector must be set loose to meet the challenge of competition by giving flexibility and freedom of movement to it.
>
> In 1961 the specific *mu'assassat* appeared and the tie between the state budget and the budgets of the economic units began. The supervision of the ministries over the *mu'assassat* began and the encroachment of the government 'system' in the economic units began.
>
> The development of the public sector can be summarized in two points:
>
> (1) the economic units must have independent budgets appended to the national budget because they are guided by methods that differ in their nature and structure from the administration of the government apparatus.
>
> (2) The hand of the minister must be taken off of the economic units because when the minister creates his ministry, he has a political plan which the People's Assembly and the Cabinet and the various Cabinet Councils work on executing (not an economic plan).[21]

Freeing the public sector meant more than independent budgets, although that was a major step. It meant distributing voting rights according to ownership, permitting the General Assembly of each company to set the wage schedule, control credit, capitalize the company, merge with other units, and so on.[22] There was a fabric of laws and regulations from the socialist period that had to be undone. Much of this reform embodied simply a shuffling of personnel with little change in the real distribution of powers. Much of it was simply an extension of the basic ideas set down in 1968, ideas which had never been implemented. Much of it was defended with the same arguments that had been mobilized in the late 1960s:

> I say in earnest, that if we mean to free our administrative units and if we want a total operation of healthy development using all our experience and technical energy and using all our resources, we must face this subject with a complete understanding and not fear the consequences. In all our talks with the leadership of the public sector, including the heads of the *mu'assassat*, they demand non-intervention in the administration of their units, declaring that they bear the responsibilities and the goals and are accountable for them.[23]

The left was alarmed by this approach. It argued that there was no effective plan to guide foreign economic activity at a moment when such a plan and careful supervision were necessary.[24] Given the increased need for planning, the left felt that the effort to restrict centralized planning in the public sector was particularly ill-considered. It believed that the public sector would be weakened by the reform and could be seriously damaged:

> The *mu'assassat* — especially the *mu'assassat* which direct industrial activity — cannot be called a bureaucratic apparatus in any sense. They are coordinating, oversight, administrative and planning apparatuses containing many of those who have the capabilities of managing the guidance of this important sector of the Egyptian economy . . .
>
> The end of the *mu'assassat* will lead to a scattering of capabilities and technical experts who are in this basic sector, which is the foundation of the Egyptian economy . . . It cannot compensate for these capabilities in any circumstances. Some may go to the private sector companies, some to foreign companies. The loss will be in a sector we call the foundation of the national economy, the public sector.[25]

On the other hand, the right was just as adamant in its support of a thorough liberalization of the economy with the public sector as a particular target of its attack. It insisted on an almost total return to free market principles by restricting the scope of the public sector and demanding the mandatory sale of shares of public sector companies on the stock market. From its point of view, no stipulation that majority ownership remain in the hands of the state was necessary.[26] Indeed, it seemed to hope that the state sector would all but disappear.

Agrarian Policy

The government policy on agrarian investment also embodied a broad approach to liberalization. It invited foreigners to invest in land reclamation as well as vegetable and export crops:

> The operation of reclaiming land is not an operation in which Arabs will invest because they do not have experience in agriculture. However, foreign investment will enter into this area because there are companies specializing in such operations. I envision, here, that the operation will be a vegetable and fruit operation and it will not enter into other fields like cotton or berseem.
>
> Production in this way needs very high technology which means, in turn, we want to raise the level of agricultural production. This leads to the entry of new machines. Thus, we find ourselves in great need of capital and very high technology.[27]

As in all other cases, this invitation was extended to Egyptians in order to avoid placing them at a disadvantage.[28]

In addition to encouraging Egyptians and others to expand their activity in the capital intensive crops, there was also an effort to 'rationalize' the organization of the agrarian sector. This constituted an effort to let market forces have a freer reign. At various times, efforts were made to free the purchase and sale of land, to raise rents, to make it easier to evict individuals in arrears on their rents and to permit individuals contractually to determine the manner of payments of rents (cash or in kind).[29] It was recognized that these were extreme steps. Agrarian reform had been one of the major ideological underpinnings of the Arab Socialist regime and to attack it in too blatant a form could cause considerable resistance.

> All of us know the existing relations between owners and renters, insofar as all owners endeavor to expel the renters by any means possible.
>
> We will have 1.5 million problems because all the owners will transfer rent from cash to crops immediately. We have broken the obstacle of rigidity which has dominated twenty-two years, but it is not reasonable to make large surprise changes because this operation can have dangerous social effects. In deference to an evaluation of the social conditions of our society and the political conditions in

which we live, we can undertake this operation in stages and not force it in this way.[30]

The left contested every effort to make these changes in the agrarian sector. The industrialization of agriculture around export crops was defined as a fundamentally anti-populist policy. From the point of view of the left, inviting foreigners to participate in these activities and encouraging Egyptians to move in this direction had carried the policy far afield and could be disastrous:

> In principle, I am against this completely and against renting barren land for reclamation as well. Perhaps I can agree to the renting of desert land for reclamation, but as for barren land I am against it because we have the ability to reclaim it. As for what my colleague Ahmed Fu'ad said in regard to industrializing and reclaiming large areas and depending on capital crops, I disagree with him. I want to make clear that the number of people who have died in countries which have settled on a path such as this and limited food crops, is double all those who died in wars since the beginning of time. I am against this because we must change the crops so that people eat and do not die.[31]

Efforts to restore a market in the sale or rental of land were seen as a direct opening to abuse.[32] Because land prices had sky-rocketed and the influx of foreigners into the market would push them even higher, only the wealthiest would benefit from this freeing of market forces. Great pressures would be brought on small landholders, directly through rising rents and indirectly through increasing inflation. In consequence, 'The left saw the whole project as "an attempt to change radically the social relations which were established in the Egyptian countryside since the issuance of their design in law 178/1952." '[33]

Import Policy

The government's willingness to allow the economic liberalization to move quite far from the original conception of encouraging the importation of advanced technology was nowhere better demonstrated than in the area of import policy. Enough openings had been created by the law on foreign investment and other policies that one could expect an explosion of commercial activity.[34] There was a strong sentiment on the right that this was the proper direction in which to move:

If we truly want to realize liberalization in our country and to return Egypt as it was to a center of trade in the whole Middle East — where the merchants of Lebanon and Syria and Jordan and all of the Arab East and Arab West had recourse to it because it had a stock market and its laws allowed all individuals to import and export everything and where companies were carrying out import/export operations by telephone or telex — then we cannot give the Minister of Commerce the right to close the market of countries, or open them, according to his understanding or ideas.

The intervention of the government in the operation of public and private companies, all this must be terminated.

If we want — as my colleagues say — a true liberalization, I believe that returning a free operation to the public and private sector will lead to competition between them which will lead to an improvement in our entire society.[35]

Thus, to the aspiration that Egypt become a financial centre the right added the aspiration that it become a commercial centre.

The left could marshal strong arguments against the freeing of imports and the equality of the public and private sectors in this area. The very same historical experience to which the right pointed as justification for the policy, the left considered evidence against it because 'there was an experiment before 1961 including an importation which was open to the private sector and in all cases, it wasn't in the national interest'.[36] Furthermore, from a practical point of view, the public sector would be seriously hurt by this approach. Above all, the intention of the liberalization policy to stimulate production would go completely astray.

We are in the shadow of socialism. We cannot return the matter to the private sector or individuals to import perfumes or luxury clothes, or spare parts or high priced products which some people benefit from. The meaning of liberalization is not the importation of anything, but its meaning is to import capital which will increase production for the interest of the people.

This law will permit a specific class of people to become wealthy, where it was possible for the public sector to gain from it. We do not want merchants, we want modern technology; we want productive profits to increase production and decrease prices; we want projects to increase currency, but we do not want merchants.[37]

Taken together, these statements present a counter-proposal. There was no doubt about the potential for a roaring, high-profit business in the importation of high-priced consumer goods. That was not the object of liberalization. If there was going to be such a trade, it should be restricted to the public sector where the revenues would be put to good public use. There was no danger of inefficiency or blockages in this trade, since it was not productive anyway. If delays occurred in this area, they truly damaged no one. Where there were blockages or potential blockages to production activities due to problems with the importation of goods, that was where the private sector could be freed.

Housing and Construction

A second area in which the government's approach moved far beyond the importation of advanced technology was in housing and construction policy. The foreign investment law invited Arabs to build luxury housing. In principle, the invitation was extended to Egyptians as well, to avoid placing them at a disadvantage. In order to attract investment into these areas, concessions had to be made. Rent control laws had to be lifted, the general exemptions for foreign investment had to be extended and other concessions on the repatriation of profits had to be made.

The argument put forward in support of these concessions was that, given the prevailing rate of profit in the Egyptian housing sector, it would be extremely difficult to attract foreign investment:

> If we examine the rate of profit which the savings of free currency achieves, we find that it reaches 13.5% . . . The limitation of rents is set on a yield of not more than 8% . . . If we strike this article we ensure the failure to attract investment to the country. Therefore, in principle, we will have to give up the idea of Arab investment.[38]

Additional arguments in support of this approach to construction included the insistence that market forces were already operating and they should be allowed to work properly; the belief that these projects would attract foreign currency; and the assertion that the responsibility for middle income and mass housing lay with the government, not the private sector.[39]

Of course, the left objected. It argued that this policy would wreak havoc on the domestic market and was a complete perversion of the liberalization goals.[40] To begin with, the use of land for construction and housing was in competition with the use of land for agriculture, particularly around cities. Egypt was consuming its most precious resource and inviting foreigners into luxury construction would only put greater pressure on that resource. Land prices had already begun to show dramatic increases. It was reasonable to assume that only Arabs and wealthy Egyptians could afford this land. One could easily envision a shift in the structure of ownership and the pattern of land use. What was true for land was true for all of the inputs in the construction sector:

> Arab investment in above middle housing and urban development will affect the wages of construction workers. It will absorb building materials, from which we already suffer a lack, in those projects at the expense of regular, or economic and popular housing projects. In addition to that, the land found in excellent areas will be owned by Arab investors.[41]

As these pressures built up on the construction sector, the state would find it more and more difficult to produce housing for the mass of the population.

Finally, there was a broader implication in this debate. The intense pressure in the construction market was certain to create a blockage for productive projects. In spite of assurances that luxury housing required imported materials, Arab and Egyptian investors were likely to scour the local market first, to keep costs down, before importing materials. Productive projects would then be placed in competition with housing projects. Even if much imported material was used, one had to consider the physical limitations of Egypt's port facilities as a blockage to the importation of other production goods.

In summary, it can be said that the government opted for a broad liberalization. It was not as broad as the right wanted, but it was much broader than the left thought was necessary or useful. Foreigners and Egyptians were to be allowed to import technologies and equipment with considerable freedom. They were to enjoy considerable tax incentives and repatriation rights. They were to have considerable freedom of banking and commercial activity. They would be free to capitalize their projects as they saw fit and to acquire resources to execute them wherever they could be found and at whatever price the market would bear. The goal of stimulating as much economic activity as possible, regardless of its nature, seems to have taken precedence over the goal of attracting foreign, advanced technology.

For the left, the attraction of advanced technology should have been the sole objective. It consistently and repeatedly criticized every aspect of the government's policy, when it strayed from that paramount goal (see Table 7.1 above for a summary of the criticism). The right argued that the stimulation of economic activity was justification enough for a broad liberalization (see Table 7.1 for a summary of the benefits attributed to such a policy).

It is interesting to note that the left and right were in fundamental agreement on the types of activities which would predominate if a broad liberalization were pursued. They agreed that financial and banking activities would be very attractive; commerce and the importation of luxury consumer goods would expand rapidly; Arabs would be attracted to housing, luxury construction and tourism. They disagreed radically about the value of these activities. Indeed, the left-right debate took on the very same pattern as the debate over economic reform in the 1967-71 period. The economists and their technocratic, white-collar supporters were on one side, the workers and those leftists who claimed to speak for them were on the other. Efficiency improvements were claimed as a universal benefit by those on the right. To those on the left, the loss of equity was an unacceptable result of the liberalization policy.

The Failure of Economic Liberalization

Until the end of 1977, economic liberalization was an utter disaster. It produced none of the benefits that the government had projected and almost every one of the negative impacts that the left had predicted. On the side of production and investment, there was a deindustrialization of Egypt — literally, a shrinking of industrial activity as a percentage of economic activity. Arabs rushed into financial activities, tourism and luxury construction. Egyptians shifted their activities into the free zones to escape the socialist laws and into commercial activities to service the expanding international trade. Very little in the way of industrial activity, not to mention advanced technology industries, was even contemplated.

On the side of consumption, there was a rapid expansion covering all commodities — especially consumer goods — in both the public and private sectors. Consumer goods inundated the market. Since the output of goods and services in Egypt was not adequate to meet the increasing demand, the whole operation had to be financed through deficits — first at home, then abroad. The extent of the debt was astounding. By 1975/6, the trade deficit was running at about 20 per cent of the Gross Domestic Product (GDP). The foreign debt had grown to equal or exceed the GDP. Debt service alone came to almost 10 per cent of GDP. Debts and deficits of this size could not be sustained for long.

The economic performance was so abysmal that it shocked even strong supporters of the policy. As *al-Iqtisadi* said in an editorial on 15 November 1976, just two months before the riots of January 1977:

Among the greatest errors we have committed is to reconcile our understanding of the intention of economic liberalization with our gleaming picture of what is called 'the Beirut contract.' The comparison was always between Lebanon the opened and Egypt the closed; between the squares of Beirut full of everything that one could desire in food, drink and the latest rage from the western fashion houses, and the squares of Egypt, empty except for base local goods . . .

The squares of Cairo were transformed into an exhibition of imported goods. But, what we had forgotten in the rush to transform from closure to an opening on the Lebanese path of opening, which we pursued in the most ignorant blindness, is that this type of opening was the primary reason for its destruction and wars. It contains within it an increasing poverty for the poor and an increasing wealth for the rich.

The consumption liberalization, and what it entails in the way of an explosive inflation, has changed the structure of Egyptian society dangerously. After being divided into a poor class, a large middle class and a rich class, it has now become composed of a destitute class and a rich class, while the middle class has been transformed into a treadmill, straining on the path to maintain a minimum standard of living.

The danger of the above mentioned development is that it leads to an increase of class hatred and a convulsion of the social system in Egypt.[42]

The remainder of this chapter examines some of the details of this economic disaster and its impact on the polity.

Investment and Production

It is abundantly clear that the central focus of economic activity conducted under the umbrella of the liberalization policy was anything but industrial activity. Table 7.2 summarizes the distribution of foreign investment approved by the authority which had been set up to oversee the execution of the foreign investment law. In both inland and free-zone investment, about 23 per cent of the total was in housing,

Table 7.2: Investment in Egypt under the Law for Arab and Foreign Investment

Type of economic activity	Location and amount (000,000 LE)		Total investment (000,000 LE)	%
	Inland[a]	Free Zone[b]		
Housing, tourism and building materials	176	80	256	23
Finance projects	84	1	85	7
Transport and storage	9	71	84	7
Petroleum	0	540	540	48
Textiles	13	106	119	10
Engineering and metals	15	138	153	13
Chemicals	25	10	35	3
Mining	1	0	1	0
Food and animal	9	5	14	1
Services/Contractors	2	45	47	4
Total	284	850	1,134	100

Sources: a. as of December 1976 reported in the National Bank of Egypt, *Economic Bulletin*, 2: 1977; b. as of November 1976 reported in *al-Iqtisadi*, 1 January 1977.

tourism and construction. Financial undertakings accounted for another 7 per cent of the total. Transportation and storage projects which were aimed primarily at servicing international trade accounted for another 7 per cent. Although investment in these activities might provide some additional hard currency, it was certainly not going to provide a real solution to Egypt's economic problems. Even investment in petroleum activities (48 per cent of the total), which would be a big plus in earning foreign currency if it were successful, could at best provide an indirect assistance to development. It would not be a major employer of Egyptian labour. It would not be a major purchaser of Egyptian manufactured goods. It was an enclave with respect to the rest of the Egyptian economy.

Investment in industrial projects that might really affect the economy was paltry. Chemicals, engineering, etc., accounted for 16 per cent of the total. Textiles accounted for 10 per cent of the total. Food production accounted for a mere 1 per cent of the total.

The above figures are for approved investment — i.e. projects which had been proposed and approved by the authority. If we consider investments that were active — i.e. investment projects that were completed or under execution — we find a somewhat different and more ominous picture.[43] To begin with, only one-fifth of the projects were active.[44] Moreover, of those projects which were active, 78 per cent of the capital was tied up in financial activities, tourism, construction and building materials. As had been predicted, the Arabs were particularly drawn to these areas. Arab capital was four times as likely to be in tourism and housing and only one-third as likely to be in industrial projects, as was non-Arab capital.

Egyptians, too, were inclined to pursue activities that were more commercial than industrial. To begin with, they seem to have flooded the free zones with a host of small transportation, storage and commerce projects intended to service the expanding international trade.[45] A list of the companies formed by Egyptians in the first nine months of 1976 gives an indication of this bias (see Table 7.3). Of the 201 companies formed, only 12 per cent were industrial. At least one-fourth and probably more than one half (if one adds the multi-purpose companies and the contractors) of the companies were oriented toward import/export activities and servicing the international sector. To this we should add another quarter of the companies which were involved in internal commerce and services. Of particular note is the absence of food companies. They account for less than one per cent of all companies and only 10 per cent of the industrial companies. Thus, it seems that neither foreigners nor private-sector Egyptians were going to provide a solution to the problem of food production and processing.

If we examine the registry in which these companies are entered, this general pattern is repeated. This registry includes all private 'moral' entities which engage in trade (since industrial companies market output it seems to include most private industrial capital) and all foreign capital. We find that the figures are quite consistent with earlier indications (see Table 7.4). The bias toward commercial activities is very striking. Between May 1974 and August 1976, commercial capital rose from 41 per cent of total Egyptian capital to 57 per cent. Of capital

Table 7.3: Companies Formed in Egypt (1 January-30 September 1976)

Type of company	Number	%
Pure commerce	68	34
Import-export	34	
Internal commerce	30	
Automobile commerce	4	
Multi-purpose		
(Import-export, contracting)	35	17
Contractors	33	16
Tourism and hotel management	14	7
Industry	25	12
Weaving and clothing	9	
Wood and furniture	8	
Plastic and shoes	4	
Food	2	
Industrial metal	2	
Other	26	13
(Hospital management, Real estate,		
Naval operations, transport, drugs)		
Total	201	99

Source: *Al-Jumhurriyya*, 4 November 1976.

Table 7.4: The Distribution of Capital Registered in Egypt, 1974-6

| Type of capital | Total registered | | | | Increment between | |
| | May 1974 | | August 1976 | | May 1974-August 1976 | |
	000,000 LE	%	000,000 LE	%	000,000 LE	%
Egyptian						
Commercial	227	41	737	57	513	64
Industrial	329	59	615	45	286	36
Foreign						
Commercial	NA		135	50	NA	
Industrial	NA		135	50	NA	

Source: *Gyareeda Isma' al-Tigariyya*, various issues.

added in that 2.5 year period, which includes not only the creation of new companies but the expansion of old companies, 64 per cent was commercial. This fits very closely with the distribution of the companies formed in the first nine months of 1976.

Foreign capital entered in this registry exhibits a similar pattern. First, the amount of capital entered in the registry under law 43/1974 is less than 20 per cent of the amount approved by the Authority. This reflects slow implementation. Half the capital registered was commercial and half was industrial. This means that there was a much higher rate of registration (hence implementation) for commercial projects, something that was clearly manifest in the earlier analysis.

Further evidence of this tendency can be found in the figures on total fixed investment (see Table 7.5). The relative share of investment directed toward industrial and production activities (excluding petroleum) declined rapidly between 1973 and 1975. From 47 per cent of the total invested in 1973 they declined to 35.2 per cent in 1975. The share of distribution and services rose sharply, from 48.2 per cent to 55.8 per cent in 1975. Investment in petroleum activities also rose dramatically.

Several other specific areas of economic activity are also noteworthy. Investment in the private industrial sector expanded much more rapidly than in the public sector and rose from 28.5 per cent of the total in 1973 to 31.3 per cent in 1975. The textile industry showed a marked relative decline in the public sector. After having represented 15 per cent of the total investment in the 1971-4 period, it fell to 4.4 per cent in 1975. Even though private investment in textiles doubled, it did not equal the drop in the public sector. Part of this may be accounted for by the fact that much private investment in textiles seems to have shifted to free zones. We observe an opposite specialization in the food sector. In the public sector investment in food production projects accounted for 8 per cent of the public sector in 1973 and jumped up to 22 per cent in 1975. Thus, the public sector seems to have been trying to fill the gap that private-sector investment had left in the food industries.

The sources of information are quite diverse and occasionally entail discrepancies in the estimate of the magnitude of investments. However, on the whole, they are quite consistent, especially in depicting the general nature of the investment that the liberalization policy had stimulated. Evidence on actual production, although similarly diverse, points in the same direction. In fact, production seems to have followed investment fairly closely, which is to be expected.

Overall, there seems to have been a serious stagnation in output. Major industrial products such as textiles recorded only small increases. Major crops, such as cotton, beans, berseem, and millet — the basic output of the peasantry — registered no increases or declines in production and very small, if any, increases in productivity.[46] Moreover, there was a failure of export performance. As a percentage of Gross Domestic

Table 7.5: (a) Fixed Investment (per cent)

Sector	1971/2	1972	1973	1974	1975
Production sectors	59.2	59.0	53.5	50.7	45.0
Industry	33.5	31.6	27.2	29.5	22.2
Petroleum	6.4	6.1	6.1	6.4	9.8
Distribution	23.3	19.4	27.3	30.7	32.3
Services	18.6	22.8	20.9	19.3	23.5
Total: (000,000 LE)	365	405.3	462.4	642.7	1,193.9

(b) Industrial Investment

	Public (000,000 LE)				Private (000,000 LE)		
	1971/2	1973	1974	1975	1973	1974	1975
Engineering & mineral	45.3	40.9	71.5	113.9	10.2	10.9	21.0
Chemical	10.4	8.5	17	47.21	4.5	2.3	17.5
Food	6.3	5.4	11.8	41.74	2.0	1.1	10.2
Textiles	7.7	12.0	21.5	9.41	1.6	5.1	12.2
Building material	5.4	3.0	5.0	1.40			
Small projects					1.6	1.4	6.1
Total	75.1	69.8	126.8	213.5	19.9	20.8	67
Per cent							
Engineering & mineral	60.3	58.6	56.4	53.3	51.3	52.4	31.3
Chemical	13.8	12.2	13.4	22.1	22.6	11.1	26.1
Food	8.4	7.7	9.3	19.5	10.1	5.3	15.2
Textiles	10.3	17.2	17.0	4.4	8.1	24.5	18.2
Building material	7.2	4.2	3.9	0.7	8.1	6.7	9.1

Source: Central Bank of Egypt, *Annual Report*, 1977; Federation of Egyptian Industries, *Yearbook*, various issues.

Product, exports rose from 12.9 per cent in 1970 to 16.9 per cent in 1974, then fell back to 11.5 per cent in 1976.[47] Furthermore, little progress was made in shifting into manufactured exports. They were constant as a percentage of the total. Petroleum exports did register large increases. One can say that Egypt did diversify a bit — from a mono-crop (cotton) export economy it moved towards being a diversified primary product exporter (cotton, fruits, vegetables, petroleum). This was an improvement to be sure, but not a particularly strong one.

From the point of view of the distribution of economic activity, expansion occurred where investment had been greatest (see Table 7.6). Six sectors increased their share of total output — petroleum, construction, electricity, trade and finance, transportation, communication and storage. Further, the shift in industrial production between the public and private sector also continued. At the aggregate level, private-sector production increased from 26.1 per cent of the total in 1974 to 28 per cent in 1975. Similarly, the private sector continued to increase its share of manufactured exports. In the decade after the 1967 war they had grown from almost nil to one-quarter of the total, a figure that is consistent with the sector's share of total output. In the agrarian sector, changes which had begun immediately after the 1967 war continued. Capital crops continued to increase their relative share of total agrarian income and fruits and vegetables continued their upward trend as export crops.[48]

Consumption and Imports

Even if there had been significant real increases in output, they would have paled against the much more rapid rate of expanding consumption. As the *Annual Review of the Middle East* published by *The Economist* described the situation in 1974-5:

> Savings had probably been negative in 1974-5 and with the taste for consumer goods in a traditional cash society there was little that banks could do with raised incentives for savings. Those with cash argued that they could afford a little self-indulgence. Demand inflation increased at the middle class level. Fixed wage earners demanded and received salary increments. Money supply was increased quietly and production was left behind.[49]

Private consumption as a percentage of Gross Domestic Product

Table 7.6: The Structure of Gross Domestic Income (at current factors)

Activity	1973 Value (000,000 LE)	1973 %	1974 Value (000,000 LE)	1974 %	1975 Value (000,000 LE)	1975 %	Rate of change 1973-5 %
Petroleum	34.3	1.1	93	2.5	120.7	2.7	252
Construction	107.5	3.3	134.9	3.6	230	5.2	114
Electricity	44.8	1.4	48	1.3	71.9	1.6	60
Trade & finance	311.4	9.7	405	10.8	478	10.9	40
Transport	158.6	4.9	167.4	4.5	221.4	5.0	33
Utilities	13.8	0.4	16.2	.4	19	.4	33
Industry	600.7	18.7	687.5	18.3	798.8	18.2	32
Agriculture	1,062.4	33	1,280.0	34.1	1,406.9	32.0	22
Services	759.4	23.6	791.9	21.1	925.0	21.0	5
Housing	124	3.9	127.1	3.4	130	3.0	37
Total	3,216.9		3,751.0		4,401.7		

Source: Central Bank, *Annual Report*, August 1976.

increased rapidly in the wake of the liberalization policy.[50] Between
1973 and 1975 it grew from 63.3 per cent of GDP to 74.8 per cent.
The rate of increase is extremely rapid, 41 per cent in two years. At
the same time, public consumption maintained its relentless growth,
albeit not as rapidly as private consumption.

With production increasing only modestly and consumption expanding rapidly, the bulk of the increase in consumption had to be from
imports (see Table 7.7). Between 1973 and 1975 imports grew almost
four-fold. They rose from about 10 per cent of Gross Domestic Product to over 30 per cent. The latter figure is certainly remarkable. Food
led the way, but all other categories rose sharply as well. Specific
figures vary according to the manner of classification, but it is safe to
say that the rising cost of food was one primary cause of the increase.
When the price of wheat moderated in 1976, food imports declined.
Still, total imports did not drop as much as food imports. Furthermore,
food imports did not drop as much as was possible. Having been placed
in a very vulnerable situation in terms of food, Egypt seems to have
paid the highest price in all instances. That is, having been caught unprepared at the outset, Egypt paid the highest price as prices rose.
Later, in an effort to insulate itself against further price increases, it
made commitments when prices were high, thus it was unable to take
advantage when prices fell.

It is remarkable that the importation of consumer goods, durables in
particular, could keep pace with the precipitous rise in food imports
and the importation of capital goods, even though this had been predicted by the left. Demand was so insatiable that it startled even the
most conservative supporters of the regime. The absolute increase in
the importation of non-food consumer goods (370 million LE) for
1975 and 1976 was larger than the absolute increase in the importation of capital goods. Consumer durables led the way. They increased
six-fold, moving from 0.3 per cent of GDP to 1.3 per cent. More cars,
televisions and refrigerators were imported into Egypt in 1974/5 than
in the previous four years.[51] Commerce had truly become the focal
point of liberalization.

A major debate immediately arose over how this rate of importation of consumer goods had been achieved. Some critics pointed to the
policy of importation without the transfer of currency (own-exchange
imports). *Al-Iqtisadi* produced figures on own-exchange imports,
attributed to a responsible source in the Ministry of Trade, that showed
food and consumer goods equalling almost 30 per cent of the total.[52]
Other categories of goods which were probably primarily for consump-

Table 7.7: Total Imports, 1970-6 (000,000 LE)

	1970	1971	1972	1973	1974	1975	1976
National Bank							
Grain	30.5	70.7	51.8	68.2	288.6	286.6	220.8
Other food	42.1	40.2	50.8	35.8	109.1	247.4	184.2
Food subtotal	72.6	110.9	102.6	104.0	397.7	534.3	405.0
Durables	7.3	11.8	6	9.1	33.2	57.7	N/A
Other	25.1	24.1	27.0	26.6	47.2	69.1	N/A
Other consumer subtotal	32.4	35.9	33.0	35.7	80.4	126.8	158.3
Raw material and capital goods	237	253	254.9	221.5	442.0	877.6	926.6
Total	342	399.8	390.5	361.2	920.1	1,539.3	1,489.9
Federation of Egyptian Industries							
Fuel	28.2	28.0	21.1	7	23.5	104.2	54.6
Raw material	45.8	79.4	66.6	80.6	294.5	289.5	240.9
Intermediate	128.6	150.0	169.5	131.8	315.8	618.7	446.8
Investment goods	79.9	81.7	77.8	79.2	124.0	260.2	404.8
Consumer goods	59.5	60.4	55.8	62.5	161.8	266.7	342.8
Total	342	399.5	390.8	361.1	920.1	1,539.3	1,489.9
GDP at factor cost (Central Bank)				3,217	3,664	4,403	5,189[a]

a. Projected.

tion (health and beauty items, means of transport) rather than production accounted for another 30 per cent.

An institution which overlapped and interacted with the own-exchange imports policy was the parallel currency market. Funds in this market were constituted by receipts from tourism, savings of Egyptians abroad, non-traditional exports and earnings from traditional exports in excess of 50 per cent above target levels.[53] Thus, the parallel market embodied two major sources of foreign currency associated with the liberalization policy, tourist receipts and repatriations.

The parallel market did become a major factor in financing imports. In 1976, almost 400 million LE were financed through the market. This is about 20 per cent of total imports. Parallel market transactions seem to have been devoted to the importation of consumer goods in about the same proportion as own-exchange imports. Roughly 40 per cent of the goods were directed towards consumption rather than production.

Between own-exchange imports and parallel market transactions, both of which were private sector in nature, we can account for about 30 per cent of the total imports. We can also account for about two-thirds of the imports of consumer goods, including all non-grain items. It seems certain that they played a major part in the consumption liberalization which *al-Iqtisadi* had lamented. The policy of freeing trade certainly had the effect that the right had expected and the left had feared.

Inflation, Finance, Foreign Debt and the Fiscal Crisis of the State

Lagging production and expanding consumption set the conditions for a roaring inflation and a massive deficit. Official figures on inflation, which run between 5 per cent and 10 per cent per year, are far too low. By 1977, even the National Bank had run out of patience with the official figures:

> Thus, the Consumer Price Index showed a rise in respect to rural areas of 12.2 percent and in the case of urban areas of 10.7 percent. Large increases were recorded in dairy products (47.7 percent), fruits (27.2 percent) and furniture durables (49.5 percent). In urban areas the increases are attributable to the rise in most items covered by the index, particularly meat, fish and eggs (22 percent).
>
> It should be noted in this respect that the above figures do not

reflect true price trends, as prices for goods and services are fixed by the authorities and thus differ widely from those prevailing in domestic markets.[54]

The Economist estimated a rate of inflation somewhere between 20 per cent and 35 per cent.[55] Radwan gives a figure of 20 per cent for rural cost of living increases in 1974.[56] *Al-Iqtisadi* gives a set of figures for twenty food items that averaged almost 40 per cent between June 1973 and June 1974 alone.[57] It is interesting to note the items for which the price increases were greatest. Food items and furniture reflect two of the most basic concerns that the left had expressed. On the one hand, no one was shouldering the responsibility to maintain food production. On the other hand, the tourism/construction business was putting a tremendous strain on local resources.

The expansion of money supply and credit can shed some light on the rate of inflation — both its magnitude and its causes. Total money supply grew 21 per cent in 1974/5 and 25.3 per cent in 1975/6. These are probably good estimates of the rate of inflation. The growth was concentrated in current money, led by private-sector current deposits and quasi-money (cheques, etc.). It is also quite clear from the figures on money supply that there had been a failure to stimulate savings. Gross domestic savings as a percentage of GDP seem to have declined from 4.7 per cent in 1970 to 0.5 per cent in 1974 and then risen to only 4 per cent in 1976. Most alarming in the money supply picture was the growth of government borrowing. In 1974 government borrowing increased 55 per cent. In 1975 it more than tripled. The figure achieved in that year was almost one-third of total Gross Domestic Product. This type of expansionary finance, essentially operating to sustain consumption, was unprecedented and, as the Central Bank noted, extremely dangerous.

> The continued dependence of the Public Treasury on the banking system as an alternative to *real* resources sufficient to meet the budgetary requirements together with the increasing rate of deficit financing, will result in augmenting inflationary pressures year after year which might lead to far reaching effects.[58]

The Central Bank was being moderate in its assessment, as was *The Economist*, as quoted earlier. This was not a quiet expansion of money supply and credit, it was an explosion. It could not be long sustained. The conditions for deficit and inflation became the elements of a crush-

ing fiscal crisis of the state. Consumption was expanding rapidly; production, investment, savings and exports lagged. Inflation was rampant
outside of Egypt, demand was strong within. The government was
affected by all of these pressures and seemed to have little power to
deal with any of them. It could not simply pass the higher external
prices on, which would have reduced demand by increasing inflation.
The social and political consequences of letting the prices of basic
consumption commodities rise were very high indeed. Further, having
liberalized, the administrative means for repressing demands and controlling goods had been given up. In addition, the state had difficulty
raising its revenues. There were a number of reasons for this. (1) It had
given concessions on customs. (2) It was retrenching on progressive
taxation to create greater incentives. (3) Much of its revenues were tied
up in price differentials of one form or another on state-produced
goods, which it could not raise without fueling inflation. The only
recourse was to deficit financing at home and borrowing abroad.

On the current account a large part of the deficit was immediately
translated into external deficit through the balance of payments deficit
for grain, food, and other inputs. On the capital account, the debt also
became foreign at the level of government to government loans.

To overcome these problems, measures were taken during the year,
at the Arab level, by the creation, in April, of the Gulf Organization
for Development in Egypt comprising Saudi Arabia, Kuwait, Qatar,
and the United Arab Emirates. The object of this organization is to
assist the economy and bolster the Development Plan by contributing towards the financing of the balance of payments deficit
whether separately or in conjunction with other Arab and international financial institutions; extending long and medium term
financing to development projects; establishing or participating in
creation of industrial, agricultural and real estate corporations.
At the international level, a Consultative Aid Group was set up,
in mid-September, under the aegis of the International Bank for
Reconstruction and Development, comprising fifteen countries
and international organizations. This group's task is to work out a
program for the provision of the necessary capital funds, estimated
at about $3 billion per year up to 1980, required for economic
program development and the adjustment of the balance of payments deficit.[59]

The dates of these emergency international and multi-national measures to shore up Egypt's foreign debt position are worthy of note. By the middle of 1976, just two years after the beginning of the push for liber- alization, the external debt had become debilitating. If we examine the balance of payments accounts we can appreciate the need for emerg- ency measures (see Table 7.8). I have included figures at the top of the table figures for Gross Domestic Product and the difference between utilizations and GDP, which the National Bank calls 'physical deficit'. The obvious point is that the physical deficit in 1975 and 1976 was huge, 28 per cent and 21 per cent of GDP, respectively. The bulk of this is in the balance of trade deficit, which was 22 per cent of GDP in 1975 and 17 per cent in 1976. This balance on current account was somewhat less: 22 per cent of GDP in 1975 and only 8 per cent in 1976. The fact that the current account imbalance was reduced in 1976 reflects a transformation in the structure of receipts. Invisibles, which were 27.2 per cent of total receipts in 1972 and 31.9 per cent in 1974, rose to 41.4 per cent in 1975 and 56.1 per cent in 1976. A dependence on invisibles to close the trade gap is a difficult path for nations in strong economic positions. For Egypt it was extremely 'weak'.

Even these figures do not fully reflect the magnitude of the prob- lem. First, there was an asymmetry in payments and receipts. Much of the exports were made to the Eastern-bloc countries; much of the imports were from Western-bloc countries. Second, and partly as a result of this, Egypt was heavily in deficit in a short-term money market, particularly suppliers' credits. As a result, direct long-term investment from abroad was very small, estimated by the IMF, which does not consider short-term capital as investment, to be less than 10 per cent of total capital investment in 1975-6. Thus, Egypt had never broken the pattern of reliance on government-to-government loans and a significant part of these loans were the worst type, short-term credits.

A third point that must be kept in mind in assessing the debt is that none of these figures properly reflects the magnitude of Egypt's mili- tary debt. It alone may have been in the order of two-thirds of the non- military debt. This debt may have been consuming the apparent trade surplus with the Eastern bloc, which was the primary supplier of weapons.

If we examine the nature of non-military loans we find another weakness (see Table 7.9). Given the deficit position, a significant part of the loans is general finance, rather than finance tied to projects. The share of non-project loans increased from 28 per cent in 1974 to 37 per cent in 1975/6. There was also a shift of borrowing toward the West, which parallels the increasing trade deficit to the West. These figures also shed some light on the size of the foreign debt, which

Table 7.8: Balance of Payments (000,000 LE)

	1972	1973	1974	1975	1976
Gross Domestic Product	3,417	3,692	3,956	4,403	5,189
Physical deficit	192	169	460	1,247	1,080
Balance of trade	−32	+83.1	−326.7	−990.7	−899.4
Exports	358.8	448.2	593.3	598.6	595.6
Imports	390.3	361.2	920	1,539.3	1,489.9
Other Merchandise Transactions	−173.5	−309.1	−272.2	−87.6	+47.8
Net Merchandise Transactions	−205.5	−226	−598.9	−1,078.3	−851.6
Invisibles (Receipts)	134.1	166.4	277.6	422.6	762.3
Insurance and shipping	5.7	6.0	8.1	23	37.8
Suez Canal revenue	—	—	—	33.2	121.8
Interest, dividends and other	46.3	47.5	107.9	176.9	323.8
Travel and maintenance	82.1	112.9	161.6	189.4	278.8
Invisibles (Payments)	131.1	163.7	211.4	312.8	336.9
Commercial	13.9	20	36.1	66.2	45.1
Insurance and shipping	8.9	8	12.8	37.1	34.3
Interest and dividends	30.4	50.5	61.1	74.5	104.7
Travel and maintenance	18.5	24	41.1	41.2	45.5
Government	27.3	22.7	30.3	40.4	41.0
Net invisibles	+3	+2.7	+66.2	+109.8	+425.4
Net Current Account	−202.5	−223.3	−502.7	−968.5	−462.2
Arab support (transfers)	128.2	253.7	405.2	421.3	263.1
Net capital transactions	66.2	85.7	157.7	695.3	255.2
SDRs	11.0	8.7	9.4	—	—
Net balance of payments	+1.3	+716.1	+30.2	+148.0	+92.1

Source: National Bank of Egypt, *Economic Review*, various issues.

must be estimated with care. Estimates of the non-military debt at the end of 1974 are about 2,000 million LE, with a debt service of about 170 million LE.[60] World Bank figures for the end of 1975 are about 3,675 million LE.[61] We find that in the thirty-three-month period from the end of the October War until June 1976, Egypt received 4,000

Table 7.9: Loans to Egypt ($000,000)

| | October-January[a] | | January-June[b] | |
| | 1973 | 1975 Non-Project | 1975 | 1976 Non-Project |
	Project	Project	Project	Project
Saudi Arabia	661	475	350	—
Kuwait	815	33	250	—
Iran	480	200	650	400
USA	170	157	250	50
United Arab Emirates	240	18	—	—
Japan	190	50	215	205
West Germany	105	100	35	166
Intl. Bank	120	70	222	40
USSR	160	—	—	—
Qatar	93	10	—	—
Rumania	100	—	—	175
France	43	53	70	100
IMF	—	40	25	100
UN	7	9	—	—
Denmark	—	9	—	13
Holland	—	6	90	26
EEC	—	—	349	131
Other European	—	—	200	99
Gulf Org.	—	—	—	250
Arab Bank for Development	—	—	240	—
Hungary	—	—	25	—
Total	3,210	1,230	2,971	1,758

Sources: a. *al-Iqtisadi*, 1 October 1975; b. press releases.

million LE in loans. The government offered a figure to the People's Assembly of 4,260 million LE for the debt at the end of 1976.[62] The figures seem consistent and they indicate a precipitous rise — a doubling of the debt in two years. At the end of 1976, the debt stood at 90 per cent of GDP, while debt service may have been in the order of 6 per cent of GDP and 50 per cent of exports. This does not seem to include military debt. This may have been in the order of 2,000 million LE, with a debt service equal to another 2 to 3 per cent of GDP and 20 per cent of exports.[63] In sum, Egypt's total foreign debt was probably somewhat larger than GDP. Debt service was probably 10 per cent of GDP and 70 per cent of exports.

To put these figures in perspective, we might recall that Mabro had argued that a balance of trade deficit of 7 per cent of GDP was too much for the economy to bear in the mid-1960s.[64] In the mid-1970s, the trade deficit was three times as large as a percentage of GDP. Debt service alone was at least that large. Economic liberalization had dealt a severe blow to the economy.

The Political Impact of Economic Failure

It is possible to construct a number of theoretical explanations for the failure of economic liberalization.[65] From the point of view of the Egyptian reality, the explanation offered, before the fact, by the parliamentary left will suffice and is the most relevant. Indeed, a precise theoretical explanation is of considerably less importance than an understanding of the political reasons that the policy was chosen in the first place and adhered to even in the face of its mounting negative impacts. With the policy failing so miserably and a ready explanation for the poor performance available in the leftist criticism, one must ask, as many Egyptians did, why the government continued to pursue it.

From one point of view, it does seem that the government continued to believe in the efficacy of the policy. It was strongly predisposed to disregarding the leftist argument that there were fundamental flaws in the policy, and it kept making minor changes in an effort to patch up what it saw as superficial and temporary difficulties. However, over time, as the evidence that the policy was having a disastrous impact mounted, one suspects that the government should have begun to ask more basic questions. For political reasons, it was not inclined to do so. This is the second point of view − the political point of view. There were specific interests in society − interests which were major supporters of the regime − that were being served by the policy, even as it produced its negative impacts.

The policy contained what was tantamount to a very regressive incomes policy: (1) a high wage policy that was certain to benefit very limited groups; (2) a direct exemption on the taxation of profits which was in the interest of a small class of entrepreneurs; (3) a general attack on progressive taxation which served the same group; (4) concessions on rent controls which served large, urban landowners; (5) a shift to capital crops while taxation was still based on land rather than income, which served the wealthiest rural farmers; (6) an effort to raise agrarian rents and expel small renters, which served the same wealthy agricultural interests. This incomes policy was a conscious effort to alter the distribution of wealth and welfare in society — a redistribution which served upper-class interests.

There can be no doubt about the effects of that incomes policy. Not only were objections raised in the parliament, resistance to the policy was being generated in the bureaucratic structure, in the moderate press, on the streets and even, occasionally, at the highest level of the government. For example, in January 1975 Prime Minister Abdul Aziz al-Hegazi, author of the plan for administrative reform in 1968, reacted strongly when he was criticized for moving too slowly with economic liberalization:

> The policy of liberalization aims first and before everything for the interests of the mass of our working people. Among its goals is not a condition for a. limited number to realize a fabulous wealth that is not shared in the welfare of the society.[66]

Thus, even moderates began to question the policy. However, their doubts were brushed aside. With this attitude, Hegazi was soon removed from the cabinet. In fact, he served the shortest Prime Ministry in the entire period after the 'Corrective Revolution' of May 1971. On this issue, it seems clear that the regime was willing to take considerable political pressures to satisfy specific interests.

Given the fact that the policy was, at heart, highly political, it was only a matter of time before it became consciously recognized as such. At the outset, the supporters of the regime tried to gloss over the conflict of interests and the basic political implications of the policy. In the long run, they could not obscure the fact that it was a highly charged, class-based issue. For example, in March 1974, *al-Iqtisadi* had argued that 'economic liberalization does not mean a change in the political system'.[67] By early 1975, it had changed its tune.

> The first observation must be that the economic opening, which general policy has called for since the victory of October and which requires for its execution scientific administration at the highest level of ability, needs as well a political opening . . .
> The general policy includes evaluative decisions. It is not necessary that all people are satisfied with them, but what is important is that these decisions reflect a political line| finding sufficient support from the large majority. Without that, the general policy decisions will merely be a series of attempts to embrace the largest number in the longest run possible. The issue will result in fumbling, and

many amendments, and many changes, and public opinion will come back to bad practices — the practice of demanding an increase from the government every day without a goal, gluttony without satisfaction, an increase of desires that will never end.[68]

By June 1976 the recognition of the conflict of interests in the policy had become explicit. The First Secretary of the Arab Socialist Union, newly appointed to oversee the transition to political parties, stated in one of his first interviews:

The policy of economic liberalization will undoubtedly lead to a deepening of the mutual contradictions between the interests of classes and we must acknowledge this, for flowing from the policy of economic liberalization we will find the interests of the worker conflicting with the interests of national capital, the interests of peasants, as well as the interests of professionals. These are the four blocks composing the society and their interests will be in conflict.[69]

Needless to say, the failure of the policy and its politicization became very important inputs into the process of political liberalization. Indeed, the kind of polity that *al-Iqtisadi* called for was, essentially, a liberal polity, one which was based on a majority, rather than an insistence that all interests and demands be represented and responded to. The Arab Socialist ideology had always insisted that politics be based on the common interests, the shared interests of all. By the time economic liberalization had been in place for a year, there could be no doubt about the conflict of interests that it entailed and the need to establish a political system to contain and moderate that conflict. The following chapters examine the efforts to find such a system.

8 POLITICAL LIBERALIZATION: CONTENT AND FORM

Critical Problems in the Liberalization Process

Perspectives on Liberalization

The *October Working Paper* had reaffirmed the regime's commitment to achieving a democratic polity along the lines laid down in the Constitution, the President's speech in September 1971, as well as the *March 30 Program*. In fact, the basic conception of a semi-liberal polity had been made clear as far back as the 'Open Society Debates' of mid-1967. That conception, symbolized in the expression 'a nation of institutions' was a fairly straightforward liberal approach to political activity. Above all else, the expression referred to an end to the capriciousness in the use of power. The holders of power were to be bound by rules and procedures in the exercise of power. There were to be clearly designated spheres of competence and clearly designated mechanisms for making decisions within those spheres. Citizens were to have a stable set of expectations concerning how power was to be used. There were to be prescribed sets of procedures for citizens to defend themselves and call power holders to account. The ultimate accountability of power holders to the citizenry was to be the basis of the 'state of institutions'. That accountability was to be ensured by free and open political discussion, debate and election.

These principles were combined with the somewhat peculiar concept of the polity which the President had articulated and to which he adhered. The concept was peculiar in the sense that the very large role of the President and the heavy emphasis on the authority of the state flew in the face of the principles of liberalization. Making the authority of the state and the role of the President so supreme made it difficult to see how holders of office would be called to account. Under these circumstances, the operation of a liberal or semi-liberal polity proved a difficult task to achieve.

Nevertheless, in the period between 1971 and 1977 there were major efforts to give meaning to the concept of a semi-liberal polity. Those efforts were intense and prolonged. They were also chaotic, lacking in a consistent plan and ultimately unsuccessful. Because the efforts failed, it is easy to dismiss them as a ruse, tolerated by the regime to keep the active political elements in society busy and harmless. To do so is to misunderstand the nature of politics and the politics of liberalization in two fundamental ways.

First, let us take the view of those involved in the political process. Even if we assume that the powerful politicians who oversaw the efforts at reform were less than forthright in their positions – i.e. they had no intention of dramatically altering basic power relations in society – we are forced to conclude that they seriously misunderstood the nature of the political game they were playing. The call to free and open debate is a powerful political appeal. Many people took it very seriously. They poured their energies into it and had their passions aroused by it. When the regime decided it had had enough and tried to cool the political flames, it discovered that the task was not so easy. For more than two years the people had engaged energetically, even desperately, in what they thought was a redefinition of the political structure. They thoroughly debated the political history of the July Revolution. Under the aegis of the debate, a new form of political organization was created. In that form the electorate was mobilized in the most intense election campaign that Egypt had witnessed in a quarter of a century. Politics and political demands were real, even though they were somewhat different than the regime had thought or intended. To fail to study liberalization is to miss the core of political developments in Egypt.

Second, let us take the point of view of the student of political science. The simple fact of the matter is that a successful liberalization is an extremely difficult political process to carry out. In 1971, Robert Dahl, one of the leading scholars of the process of liberalization, listed only thirty polyarchies (roughly meaning democracies or liberal polities) out of one hundred and fifteen politically independent states existing at that time.[1] Of those thirty, only half had emerged through a process of internal evolution. Only one or two had done so in the twentieth century. The fact that Egypt failed need not be an indication of the meaninglessness of the efforts, rather it can be taken as testimony to the difficulty of the process.

Conceptualizing Liberalization

Dahl's analysis can be used both to define liberalization and to measure its difficulty. Here it is important to note that the calculus for measuring events and changes in the polity is decidedly less precise than the calculus for measuring events and changes in the economy. On the surface at least, the basis for the accounting of economic value – money – is neater than any available equivalent for measuring values in the polity — power, influence, and so on. Of course, as the previous chapter shows, simple money accounts may not properly represent the true complexity of the economy. One must look at the types of money (short-term versus long-term, current versus time accounts, real assets versus debt), the uses and flexibility of assets (project versus general finance, invisibles versus tangibles) and relative economic parameters (terms of trade, shares in value added, rates of exchange, and so on), among other things, in order to appreciate the true nature of economic activity. Still, money is a very handy least-common-denominator for discussing these features of the economy.

Political analysis must deal with a complexity of similar, if not greater magnitude than economic analysis, without the benefit of even an oversimplified calculus such as money. One must draw up a balance-sheet, without an arithmetic that is amenable to addition and subtraction. In the following analysis, I will examine the pluses and minuses of political liberalization in the same — even greater — detail that I have examined the nature of economic liberalization. The arithmetic is not as simple, but I believe the analysis is just as rigorous. I begin with some basic definitions.

A liberal regime conducts the basic political activities identified in chapter 2 in specific ways. Liberalization means a change in political activity in the direction of a liberal regime. Dahl defines liberal regimes as societies in which there is an opportunity to formulate and state preferences and to have those expressions weighted equally in the making and execution of decisions (see Table 8.1). He identifies eight conditions or institutional guarantees required for a liberal polity:[2] (1) freedom to form and join political organizations; (2) freedom of expression; (3) right to vote; (4) eligibility for public office; (5) right of political leaders to compete for support; (6) alternative sources of information; (7) free and fair elections and (8) institutions for making government policies depend on votes and other expressions of preference.

Over the period between 1967 and 1977 Egypt did liberalize in terms of several of these conditions. From one party defined as the sole political organization, it moved to several platforms within the party and then to a small number of parties. From a very tightly controlled press, it moved toward greater freedom in the press, but it stopped far short of permitting complete freedom to publish. From certification of candidates for political office by the Arab Socialist Union it moved to an almost complete freedom of candidacy. From rather rigidly controlled elections it moved to rather free and competitive elections.

Table 8.1: Dahl's Requirements for a Democracy with Advice to Liberalizers

Opportunity to:	Institutional Guarantees are Necessary	Advice to Liberalizers	Basic Political Activities
Formulate preferences	1. Freedom to form and join organizations 2. Freedom of expression 3. Right to vote 4. Eligibility for public office 5. Right to compete for support 6. Alternative sources of information	Avoid Fragmentation; Use subnational governments as training grounds	Recruitment and enforcement
Signify preferences	1. Freedom to form and join organizations 2. Freedom of expression 3. Right to vote 4. Eligibility for public office 5. Right to compete for support 6. Alternative sources of information 7. Free and fair elections	Implement mutual guarantees	Consent
Have preferences weighted equally in the conduct of government	1. Freedom to form and join organizations 2. Freedom of expression 3. Right to vote 4. Eligibility for public office 5. Right to compete for support 6. Alternative sources of information 7. Free and fair elections 8. Institutions for making government policies depend on votes and other expressions of preference	Balance executive authority	Resource allocation

Source: Robert A. Dahl, *Polyarchy* (Yale University Press, New Haven, 1971), pp. 3, 217-26.

Finally, there were a number of battles in which major institutions attempted to call officials to account, i.e. to make them responsive to the preferences of different interests.

None of this was particularly successful; all of it was intense and energetic. How Egypt got to the semi-liberal structure of the late 1970s and why it failed is the story of the next five chapters.

The Difficulty of Liberalization and the Causes of Failure

In addition to examining the behaviour of the major political institutions, I will discuss the major stumbling-blocks to a successful liberalization. Dahl identified these stumbling-blocks by choosing to give advice to liberalizers in four key areas.

1. One must place checks on a powerful executive, while also ensuring an effective executive:

> When barriers to public contestation and participation are lowered, interests and demands will appear which the government has hitherto ignored. If public contestation and participation are to be effective, the authority of political institutions responsive to these new interests and demands must be increased. But to reduce the likelihood of immobilism and deadlock, the executive must retain a considerable measure of power for rapid and decisive action, especially in emergencies. Thus the executive must have authority that in a realistic sense is beyond the capacities of transitory majorities in parliament to curtail and yet not beyond the reach or influence of substantial and persistent coalitions, whether minorities or majorities.[3]

2. One must find arenas of politics that run counter to the major political divisions, but which also permit individuals to build skills that will be used in the struggle across those political divisions:

> Since somewhat autonomous representative institutions below the national level can provide opportunities for the opposition to acquire political resources, help to generate cross-cutting cleavages, and facilitate training in the arts of resolving conflicts and managing representative governments a strategy of toleration requires a search for ways of developing subnational representative governments.[4]

3. One must avoid fragmentation, while permitting adequate political expression:

Since the costs of toleration are raised by excessive fragmentation into competing political parties, a strategy of liberalization requires a search for a party system that avoids a great multiplication of parties.[5]

4 One must permit contestation for power while limiting serious damage to losing parties:

Opponents in a conflict cannot be expected to tolerate one another if one of them believes that toleration of another will lead to his own destruction or severe suffering. Toleration is more likely to be extended and to endure only among groups which are not expected to damage one another severely. Thus the costs of toleration can be lowered by effective guarantees against destruction, extreme coercion, or severe damage. Hence a strategy of liberalization requires a search for such guarantees.[6]

These are delicate balances that were not achieved in Egypt. In general, I believe that the failure can be attributed to the interplay of the three basic factors which I have referred to repeatedly throughout this work: institutions, interests and individuals.

First, I believe that the distribution of power between institutions was so skewed that it was extremely difficult to shift political accountability and responsiveness. This essentially accounts for the failure to solve the first and second problems that Dahl has identified.

Second, the class interests present were very sharply formulated. This made it extremely difficult to achieve a moderated political conflict that could be contained within the political institutions. This accounts for the failure to solve the third and fourth problems that Dahl has identified.

Finally, I recognize that individuals played a part, although I relegate them to the lesser position. It is clear that the individuals involved in the process lacked the political skills and the clear political conception of liberalization necessary to execute the change in the polity successfully. They mismanaged the process, limiting and dissipating whatever prospects there were for success. This contributed to the failure to solve all four problems.

Form: The Process of Semi-Legal Revolution

If liberalization is such a difficult process, an obvious question to ask is *why* and *how* does it come about? In earlier chapters I have addressed the question of why the regime chose liberalization. In brief, the pressure on the regime and the particular way that interests were juxtaposed, especially in the tension-filled moments after the June 1967 defeat and the death of Nasser in September 1970, pushed toward liberalization. To these can be added the pressures of a failing economic policy that demanded the ability to build a consensus around specific goals. In the following chapters I will note a number of additional political considerations that pushed towards liberalization.

The question of how liberalization comes about can be answered with reference to the same pressures and institutions. I have said that the political process in Egypt entailed a chaotic drift in the direction of liberalization, rather than a carefully planned march toward it. Earlier, I referred to a continuing deadlock in the polity in which no particular force seemed to be able to take decisive action. These factors combined to create a process I call semi-legal revolution,[7] a process which I believe sustained the liberalization.

Conceptualizing Semi-Legal Revolution

A semi-legal revolution is defined as a change of regime by use of legal procedures against the spirit of the laws. The definition of semi-legal revolution rests on a fine distinction between legality and legitimacy. Legality is defined as a set of obligations imposed by existing law. Legitimacy is the principle which justifies those obligations — in Weberian terms, the basis of the claim to being obligatory.[8] Semi-legal revolution accepts, *pro forma*, existing legality on the basis of jaundiced interpretations of existing legitimacy principles. In the course of the revolution, legality is manipulated to such an extent that the sense of existing legality is changed — obligations are changed within the existing justifications. Ultimately, however, the justifications — the legitimacy principles — are also changed. This is in sharp contrast to typical political revolutions. In most cases of revolution, the legitimacy principles are changed first — i.e. they are overthrown directly — and the legality is worked out later.

The process of semi-legal revolution will be described at three levels — pre-existing legality, alternative legality, and alternative legitimacy (see Figure 8.1). These are roughly the stages of the semi-legal revolution, but there is overlap between them and it is important to stress

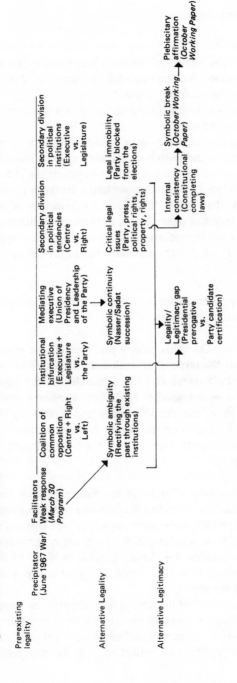

Figure 8.1: A Model of Semi-Legal Revolution

their interconnectedness.

Pre-Existing Legality

Pre-conditions. The semi-legal revolution appears in a condition of social fragmentation. The fragmentation of social forces creates a deadlock that makes the revolution possible.

1. Fragmentation means that social forces lack the necessary power to mount a direct challenge in the polity.

2. Fragmentation also implies a certain ambiguity in the existing structure of legality and legitimacy. Legality must be loose enough and the revolutionary ideology vague enough to permit the two to co-exist.

3. As a corollary to the above, we find a tentative commitment to existing legality that makes it difficult to block the revolutionaries directly and a tentative commitment to the regime that makes groups on the inside of the regime unwilling to bear the costs of repressing the challenge. This is roughly the situation that I have described in Egypt in the late 1960s.

The precipitator. The deadlock is dislodged by an 'external' crisis — the crisis of the June 1967 war.

A weak response. The crisis creates pressures on the regime to take some action, but the response is weak and only exacerbates the problem. In Egypt the attempt at reform embodied in the *March 30 Program* was such a weak response. The efforts at reform serve to underline the weakness of the existing regime and further sap its strength. They also serve to give an opening to the forces of change which gained an indispensable note of acceptability, a point of legitimate entry and a point of leverage.

Facilitators. The ability to push the opening depends on the interplay between the interests present and the structure of institutions.

1. A coalition based on common opposition: the entry of the revolutionaries means the sharing of power by inherently antithetical groups. The impetus to making this sharing possible is likely to be a strong common opposition to a third party. In Egypt it was a centre/right coalition against the left.

2. An institutional bifurcation: a key element in permitting the strange bedfellows to co-exist appears to be a separation in their institutional bases of support. Each has a different type of social power concentrated in a different institution and the interpenetration of

institutions is low. This permits the revolutionaries to consolidate their bases of support while it disguises the nature of the threat. In Egypt we find the executive and the legislature on one side and the party on the other.

3. A mediating role for the executive: a direct assault on power will raise political stakes too high at the outset. The executive must be able to mitigate the initial impact by either absorbing political pressures or camouflaging political consequences. In Egypt an essential element was the convergence of the Presidency and the leadership of the party in one person.

4. A secondary division: with the revolutionaries 'inside' the political structure and gaining strength, a division within the revolutionary coalition occurs. This is between the centre of the coalition and its extreme wing. It is both political and institutional. In Egypt it was between the moderate centre (in the executive and the legislature) and the right (in the legislature). The extreme partner wishes to push the revolution farther and faster. This threatens to undermine the balance of forces that sustains the revolutionary process. As the extreme partner becomes more assertive, the 'intentions' of the revolutionaries become clear and more threatening. Old lines of opposition are reinvigorated as the opposition comes back to life. In Egypt, as political and economic liberalization proceeded and the right tried to push it farther, there was a resurgence of the extreme left, with the Communist party reconstituted after a decade of non-existence.

The function of these secondary divisions seems to be to keep the revolution on its course. Goaded by its extreme partner, it is not permitted to stop short in the process. Threatened by its 'old' opposition, it does not rush ahead too rapidly. It remains both revolutionary and semi-legal.

Alternative Legality

At this level a series of legal actions begins to erode the principles of legitimacy on which the regime is based.

Symbolic ambiguity. The weak response, which provides the structural factor of a point of legitimate entry, also has a major impact at the symbolic level. It introduces a fundamental ambiguity into the legitimacy/legality structure. It shakes the principles on which the regimes stand. The reform creates a split symbolism. It criticizes the errors of the past while making a commitment to similar or the same institutions in the future.

Symbolic continuity. The moderating role of the executive, noted above, has a symbolic dimension to it expressed in continuity at the top. Sadat was chosen by Nasser. Thus, those who oversaw the revolution were the legitimate inheritors of power. This appears to commit a certain number of people to the revolution, or at least to inaction in face of the revolution, for purely legalistic reasons.

Critical legal issues. The reform, as a response to weak points in the existing regime and by opening criticism of the past, provides the basic line along which the revolutionaries push. A set of highly symbolic issues becomes the focus of concern, issues which tear at the fabric of the existing legitimacy/legality structure. The issues were the extension of political rights and the freeing of political activity. Specifically, the issues were the role of the party and the legislature, freedom of the press and definition of crucial rights.

Legal immobility. In this ambiguous position, those who wished to resist the revolution seemed to be immobilized. The party tried to slow the revolution down — to restrict candidates for election, to 'steal' the local government elections — but it was unable to do so when faced with the growing alternative legality.

Alternative Legitimacy

Legitimacy/legality gap. Eventually, 'legal' actions become separated from the principles legitimizing them because intervening justifications have been set up. The party did have the right to certify candidates and the President did no more than insist that it do so. The party could not produce a set of criteria by which to exclude the candidates it wished to. Those who wanted to slow the process could not operationalize their own principles. The idea of political reform stood in their way.

Internal consistency. Within this legitimacy/legality gap, the revolutionaries begin to build an alternative sense of legitimacy by citing the intervening justifications.

A symbolic break. This alternative legitimacy still requires a break with the existing legitimacy principle, and hence with the past. This final break must be sharp. The plebiscite held on the *October Working Paper* was of particular importance. The paper drew a direct line between the semi-legal revolution and the victory:

The corrective measures of May, 1971 were fundamentally necessary — although the intrigues of some of the centers of power expe-
dited it — in order to put our people in a position better suited to
carry the burdens of the battle and to participate in achieving the
victory.[9]

The victory and the liberalization were inseparably intertwined in the
push to an autonomous legitimacy for the 'Corrective Revolution', as
the semi-legal revolution came to be called.

Plebiscitary affirmation. Since semi-legal revolutions are semi-parliamentary, semi-elective games, elections play a key role. While parliamentary elections are important, plebiscites are all important. It is
through the plebiscite that semi-legal revolutionaries tap into the 'will
of the people'. The plebiscite on the *March 30 Program* began the
process and that on the *October Working Paper* sealed it. In addition,
there were key parliamentary elections in 1971 and 1976.

Landmarks in the Process of Change

The stages in this process can be easily marked with a variety of events,
acts and laws in just about every sphere of political and economic
activity (see Table 8.2). Each stage possesses a major document which
was subject to a plebiscite and defined the basic nature of that stage.
Following that document came a series of laws which filled in the
details. I have already discussed the major changes which took place in
the economy — especially those in the public, foreign and agrarian
sectors. The major changes in the legislature, local government and the
press will be discussed in subsequent chapters. To illustrate both the
general pattern and the content of the semi-legal revolution in this
chapter I will briefly examine two areas of activity that are largely
symbolic and are not treated elsewhere in this work. Because they are
symbolic, they exhibit the patterns of the semi-legal revolution with
particular clarity.

I have chosen to track two sequences of laws — those dealing with
the return of property and those dealing with the return of employment rights (see Table 8.3). As suggested by chapter 2, the symbolic
significance of these laws is very great. State capitalism had developed
by expropriating specific classes of individuals and by manipulating
employment in the state. To reverse these was to redress the major

Table 8.2: The Structure of Liberalization in Egypt: June 1967 – September 1976

Stages	incipient	Pre-existing legitimacy	Alternate legitimacy	Effort to stabilize semi-liberal political economy
	Pre-existing legitimacy	Alternate legality	Alternate legality	
	Pre-existing legality			
Founding Document	*30 March Statement* (1968)	July 1971 Constitution	*October Working Paper* (April 1974)	
Supporting Acts				
A. Political				
Legislature/party	Elections (August 1968, January 1969)	Law 38/September 1972	Law 109/September 1976	
Judiciary	Law 89/1969	Law 34/November 1971	Legis. Report (January 1975) (Socialist Pros. Gen.)	
Local government	—	Law 57/November 1971	Law 52/June 1974	
Political rehabilitations	'Releases', November 1967	Law 51/November 1971	Law 51/June 1974	
The press	'Open Society', October 1968	Legislative Debate, February 1972	Presidential Decree, February 1974	
B. Economic				
Sequestrations	Land de-sequestration, Summer 1967, Summer 1970	Law 49/November 1971	Law 69/July 1974	
Public sector	Hegazi Scheme/June 1968	Law 60/November 1971	Law 111/September 1975	
Foreign sector	Decision 364/June 1968	Law 65/November 1971	Law 43/May 1974	
Agrarian	Reform Law 50/69	Law 75/November 1971	Law 67/July 1975	
Major events	(Development of necessary conditions) → (Corrective revolution entre) →	(Legal Revolution) →	(October War, 1973) →	(Free elections, November 1976)

Table 8.3: The Pattern of the Semi-Legal Revolution in the Reversal of Sequestrations and the Return of Employment Rights

Stage of the semi-legal revolution	Type of action	Date of retroactivity	Law number	Type of law	Discretion	Time taken to enact (number of days)
Incipient phase						
Sequestrations	Some *ad hoc* desequestrations	?	NA	Presidential decision	NA	NA
Employment rights	None					
Pre-existing legality						
Sequestrations	Implementing those which had already been reversed	none / 1964 or later	34/71 / 49/71	Project / Decree	Discretion / Discretion	6 / 174
Employment rights	Major political categories: legislators / judges / political prisoners	1963 / 1969 / 1965	51/71 / 85/71 / 101/71	Decree / Decree / Decree	Discretion / Discretion / Discretion	149 / 110 / 100
Alternative legality						
Sequestrations	Reversing those which violate the new legality, in particular the right of judicial recourse	none / 1964 or earlier	52/72 / 53/72	Decree / Decree	Discretion / Mandatory	355 / 373
Employment rights	Non-political state administrators: military / judges	open / 1969	26/72 / 43/73	Project / Proposal	Discretion / Partial discretion	23 / 13
Alternative legitimacy						
Sequestrations	Integrating and reversing all which violate new legality, including foreigners	1958 / 1958	69/74 / 114/75	Project / Project	Mandatory / Mandatory	5 / 20
Employment rights	General categories of personnel: workers / diplomats / police / educators	1963 / 1963 / 1955 / 1954	28/74 / 30/74 / 38/74 / 51/74	Proposal / Proposal / Proposal / Proposal	Mandatory / Mandatory / Mandatory / Mandatory	108 / 27 / 400 / 93

'injustices' of Arab Socialism.

The period between the 1967 war and the issuance of the *March 30 Program* had seen some activity. In the wake of the defeat of June 1967, a sequestration debate was opened and by mid-summer of 1968 some minor desequestrations had actually taken place. Similarly, a number of political prisoners had been released, but they had not been accompanied by the return of either political or employment rights. Once the major opposition had been removed by the purges of May 1971, the semi-legal revolution began to take on a clearer form. On 31 May 1971 the President personally participated in a public burning of police surveillance tapes. It was a highly symbolic act intended to demonstrate that the Corrective Revolution had begun in earnest. On the very same day the legislature passed the first law regulating sequestrations. The symbolic significance of this was stressed. As the memo attached to the law stated:

> Among the primary tasks of the victorious stage through which we are passing, and which the heroic leader Gamal Abdul Nasser set out in the *30 March Program Statement*, was guaranteeing the protection of the revolution in the shadow of the rule of law. This issue was among those which the leader gave a good deal of thought to and gave his call to the legalization of the revolution, which would base permanent steps on theoretical and legislative roots supporting all guarantees of rights and freedoms for citizens, in the limits of maintaining national security and the basic principles and lines of the revolution.[10]

The circumstances surrounding the law are of interest. This was the very first law presented by the 'post-coup' government to the Assembly. It was the first official document generated by the government. It was presented to the legislature in the form of a letter. So far as I can tell, in the decade between 1967 and 1977, this is the only law presented in this form. The reason for this is a legal technicality. Letters are read into the legislative record first. This suggests a good deal of haste. The law was also presented with a request for immediate consideration, reinforcing the sense of urgency. Presented on 25 May, it was studied in committee, debated in the Assembly, and passed in just six days. It was by this extraordinary route that, on the very same day that the President publicly burned police tapes, the Assembly came to pass its first law to regulate sequestrations.

The significance of the law was not overlooked by the members of the Assembly, as one of the members pointed out: 'It is not strange at all that this law to organize sequestration of funds is among the first laws which is presented to the National Assembly, this law which guarantees the humanity of the individual.'[11]

The ideological theme of honouring the individual became one of the centrepieces of the semi-legal revolution. Over time, the ideology became better defined and more complete. Careful explanations of the precise reason for overturning past acts were worked out. What started as an *ad hoc* series of actions became a detailed historical and ideological explanation. Ultimately, there was a fully-fledged attack on the past:

> In 1961 when the crime of the split between Syria and Egypt occurred, those who had failed wanted to cover their failure and they fabricated that the feudalists and reactionaries began the movement to overturn the gains of the revolution and the gains of the workers and peasants and they began sequestrations. Then in 1965 another farce was perpetrated ... Therefore, the principle of sequestration and the principle of seizure are illegal and unconstitutional and unjust.
>
> If we, in our meeting today, correct these errors, then we correct the oppressive errors that affected the July 23 Revolution.[12]

The change in ideology was coupled with an increasing symbolic specialization in the area — the Socialist Prosecutor General specialized in sequestrations; the legislature specialized in return of employment rights. In both cases we find a continual expansion to incorporate other aspects of the social structure — i.e. new categories of people. We can also note some patterns in the technicalities of the laws which correlate very closely with their substance. First, and of paramount importance to the present discussion, is the shift in the dates of retroactivity of the laws. In the stage of pre-existing legality or alternative legality, the laws were confined to the mid and late 1960s. In the third stage, the dates of retroactivity were pushed back to the very beginning of the socialist revolution. In this stage the socialist revolution was being undone.

Another shift is in the origin of the laws. The initial laws were largely Presidential decrees. In the final stage for sequestrations and in the second stage for employment rights, we find project laws. These are laws which originate in the government. The final employment rights laws were all proposals. These originated in the legislature, indicating a full legislative process. This reflects a shift into semi-parliamentarianism that typified the semi-legal revolution in Egypt.

Fourthly, there was a shift from the 'discretionary' return of property or employment rights to the mandatory return. This shift parallels other changes in its timing and reflects the increasingly explicit liberal concept of the absolute guarantee of rights.

A fifth observation of significance can be drawn from the categories of people to which the laws apply. The President, by decree, and the government, by project, initiated a rehabilitation of what the Marxists would call the 'state repressive apparatus', what the Weberians would call the administrative staff. The legislature expanded this to broader categories of people — workers, diplomats, educators. Though there are a couple of exceptions, it can be said that the political transformation had a steadily broadening social impact in the categories of people it 'brought back' into the polity. Further, it was the legislators who had broken the barrier between the state administration and the broader categories, again reflecting the shift into semi-parliamentarianism.

As efforts continued to reverse the past there were those who objected; arguing that some steps in the past to overthrow the monarchy and secure the July Revolution had been necessary.

> The July Revolution, which overthrew the king and changed the political and social system in Egypt, this revolution in its early stages of creation, demanded steps to protect itself . . . These measures in the beginning of the Revolution are not like those which it witnessed in the following years and especially after 1963. But these steps were for truth and history in the shadow of the revolution. The army undertook, in the name of the people, at that time, legal, or semi-legal measures because it issued a law organizing the review of the circumstances of citizens and that law was 171/1952.[13]

As we examine the political activity in each of the institutions, we shall find that there is a basic commonality with this unfolding of the ideology of the semi-legal revolution.

The phases and sequences will be similar. However, the development of political institutions does differ from the development of ideology. It was far more difficult to establish operational relationships between institutions to support a liberal polity than it was to simply express a liberal ideology.

9   THE EXECUTIVE BRANCH

The Significance of the Cabinet

Making the executive branch responsive to the preferences and demands of various interests when it has been extremely powerful constitutes a major task for liberalization. For purposes of this analysis, the task of altering executive power is considered to have two aspects. On the one hand, recruitment to the executive must be routinized. That is, access to executive power should be regularized. On the other hand, the executive must become responsive to the institutions which claim the right to oversee its routine activities. The various interests represented in other political institutions should be able to call the executive to account.

In this chapter, I address the first of these two aspects – recruitment to the executive branch. Recruitment to the Presidency, with its peculiar blend of indirect and plebiscitary elements, has been commented upon in chapter 5. In this chapter, I concentrate on recruitment to the cabinet.

Patterns of recruitment to the cabinet are one of the ways that social scientists categorize and describe regimes. The assumption is that the structure of the cabinet and the class, educational and occupational backgrounds of ministers reflect the nature of the regime.[1] Those at the top of the state may represent certain groups in society or be particularly responsive to the demands of the social groups from which they come. Background characteristic may also be a good indicator of the style of rule. Education, training, age, occupational careers, and so on, all indicate how decision-makers think; how they organize to approach problems; how they issue orders and use subordinates. The institutional background of ministers may reflect the importance of various institutions in society, for the connection of institutions through individuals at the top of the state may be a good indication of which specialized constituencies must be consulted, which command power, which command resources, and so on. The discussion of the process and content of liberalization above certainly suggests that some form of institutionalization of civilian power in the cabinet is a necessary condition for the creation of a state of liberal institutions.

An Overview of Change in the Cabinet

In Table 9.1, I have represented the composition of the Egyptian cabinet in the entire post-revolutionary period. My central concern is with the post-1967 period. However, some comparisons with the earlier period are extremely useful.

The 20 March 1968 cabinet was a direct response to the riots of February. It was immediately followed by the promulgation of the *March 30 Program*. The reform was certainly forecast in this cabinet in which the military presence declined. At the same time, academics increased their presence sharply. This cabinet begins a group that I consider transitional. Nasser died in September 1970, and Sadat formed his first cabinet in October of that year under the pressures of the succession crisis. May 1971 witnessed the purge of leftists and the cabinet established in that month was thrown together hastily under extreme pressure. It was in late 1971 that the situation finally stabilized. Therefore, it is the post-1971 cabinets that can be considered the fully Sadat cabinets. This corresponds to the beginning of the second period of the semi-legal revolution.

This division of the cabinets into groups around political events is clearly reflected in their composition. Above all, it is reflected in the military presence. In the transitional period the military presence is in a middle range between the early 1960s and the late 1970s. With the January 1972 cabinet the military declined to a level below any other cabinet since 1952 and it continued to decline, with the exception of the March 1973 cabinet. Given the fact that this was a war cabinet, it is not much of an exception. There are also civilian patterns that are of interest in distinguishing the periods. Lawyers, business professionals and engineers grew to considerable prominence in the cabinet by the later Sadat cabinets.

If we look at the sources of recruitment of ministers in the aggregate, the differences between Nasser and Sadat are quite striking (see Table 9.2). Of 131 ministers who served under Nasser, 20.6 per cent were officers and 13.9 per cent were officer technocrats. Under Sadat, of 127 ministers, 7.5 per cent were officers and 7.5 per cent were officer technocrats. If we restrict ourselves to the 'Sadat period ministries', officers represent only 3.8 per cent, while officer technocrats rise to 9.0 per cent. Unfortunately, I do not have the data to examine Nasser's pre-transitional ministries, but it seems clear that the military presence in that group of ministers would be higher than for the entire period.

Table 9.1: Occupational Sources of Recruitment of Cabinet Members (1952-77)

Cabinet	Military		Bureaucracy		Business Prof.		Law		Academia		Diplomacy		Engineer		Police		Total	
	No.	%	No.	%	No.	%	No.	%	No.	%	No.	%	No.	%	No.	%	No.	%
7 Sept. 52	1	6.2	3	18.8	3	18.8	4	25.0	3	18.8	2	12.5	–	–	–	–	16	–
8 Dec. 52	1	5.9	3	17.7	1	5.9	5	29.4	4	23.5	2	11.8	1	5.9	–	–	17	–
18 June 53	5	26.3	2	10.5	1	5.3	5	26.3	3	15.8	1	5.3	2	10.5	–	–	19	–
4 Oct. 53	9	40.9	1	4.6	2	9.1	4	18.2	3	13.6	1	4.6	2	9.1	–	–	22	–
17 Apr. 54	11	45.8	1	4.2	2	8.3	4	16.7	3	12.5	1	4.2	2	8.3	–	–	24	–
1 Sept. 54	12	52.2	1	4.4	1	4.4	4	17.4	2	8.7	1	4.4	2	8.7	–	–	23	–
30 June 56	8	36.4	1	4.6	2	9.1	4	18.2	3	13.6	1	4.6	3	13.6	–	–	22	–
5 March 58	8	38.1	–	–	2	9.5	3	14.3	4	19.1	1	4.8	3	14.3	–	–	21	–
7 Oct. 58	16	48.5	1	3.0	2	6.1	2	6.1	7	21.2	1	3.0	4	12.1	–	–	33	–
17 Aug. 61	16	51.6	1	3.2	2	6.5	1	3.2	5	16.1	1	3.2	5	16.1	–	–	31	–
19 Oct. 61	15	51.6	1	3.5	1	3.5	1	3.5	6	20.7	1	3.5	4	13.8	–	–	29	–
29 Sept. 62	17	47.2	3	8.3	2	5.6	1	2.8	7	19.4	1	2.8	4	11.1	1	2.8	36	–
24 Mar. 64	16	36.4	2	4.6	2	4.6	3	6.8	10	22.7	1	2.3	9	20.5	1	2.3	44	–
2 Oct. 65	19	46.3	2	4.9	1	2.4	2	4.9	7	17.1	1	2.4	8	19.5	1	2.4	41	–
10 Sept. 66	21	55.3	2	5.3	1	2.6	2	5.3	3	7.9	1	2.6	7	18.4	1	2.6	38	–
19 June 67	19	65.5	–	–	2	6.9	1	3.5	4	13.8	1	3.5	2	6.9	–	–	29	–
20 Mar. 68	13	39.4	2	6.1	2	6.1	2	6.1	9	27.3	1	3.6	4	12.1	–	–	33	–
28 Oct. 68a	13	41.9	2	6.5	3	9.7	2	6.5	7	24.0	–	–	4	12.9	–	–	31	–
21 Oct. 70a	13	39.4	1	3.0	5	15.2	1	3.0	8	24.2	2	6.1	3	9.1	–	–	33	–
18 Nov. 70	11	33.3	3	9.1	3	9.1	3	9.1	8	24.2	2	6.1	3	9.1	–	–	33	–
14 May 71	11	30.7	3	8.3	4	11.1	3	8.3	11	30.7	2	5.6	2	5.6	–	–	36	–
20 Sept. 71	15	41.7	4	11.1	2	5.6	1	2.8	9	25.0	2	5.6	3	8.3	–	–	36	–
19 Jan. 72b	8	23.5	4	11.8	3	8.8	3	8.8	10	29.4	1	2.9	4	11.8	1	2.9	34	–
27 Mar. 73c	11	30.5	2	5.5	2	5.6	3	8.3	11	30.5	2	5.5	5	13.9	–	–	36	–
25 Apr. 74c	7	20.0	5	14.3	5	14.3	2	5.7	8	22.9	2	5.7	6	17.1	–	–	35	–
25 Sept. 74a	6	17.1	5	14.3	4	11.4	2	5.7	10	28.6	3	8.6	5	14.3	–	–	35	–
16 Apr. 75a	6	17.6	5	14.7	5	14.7	3	8.8	6	17.6	3	8.8	6	17.6	–	–	34	–
20 Mar. 76b	4	12.5	3	9.4	5	15.6	4	12.5	7	21.9	2	6.3	6	18.8	1	3.1	32	–
10 Nov. 76a	3	9.4	8	25.0	3	9.4	4	12.5	5	15.6	2	6.3	6	18.8	1	3.1	32	–
2 Feb. 77a	3	9.1	5	15.2	4	12.1	5	15.2	5	15.2	2	6.0	6	18.2	3	9.1	33	–
25 Oct. 77a	3	9.7	3	9.7	3	9.7	5	16.1	7	22.6	2	6.5	6	19.4	2	6.5	31	–

a data missing on 1 individual
b data missing on 3 individuals
c data missing on 2 individuals

Source: Dekmejian, Egypt, for 1952-72.

Table 9.2: Comparison of Ministers under Nasser and Sadat

Occupational/Educational speciality	NASSER Number	%	SADAT Number	%
Officers				
Pure officers	27	20.6	9	7.5
Technocrats				
Engineering	7	5.2	5	4.0
Physics	1	0.8	1	0.8
Political Science	3	2.3	2	1.7
Law	2	1.5	1	0.8
History	2	1.5	—	—
Medicine	1	0.8	—	—
Civilians				
Law	19	12.2	28	23.3
Engineering	19	12.2	22	18.3
Economics	12	9.3	18	15.0
Agriculture	9	6.9	8	6.7
Science	4	3.1	5	4.2
Medicine	3	2.3	6	5.0
Criminology	3	2.3	3	2.3
Islamic	3	2.3	2	1.7
Other	13	10.0	8	6.7
No college	1	0.8	1	0.8
Political Background				
Party or legislature				
Prior to cabinet		8.0		29.2
During cabinet		13.0		NA
Political bureaucracy				
Prominent 1968-71		NA		13.3
Cabinet Stability				
Number of cabinets		18		11
Average duration in months		8.7		7.6
Number of ministers		131		127

Further, though officer technocrats are roughly equal in percentages in the Nasser and Sadat periods, the soft specializations, such as law, political science, medicine and history, declined in the Sadat period. Taken together, the decline is from 6.9 per cent to 2.5 per cent. Small in size, perhaps, it is significant in what it indicates in terms of de-militarization. The cabinet posts which the military came to occupy were technical and could be directly related to the nature of military expertise. The extraneous military presence was being weeded out and the decline of the officer technocrats with degrees in the humanities was an indication of this.

In this light, two increases in specific civilian occupations during the Sadat period are notable. First, as noted above, lawyers rose from 12.2 per cent to 23.3 per cent. Second, economists rose from 9.2 per cent to 15 per cent. Both of these changes would be highlighted by the fact that lawyers and economists were concentrated in the 'early' Nasser period and the 'late' Sadat period. The presence of these specialities in the early Nasser period was a 'hangover' from the prior, semi-liberal regime. The presence of these specialities in the late Sadat period was part of the movement towards a semi-liberal regime.

Another indication of change presented in Table 9.2 is the categorization of the political background of ministers. The Sadat ministers are much more political with the percentage rising from 24.1 under Nasser to 40.2 under Sadat. Moreover, we find that 13.3 per cent of the Sadat ministers rose to or held political prominence in the 1968-71 period, prior to being recruited into the cabinet. For these purposes, political prominence is defined as election to the National Assembly (4) or service at the highest level of the Arab Socialist Union (as a province secretary (4), membership on the Central Committee (4) or on a major national political committee – the Committee of One Hundred or the Committee of Fifty (6)). A second category of individuals, which was not considered politically prominent, but which might have been defined as such, consists of those who were appointed to very high level administrative posts that are political in nature, i.e. governors (5), ambassadors (4), members of the National Councils set up by the *March 30 Program* (4).

Three years of political reform had produced a group of political actors on whom Sadat could draw to fill his ministries. They might have been trained under Nasser but their political proclivities were with the reform. Sadat found them ready to move into positions of power within the cabinet to carry out the policies of liberalization and reform.

While the occupational, educational and political backgrounds of the ministers suggest changes in the cabinet that are consistent with the creation of a more liberal political regime and a state of institutions, there is one indicator of change that points toward difficulties. Under Sadat, cabinets were extremely unstable. In 18 years Nasser (the Revolutionary Command Council at the outset) formed 18 cabinets containing a total of 131 different individuals. In just seven years, Sadat formed eleven cabinets containing a total of 127 different individuals. Cabinets and ministers lasted about one half as long under Sadat as they had under Nasser.

Figure 9.1: The Pattern of Recruitment to Ministries

Group	Ministry	16 May 71	19 Sept 71	17 Jan 72	27 Mar 73	25 Apr 74	25 Sept 74	16 Apr 75	30 Mar 76	10 Nov 76	2 Feb 77	25 Oct 77
					Cabinet							
Military	War	Off										
	War Production	Off/Eng	Off		Off/Eng	Off		Off		Off/Eng		
	Maritime		Off		Off					Off/Eng		
	Transport	P.S./Eng		OffT/Eng ?	P.S./Off			OffT/ManPwr	P.S./Eng →			
	Communications	Off		Min/Eng			Min/Eng →1		Off/Eng →2			
Foreign Affairs	Civil Aviation	OffT/Eng			OffT/Eng						Pol/Eng	
	Tourism	?	Min/Eng / Dip/Hum	Law/Law	Dip/Hum							
	Foreign Affairs	Min/?	Dip/Hum	Law	Dip/Law							
Information	Information	OffT/PolS				Dip/Law			Pol/Law		Pol/Hum	
	Culture	Acad/Law			OffT/Lit							
Economy	Planning	Acad/Law	Acad/Econ				Acad/Econ	Acad/Sci	Min/?	Min/Econ		
	Finance					4	Prof/Econ	Pol/Econ		P.S./Econ		
	Economics	P.S./Econ										
	Trade	Econ	P.S./Law		Off	P.S./Econ	Min/Econ	Min/Agic				
	Supply											
Industrial	Housing	OffT/Eng	P.S./Eng	P.S./Eng	Acad/Eng	Prof/Eng				P.S./Eng		Min/Eng
	Manpower	P.S./Econ	P.S./Econ	Econ				?				Pol
	Industry	Min/Eng	Min/Econ	Econ	P.S./Eng	P.S./Eng						none
	Petroleum	Min/Eng	5	Min/Eng	P.S./Eng							
	Power	P.S. Eng										

Table — Cabinet ministers by group, ministry, and cabinet date.

Group	Ministry	Cabinet										
		16 May 71	19 Sept 71	17 Jan 72	27 Mar 73	25 Apr 74	25 Sept 74	16 Apr 75	30 Mar 76	10 Nov 76	2 Feb 77	25 Oct 77
Agriculture	Agriculture	Pol/ Eng →		Acad/ Agric	Pol/ Agric →		P.B./ Agric				Min/ Agric →	
	Land Reclamation			Acad/ Agric					→			
	Irrigation	Min/ Eng →		Min/ Eng →		Min/ Eng		Min/ Irrig				→
Inter-Governmental	Local Govt. & Popular Orgs.	Off -		-	P.B./ Med →		P.B./ Law →					→
	People's Assembly	Offr/ — 6		-	Pol/ Law				7			
		Law →		-								
Administrative	Follow-up	-		Law/ Law	-	Law/ Law	→					
	Cabinet Affairs	Dip/ Law →		P.S./ Law →	OffT/ Eng →	Law/ Prof/ Law			Acad/ Econ			P.S./ Eng
	Presidential Affairs	Off →		-	-		-	-	-	-	-	Acad/ Law
Education	Higher Education	Acad/ Hum →		Acad/ Law →	Acad/ Law →			→				→
	Education	Acad/ Law		Acad/ Hum	→	Acad/ Law	Acad/ Sci →					
	Scientific Research	Acad/ Med		-	-		-	Min/ ?				
	Social Development	-		-	-	-	-	-	-	-	-	-
Social Affairs	Health	?	23 →	Acad/ Med →		→	P.B./ 9 Med →		Acad/ Med →			→
	Social Affairs	-		?/ Med								
	Social Insurance	-		-	Acad/ Econ	→		Acad/ 10 Econ				
Interior	Interior	Min/ Police →		→	→		→	Min/ Police →			Min/ Police	
											Pol/ Law →	
Justice	Justice	Law/ Law →		Law/ Law →			P.B./ Law →	Acad/ Law →	Law/ Law		Law/ Law	
Religious	Awqaf	P.S./ Eng →		Acad/ Hum			Acad/ Hum →		Acad/ Hum →			→
	Azhar											Acad/ Hum

Figure 9.1 (cont'd)

Notes:

Occupational Sources of Recruitment*			Educational Sources of Recruitment*			Other		
Acad	=	Academic	Agric	=	Agriculture	–	=	Post not filled
Dip	=	Diplomat	Econ	=	Economics	1	=	to State for Foreign Affairs
Law	=	Practising Lawyer	Eng	=	Engineering	2	=	from Cabinet Affairs
			Hum	=	Humanities	3	=	from Tourism
Min	=	Ministerial Bureaucracy	Irrig	=	Irrigation	4	=	to Prime Ministry
			Law	=	Law	5	=	to Prime Ministry
Off	=	Officer	Lit	=	Literature	6	=	to Deputy Prime Minister with similar duties
OffT	=	Officer Technocrat	ManPwr	=	Manpower	7	=	from Health
Pol	=	Politician	Med	=	Medicine	8	=	with Industry
P.B.	=	Political Bureaucracy	Police	=	Police	9	=	from Local Government
			PolS	=	Political Science	10	=	from Finance
P.S.	=	Public Sector Bureaucracy	Sci	=	Science	11	=	to Prime Ministry
Prof	=	Business						

*see text for a description of the categories.

Thus, an overview of cabinet changes reveals a marked demilitarization of the cabinet, paralleled by civilian changes pointing toward a liberalization. However, the very rapid turnover in the Sadat period suggests some difficulties with the institutionalization of the cabinet. I next examine the process of demilitarization (which seems to have gone quite well) and the process of institutionalizing civilian patterns (which seems not to have gone very well).

The Process of Demilitarization

In Figure 9.1 I have depicted the full array of ministerial posts after the Corrective Revolution of May 1971 in terms of the occupational sources of recruitment and educational specializations of the ministers. I have organized the ministries into what appear to be their operational groupings. The idea behind the groupings is the functional inter-relatedness of the ministries. Occasionally this was made explicit in the formation of the cabinet. By and large, it was not explicit and I have extracted it from the patterns of appointment and unification of the ministries through joint appointments. As I have grouped the ministries, there are 136 joint or sequential appointments and only eleven appointments that cut across groupings. I believe that there is no grouping of ministers that would lead to a more consistent categorization.

One of the most striking patterns is the steady reduction of officers to a few ministries — those which I have called the military group. Over the period, the military presence was rooted out of the cabinet and concentrated in a few lines. At the end of the period, the group of military ministers consisted of two lines: Maritime, Transport and Communications under an officer technocrat (Abd al-Satar Megahid); and War and War Production under a pure officer (Muhammad al-Qamasi). The essential question is, how did the number of ministers recruited from the military decline from eleven to two and the number of portfolios held by military men decline from fifteen to five?

The first step seems to have occurred with the January 1972 ministry, a ministry which I have designated the first fully Sadat ministry. Here the military is eliminated from intergovernmental affairs, both Local Government and People's Assembly Affairs. A new Assembly had been elected in October, 1971 and a new local government law was in the offing. At this moment, the military was eliminated from the central points of political interface. When they are filled, the posts are turned over to civilians with strong political credentials (in March 1973, Ahmed Fu'ad Muhyi-al-Din in Local Government and Popular Organizations and Albert Barsum Salamah in People's Assembly Affairs). Both politicians were recruited from the upper echelons of the ASU. Both had served in prominent positions in the period since 1967. One, the Minister of Local Government and Popular Organizations, had also served in the political bureaucracy as a governor. At this time, too, the Housing Ministry passed from a military to a civilian engineer (Mahmud Abd al-Hafiz).

The 1973 cabinet represents a bit of a hiatus in demilitarization, with the military presence rising from 23.5 per cent to 30.5 per cent. This was the cabinet which presided over the October 1973 war, yet the military presence in it was lower than at any other time since 1953. Given that fact, it can hardly be seen as a real break in the demilitarization process. In fact, it demands close attention as a lesson in how to carry out a war without militarizing the cabinet.

First, we should note that Sadat held the Prime Minister's portfolio in this cabinet. This significantly increased the importance of the cabinet. Second, we note that the core of the military group — War (Ahmad Isma'il Ali), War Production (Ahmad Kamal al-Badri) and Maritime (Ahmad Isma'il Arabi) were all filled with new appointees. This could well represent an effort to bring the makers of war into line. Old ties and proclivities were eliminated and a like-mindedness was recruited. Third, Internal Trade and Supply was placed under an officer (Ahmad Muhammad Thabit). This clearly could give the military effort the ability to command societal resources. Finally, Cabinet Affairs was placed under an officer (Abd al-Fattah Abdullah). This is a coordinating ministry that could provide an internal coherence to the effort. Without inferring any conscious coherence to these changes, though there is evidence that there may have been a good deal of that, it seems that the military was being given the means to conduct the war.[2]

The first post-war cabinet suggests the 'intentionality' of the war cabinet. Trade and Supply was immediately returned to civilian hands (Muhammad Abd al-Hadi al-Maghribi), as was Cabinet Affairs (Yahya Abd al-Aziz al-Gamal). At this point, another ministry was demilitarized in a most interesting fashion. After almost a decade of continual air warfare over Egypt, the Ministry of Civil Aviation was tied to Tourism and put in civilian hands (Ibrahim Nagib Ibrahim). The move is quite relevant, for the first Sinai Disengagement Agreement had taken hold and this was the eve of economic liberalization. Linking Civilian Aviation to Tourism shows the direction in which the regime was moving. Aviation became an aspect of civil society rather than an aspect of the military situation.

Two officers who came into the war cabinet of 1973 remained outside of the military group until 1975. One moved around in the administrative group and later served to 'militarize' the Transportation and Communication Ministries (Abd al-Fattah Abdullah in the second 1976 cabinet). The other (Yusef al-Sibai) was removed from the Culture Ministry in the first cabinet of 1976. The Culture and Information Ministries were joined in 1976 and placed under a civilian with considerable political stature (Gamal al-Oteify). In fact, both of the posts vacated by the military in 1975 were under civilian politicians at some point.

Culture and Information were always under a politician once the military was replaced (first Oteify, then Abd al-Munam al-Sawy). Cabinet Affairs was under a politician in the second 1976 and first 1977 cabinets (Albert Barsum Salamah).

By the end of the period, the military was limited to and could expect two posts combining five portfolios. In these, it could rightly claim expertise. One seems to be logistical in nature (Maritime, Transport and Communications) and one is purely military (War and War Production). Moreover, there does seem to have been a careful process of demilitarization. The civilians who were used to replace officers and to put portfolios into civilian hands tended to have very long tenures and to be powerful political figures. If we count the number of politicians who served in the cabinet, we observe that five of the nine occur in lines that were demilitarized. This is in addition to the fact that the timing of the demilitarizations seems to have been very careful. When a portfolio was changed, it was changed at a moment that fitted the thrust of events and general policy directions. Thus, demilitarization occurred at crucial moments, with powerful civilian alternatives and in the context of coherent policies.

Whether or not this process was carried out as a conscious strategy or merely a series of *ad hoc* responses to specific events is difficult to say with precision. However, it can be said with absolute certainty that an intense ideological campaign to put the military permanently back into the barracks accompanied these changes in the cabinet. The October war had been defined as a victory for the reformed, liberalized and institutionalized society. The politicians had decided on war and the military men had been given the means to carry it out. Now the military was to take up its role of protecting the nation and defending the Constitution and nothing more.

While these indications are certainly in the direction of a careful and successful demilitarization of the cabinet, a discordant note must also be sounded. The appointment of Hosni Mubarak an air officer who gained considerable recognition for his role in the October war, to the Vice-Presidency suggests the continuing importance of the military. While the Vice-Presidency is not a very powerful role in the Egyptian polity, it certainly is strategically located to ensure communication between the government and the military. It is also very strategically located to give the military leverage should a transition in leadership become necessary. Thus, though the military presence in the cabinet had been sharply restricted, the presence of a military man in the Vice-Presidency (by appointment) clearly suggests that the military continued to play an important political role, though not one in which it would have influence over day-to-day politics.

Civilian Patterns

Demilitarization is only part of the overall process of the transformation of the cabinet. Its inverse is civilianization and here things did not go as well. Simply replacing military with civilian ministers is not enough. One should also create stable and logical civilian patterns as well. This was not the case. Some key points follow.

1. The administrative group was not only unstable in terms of tenure, but just about every occupational and educational specialization was tried. This group of ministers represents executive coordination and no formula for carrying out the routinization of administration in the liberalizing polity seems to have been found.

2. The information group shows a different pattern of instability. The Ministries of Culture and Information were joined and split at a number of times. In the first 1976 cabinet they were joined and placed under a politician (Oteify). In the February 1977 cabinet, which was a response to the riots of January of that year, the portfolio was turned over to another politician (Sawy). Both of these civilian ministers had been legislators serving as Underspeaker of the Assembly. Thus, both were powerful, political figures. Both had difficulty dealing with the problems of these ministries. In the semi-liberal atmosphere, the press was a matter of continual debate and this office was under constant pressures.

3. In the economics group we find a fundamental instability. While Trade and Supply are consistently bureaucratic, Economics has five

different occupational sources of recruitment as does Housing. Further, we see a shifting pattern of joining and separating ministries. Particularly notable would be the appearance of the first (and only) politician in this group (Ahmad Abu Isma'il, Finance, 1975-6). This minister was recruited from the chairmanship of the Economics Subcommittee of the People's Assembly and was heralded as the tough-minded economist/politician who would finally get economic liberalization off the ground. In his capacity in the legislature, he had been the signatory of many of the reports criticizing the implementation of the liberalization policy. He knew the errors of the past, but the problems proved not to be so easily solved.

4. The Ministry of Justice provides an interesting contrast between stability and change. The post was always filled by a lawyer, but it was among the least stable of all ministries. Needless to say, the problem of legality was critical in the transition between political systems and it proved extremely difficult to resolve. Ministers tended to come and go over public issues in which legality was at stake. One can well ask how a sense of legality can be created when one cannot hold on to a Minister of Justice for more than a year.

5. The Interior Ministry is uniform in recruitment and the changes in personnel are quite notable. The Interior Minister from 1971 to 1975 moved into the Prime Ministry in 1975 (Mamduh Salem). In the wake of the January 1977 riots, he took back the Interior portfolio and he had two Deputy Ministers of the Interior. Each of these had made major career moves in 1971 in connection with the May 1971 purges (at the same time that Salem became Minister of the Interior). In the second 1977 cabinet Salem turned the Interior portfolio over to one of his deputies (Muhammad Nabwi Isma'il), while he remained Prime Minister.

6. Finally, the Foreign Ministry is of note. It stabilized early and was consistently filled by a diplomat with a non-technical background. The Foreign Minister in October, 1977 (Isma'il Fahmy) had the second longest tenure of any minister. He had been recruited to negotiate with the Israelis in 1974 and later resigned over the question of Sadat's trip to Jerusalem in November 1977. The resignation takes on significance, not only because he was originally recruited for this task and because of his long tenure, but also because a replacement could not be found within the routinized pattern of recruitment. The portfolio was offered to a Minister of State for Foreign Affairs (Mahmoud Riyadh) who fitted the pattern, but he turned it down.[3] Finally, another Minister of State (Boutros Ghali) took the portfolio temporarily. It took several

Table 9.3: Prime Ministers and Super-Ministers

Minister	16 May 1971	19 Sept. 1971	17 Jan. 1972	27 Mar. 1973	25 Apr. 1974	25 Sept. 1974	16 Apr. 1975	20 Mar. 1976	10 Nov. 1976	2 Feb. 1977	25 Oct. 1977
					Cabinet						
Fawzi	PM	PM									
Sidqi	DPM Ind+ Pet.	DPM Ind+ Pet.	PM								PM
Sadat				PM	PM						
Hegazi	Fin.	Fin.	Fin.	DPM Fin.	DPM Fin.	PM	PM	PM	PM	PM Int.	
Salem	Int.	Int.	Int.	DPM Int.	DPM Int.	DPM Int.					
Marziban	Econ. Trade	Econ. Trade Supply	DPM Trade Supply								
Kaisouni									DPM Econ.	DPM Econ.	DPM Econ. Plan.
Sadiq	War	War		War							
Ali			DPM War War Prod.		DPM War War Prod.	DPM War War Prod.					
Gamasy							DPM War	DPM War War Prod.	DPM War War Prod.	DPM War War Prod.	DPM War
Riyadh	For.	DPM For.									

Fahmi				Tour.	For.	For.	DPM For.	DPM For.	DPM For.	DPM For.	DPM For.
Sultan	Pwr.	Pwr.	DPM Pwr.	Pwr.	Pwr.	Pwr.	DPM Pwr. Prod.	DPM Pwr.	DPM Pwr.	DPM Pwr.	DPM Pwr.
Hatem	DPM Info.	DPM Info. Cult.	DPM Info. Cult.	DPM Info. Cult.							
Kamil	Waqf Azhr	Waqf Azhr		DPM Waqf	DPM Waqf	DPM Waqf					
Zayyat	PA	PA	DPM								
Ghanim	Ed.	Ed.					DPM H.Ed.	DPM SD	DPM SD	DPM SD	DPM SD
Marei	DPM Ag. Ind.	DPM Ag. Ind.									Cab. A. Sudan

PM = Prime Minister, DPM = Deputy Prime Minister, Ind. = Industry, Pet. = Petroleum, Fin. = Finance, Int. = Interior, Econ. = Economics, PA = People's Assembly Affairs, Info. = Information, Cult. = Culture, SD = Social Development, For. = Foreign Affairs, Cab. A. = Cabinet Affairs.

weeks to find a replacement within the diplomatic corps (Kemal Ahmad). He, in turn, would resign after the Camp David Summit and Boutros Ghali would be appointed. Ultimately, in terms of career pattern, no suitable replacement would be found. One can certainly interpret this as a case of an institutional constituency expressing a certain conception of the problem, one which differed from that of the President in an area in which he tended to take firm personal control.

Recruitment to the higher level positions in the cabinet (Prime Minister and Deputy Prime Minister) is also of note (see Table 9.3). The Prime Minister in the first two cabinets was a respected apolitical figure intended to smooth the transition between Nasser and Sadat. Thereafter, ministers build tenure, add ministries, and are awarded the Prime Ministry or a Deputy Prime Ministership. This reveals a certain administrative approach to power, one which is consistent with the general pattern of recruitment to the cabinet. It would seem that administrative expertise commanded more power and recognition than political expertise.

Similarly, the willingness to manipulate the Prime Ministry as political events dictated is a negative indication. For about two of the seven years covered in Table 9.3, the Prime Ministry was combined with another office. First, Sadat was President and Prime Minister from early 1973 until early 1974. This was an extremely awkward situation from the constitutional point of view and it served to impose considerable constraint on the domestic political scene. Second, from early February until late October 1977, Mamduh Salem was Prime Minister and Minister of the Interior. This was part of the rather harsh response to the rioting of January 1977. It is interesting to note that in both instances these moves were responses to perceived threats to security (external and internal). These seem to be emergencies in which forceful executive action was deemed necessary. Nevertheless, they could easily be interpreted by domestic political actors as heavy-handed attempts to use the executive to quiet legitimate opposition.

Perhaps the most important negative indication from the political point of view would be the November 1976 cabinet. An election had just been held which was considerably 'freer' than any since the 1952 revolution. The principle of cabinet responsibility to the electorate had been widely proclaimed. Here was an opportunity to politicize the cabinet systematically and decisively by appointing as ministers only individuals who had been elected to the Assembly. The actual pattern of appointments made little sense. Some ministers who had been elected were dropped from the cabinet and others who had not stood for election were appointed. A much clearer message about the meaning and significance of being elected could have been given.

An Assessment of Cabinet Changes

Reaching a judgement about the impact of these patterns on liberalization is a difficult task. Exactly what should have happened in a successful liberalization is not known with any precision. The implications of what did happen in Egypt are mixed.

With respect to the military, its presence in the cabinet was reduced and routinized. This reflects broader trends in society and probably contributed considerably to those trends. Further, the ability to execute difficult political and diplomatic manoeuvers while reducing the role of the military in the cabinet is no small feat. Finally, there does seem to have been a considerable weight created against a resurgence of the military role in day-to-day politics. On the other hand, we should not overlook the fact that the military was well represented in the executive, even with its restriction to a small number of cabinet posts. Sadat in the Presidency was a military man, as was Hosni Mubarek in the Vice-Presidency. Throughout the post-1973 period, one of the four Deputy Prime Ministers was a military man. In addition, after 1974, a policeman was Prime Minister. This is hardly an indication of civilian political control over the government.

With respect to civilian patterns there was a great deal of difficulty in establishing stability. There was a constant turnover in the cabinet, especially in the ministries at the centre of the process of liberalization — Justice, Information and the administrative group.

The regime seemed unable to give up its administrative conception of power and control over decision-making. There never was a transference of power from technicians to politicians. The idea that a politician could sit atop a technical ministry, making decisions that reflected the preferences of political groups, rather than the exigencies of technology, was not entertained.

At the same time that this technocratic concept held sway, the politicization of the cabinet that did occur was a matter of expediency. This may have had a particularly high cost in terms of institutionalization. Inserting a politician here or there as the momentary demands of the situation dictated, for reasons that were blatantly in the interests of the regime, does not build the sense of responsibility on the part of powerholders or confidence on the part of the citizenry that institutionalization would seem to require.

To leave the top levels of the cabinets as bastions of administrative expertise and accumulated power was also another aspect of civilianization that did not contribute to the prospects of stabilizing the liberal polity. Powerful administrators are responsive to their administrative apparatuses, since that is how they gain power, not to the inputs of political groups.

Finally, the instability in the cabinet as a whole had negative implications for liberalization. There was a pattern of strife and political churning in society — annual riots, continuous economic crises, repeated reorganization of political institutions, and so on — and these are reflected at the top in cabinet instability. Here we should not underestimate the impact that the effort to create a liberalized political system with a cabinet that is, at least partially, responsible to the people or the Assembly can cause. As the next chapter makes clear, individual ministers and their policies were under much more scrutiny in the press and the Assembly than they had been during the Nasser period. Caught between political systems, certain ministers were repeatedly faced with problems that would have been small matters under the old system, but which took on much greater importance under the new system. Under these circumstances, ministers and cabinets wear out quickly and need to be replaced. While a certain amount of instability is to be expected during a transition, the turnover of Sadat ministers and cabinets was extremely rapid, giving the semi-liberal political regime an air of chaos. Turnover also breeds frustration and cynicism. Each time a cabinet is changed, one must make glowing predictions about the work the new cabinet will carry out. When cabinet after cabinet is dismissed in failure, a fundamental disillusionment sets in.

In sum, the changes that had taken place in the recruitment to the cabinet did not add up to a large positive factor contributing to a successful liberalization.

10 THE LEGISLATURE AND OTHER POLITICAL INSTITUTIONS

The Legislature and the Executive: Constitutional Arrangements

The second major aspect of placing constraints on the executive deals with its relationship to other political institutions (especially the legislature), which claim some right of control or supervision over its routine activities. I have suggested above that these relationships were not worked out effectively and that part of the problem stemmed from the distribution of power between the institutions. The failure to resolve this relationship is, to all intents and purposes, synonymous with the failure of liberalization.

There is no better indication of the difficulty that a successful resolution to this relationship presented than in the Constitution itself. On the one hand, the Constitution establishes the typical powers for a legislature in a parliamentary system.[1] On the other hand, it creates an extremely strong Presidency. This blend proved to be difficult to manage. Let us begin with the Presidential powers, since they are the rarer of the two.[2] In reviewing them, it should be recalled that Sadat had repeatedly articulated a conception of the Presidency which placed it above the other political institutions.

The President had certain powers to rule by decree. In the absence of the Assembly and under 'conditions which cannot suffer delay' he may issue decrees (article 147). By authorization of the Assembly for a stipulated period, he may issue decisions which have the force of law (article 108). These powers had been frequently used, most notably in September 1971, as described in chapter 5. There is a second set of powers which gives the President direct recourse to the people. As Head of State, 'if any danger threatens the national unity or safety, or obstructs the Constitutional role of state institutions', he may take urgent measures which must be submitted to referendum within 60 days (article 74). In early 1977 Sadat invoked these powers. As Supreme executive, he may 'call a referendum of the people on important matters affecting the supreme interests of the country' (article 152). These powers, too, had been invoked, most notably in the plebiscite on the *October Working Paper*.

The President also exercises executive power. He appoints and dismisses the government and sets policy (article 137). He can call and preside over cabinet meetings (article 142). He can even serve as Prime Minister, as Sadat had done from early 1973 to early 1974. In this sense, the government is responsible to the President.

It is important to note that the government is also responsible to the Assembly and the President is intertwined in the relationship between the two. The Assembly can withdraw confidence in a minister after an interpellation, but the President can intervene and ask the Assembly to reconsider. If the Assembly persists, he can submit the dispute to a plebiscite. If the referendum supports the government, the Assembly is dissolved.

Similarly, both the President and the Assembly have the power to charge a minister with a crime, but the Assembly holds the power of impeachment. While these extreme measures were never invoked, there was a great deal of posturing about them. The Assembly did interpellate a minister for the first time since 1957. At one point the President admonished the Assembly for what he believed was an irresponsible interpellation of a minister (Ossman Ahmed Ossman, a close associate of the President). While no ministers were charged with crimes, there was a protracted debate about charging former ministers.

The Assembly also has the normal powers of a legislature – the right to reject laws proposed by the government or decreed by the President; the right to propose laws of its own; oversight over the government through the right to pose questions or conduct fact-finding hearings; and close control over the budgetary process. These normal powers of the Assembly constitute the central concern of this chapter. The ambiguous constitutional relationship between the two institutions meant that actual power relationships would be defined in routine political practice.

Legislative Activity

As the polity liberalized, there is no doubt that the Assembly expanded its role. There are a number of ways in which this expansion occurred. To begin with, it seems that the Assembly expanded and refined its internal structure in order to be able to execute a larger role.[3] The number of leadership positions in the Assembly increased and the committee structure became larger and more specialized. Assembly leadership roles have a particular significance because they constitute an elected leadership. This establishes some legislators as popular and powerful political figures. The Speaker became quite powerful as did the chairmen of the major committees, especially the committees on legislation and economics. To some extent, such individuals could not be ignored. They were major personages with access to the media and control over the legislative process. They also became a source of recruitment to the cabinet.

A second feature of the structure of the Assembly that is of note is the interaction between its corporate structure and leadership positions. In law, three categories or groups of people are identified – workers, peasants and others (professionals). The constitution reserves at least half of the seats for workers and peasants (the 50 per cent rule). There seems to have been a specialization of corporate groups within committees. Workers were over-represented on the economic and industry committees; peasants were over-represented on the agriculture committee; and professionals were over-represented on the legislation committee. The latter is particularly noteworthy because the legislation committee had the function of deciding on the constitutionality and correctness of all laws. This gave professionals a special power in the Assembly. In fact, professionals held a disproportionate number of leadership positions in the committees (65 per cent) and chairmanships of committees (72 per cent). Put another way, 39 per cent of the professionals held leadership positions, while only 11 per cent of workers and peasants did.

The redefinition and expansion of leadership was paralleled by an expansion of legislative activity. Between the last term of the National Assembly (1970-1) and the first term of the People's Assembly (1971-2) the number of laws considered and passed tripled, while supervisory activity seems to have at least doubled (see Table 10.1). Moreover, the members of the Assembly became particularly active in proposing laws. From 10 per cent of all laws considered by the National Assembly, proposal laws (i.e. those coming from members) increased to 50 per cent of all laws considered by the People's Assembly. However, as a percentage of laws passed by the legislature, those proposed by the members only increased from 7 per cent to 18 per cent. Thus, the Assembly remained relatively unimportant as a source of laws that were passed. In addition, the Assembly never was much more than a rubber stamp with respect to the executive branch. Only in 1971-3 did it offer any resistance, failing to pass 10 per cent of the President's decree laws. Thereafter, every Presidential decree law was passed. Similarly, with respect to the government, it failed to pass 28 per cent of its project laws in the 1971-2 session, but thereafter it passed more than 90 per cent of the government's project laws in every session.

Table 10.1: (a) Legislative Activity on Laws

	Decree laws		Project laws		Proposal laws	
	considered	passed	considered	passed	considered	passed
Number						
1969-71	47	46	188	137	26	14
1969	41	40	67	44	10	7
1969-70	3	3	72	57	5	5
1970-1	3	3	49	36	11	2
1971-6	104	97	494	462	589	119
1971-2	62	56	36	26	69	16
1972-3	11	10	82	80	110	28
1973-4	17	17	117	109	111	27
1974-5	4	4	136	120	124	26
1975-6	10	10	123	127	175	22
% of all laws						
1969-71	17	23	72	70	10	1
1969	35	44	57	48	8	8
1969-70	4	5	90	88	6	8
1970-1	5	7	78	88	17	5
1971-6	9	14	42	68	50	18
1971-2	37	57	22	27	41	16
1972-3	5	8	40	68	54	24
1973-4	7	11	48	71	45	18
1974-5	2	7	52	80	47	17
1975-6	3	6	40	80	57	14

Rate of passage (Passed/Considered)	Decree	Proposal	Project
1969-71	98	73	54
1969	98	66	70
1969-70	100	79	100
1970-1	100	73	18
1971-6	93	94	20
1971-2	90	72	23
1972-3	91	98	25
1973-4	100	93	24
1974-5	100	88	21
1975-6	100	100	13

(b) The Control Activities of the Legislature

Activity	1971-2	1972-3	1973-4	1974-5	1975-6	Total
Questions						
Total presented	90	94	62	62	124	423
Total considered	90	86	28	52	85	341
Sent to committee	37	104	8	28	15	192
Written response	24	40	28	33	28	153
Requests for information						
Total considered	9	4	4	18	49	84
Sent to committee	3	4	4	3	2	16
Requests for debate	5	1	—	6	2	14
Interpellation	1	2	—	3	1	7
Committees						
Special	3	4	2	3	5	17
Fact-finding	2	2	3	3	1	11

Sources: Pre-1971 figures are from annual reports. Post-1971 figures are from *Accomplishments*, passim.

Figures on the activity of the Committee for Proposal and Complaints shed some light on the activity of the Assembly with respect to the proposal of laws (see Table 10.2). Members of the Assembly receive complaints from their constituents and pass them on to the government through this committee. Theoretically, complaints which go unanswered point to legal problems. The result is the proposal of laws. The number of complaints was quite large and rose steadily over time. However, the peak in terms of getting a response from the government was the 1972-3 session. Thereafter, the government reduced its response rate dramatically.

Table 10.2: Handling Complaints

Year	Complaints	Held because improper	Passed to ministries	Answered by ministries	Rate of response (%)
1971-2	15,068	1,360	13,708	7,179	52.3
1972-3	22,621	2,150	20,471	12,447	60.8
1973-4	24,647	3,984	20,663	5,623	27.2
1974-5	40,074	1,222	38,852	6,968	8.2
1975-6	29,107	6,515	22,592	7,074	31.3

Source: *Accomplishments*, p. 25.

Oversight activity also expanded. The Assembly seems to have been able to force some changes in the government with this activity. In 1972, the attack on the Sidqi government, revolving around its manipulation of the budget, seems to have played a part in moving Sadat to dismiss Sidqi and take the Prime Minister's portfolio. Something similar seems to have happened in 1975 to Hegazi in the Prime Ministry over the issue of economic liberalization. The interpellation of the Minister of Justice who had harassed a member of the press (which, in turn, was related to the investigation of water pollution in Cairo) seems to have led to the separation of the offices of Minister of Justice and Socialist Prosecutor General. Constant pressure on the Minister of Housing seems to have forced him out of the cabinet. Investigations into the Ministry of Waqfs led to shake-ups in leadership and changes in policy. In these cases the Assembly seems to have been able to raise the cost of retaining a minister who had acted improperly, if not illegally, by embarrassing him publicly.

Similarly, special investigatory or hearing committees played some role (see Table 10.3). The work of every one of the major committees appears in this book at one point or another and I think it is fair to say that they focused public attention and mobilized the legislature on a number of issues. Some were investigative in nature, such as the committee investigating the public sector. Others were a form of hearing committee, such as that on sequestrations. Others were tied to specific pieces of legislation, such as the Committee on Economic Liberalization. They could even be political, such as the committee on the ASU, which will be discussed in the next chapter. Regardless of their precise nature, they all built evidence through testimony and debate that justified and occasionally created pressure for legislation or policy changes. They also served to air issues, test out ideas and new approaches to problems, or release tensions over hot political issues.

The overall impact of the activity of the Assembly was not entirely positive from the point of view of establishing its role as a political institution. It did not gain control over legislation. Overall, the pattern of legislative activity can be interpreted as one in which the Assembly was trying to establish a larger role, but was ultimately unable to do so. If it had been successful, we would have expected to see a higher rate of passage of member-initiated laws and more government laws rejected. Nor does there seem to have been a developmental process in which the balance was slowly shifting in favour of the Assembly. If anything, the Assembly seems to have peaked in 1972-3.

Table 10.3: Special Action for Oversight and Control

Topic	Interpellation	Fact-finding committee	Special committee
Economic Corruption Foreign dealings	Sumed pipeline Housing supplies	Iranian buses	
Domestic dealings	Drug *Mu'assassa*	Alexandria Oil Co. Waqf Ministry Agrarian Co-ops	
Internal supply and inflation	Poor distribution	Steel prices	Basic goods short- age Inflation
Agriculture		Effects of high dam	Distribution of pesticides Distribution of crops Future of new lands
Public sector			Nasr Car Co. Losing public sector Companies
General			Economic liberaliza- tion
Social Problems		Water pollution in Cairo	Graduates of agri- culture and commerce Merchants Union Families of war dead Mental hospitals
Political	Violation of Constitution in budgeting matters (72, 76) Behaviour of Minister of Justice vis-à-vis members of the press Minister of Interior over local government elections	Student demon- strations Sporting event riot	Sequestrations Egyptian represen- tatives abroad Arab Socialist Union

Source: *Accomplishments, passim* and local press.

With respect to its oversight activity, obstruction, criticism and embarrassment of the government could be quickly defined as a nuisance and proof positive of an inability to act. Even where it was most productive in airing issues and pursuing corruption, the results did not rebound to its credit. It was rarely seen as the initiator of the action. A process of negotiation that led to some positive result did not seem to be operating. It seemed to be left with the task of conducting very bitter debates that came to no decisive conclusion and left everyone frustrated. Its single largest task, investigating corruption, was thankless in a society where corruption was widespread at all levels.

Nor could the legislature demonstrate any direct connection between its activities and policy. The number of times that action on the part of the Assembly led to action by the government was small. On major points it seemed miniscule. On a number of occasions, as soon as the Assembly had approved the government's general policy, the government or the policy was changed. Further, the turnover in the cabinet, described in the previous chapter, was certainly not at the discretion of the Assembly. We can account for only four or five changes that were pushed by the Assembly out of well over one hundred. Ministers came and went at the discretion of the President or the Prime Minister, not the Assembly.

Secondary Institutions

There are many other political institutions in society. Two that are of particular note are local government and the press. As it turned out, the Assembly more than the President became repeatedly involved with these two institutions. This happened partly because it had the legal duty of legislating the arrangement for these institutions and partly because the members of the Assembly wanted a say in the organization and operation of these institutions. In fact, these were areas where the Assembly became quite active.

Local Government

There were two important factors at work in the relationship between the local government units and the other political institutions. First, the new local government councils were to replace the ASU in certain functions. This gave them some importance and considerable jockeying went on about how to create them. The Constitution stipulated that elections were to be held for the Councils. However, the government proposed a law which would have appointed ASU secretaries as the heads of these councils. Such appointments were by Presidential decree and would have preserved a significant point of leverage for the President. As noted in chapter 5, the President had used this power effectively in 1971. The government defended this act as a matter of expedience and efficiency:

> Among the basic tasks of the ASU and the governate councils is to study the problems of the masses and to present solutions for them. These fundamental tasks are to be those of the Popular Councils. This law envisions creating these councils by direct election. By this we create a conflict between these councils and the governate councils [of the ASU], especially since the tasks of the two will be the same. Therefore, we thought to benefit from the existing organization in creating another popular organization. This is not a final configuration, but we have said it is a temporary step to permit the government to work with all energy and seriousness toward transferring the duties and responsibilities and employees from the central government to the local government.[4]

This proposal was blatantly unconstitutional and members of the Assembly objected. This led the government to withdraw the law. It also leads us to the second key factor operating on the local government councils. They were also clearly competition for the members of the Assembly. That is, they would be elected by popular vote. They would have an arena to discuss and debate political issues. They would have at least some powers to affect the lives of their constituents. Moreover, 'Most of them were people who failed in the People's Assembly elections and therefore there appeared numerous and major conflicts between the members of the People's Assembly and the members of the Popular Councils.'[5] At a minimum, local government was viewed as a political resource over which none of the other political institutions wanted to lose control.

These were the basic elements that were at work in the development of local government. The government did not finally present a law until 1975, though it was repeatedly taken to task for having failed to do so. As one member of the Assembly argued, it had maintained 'the operation of the Popular Councils for a period of three years in contradiction with the Constitution.'[6]

When the elections for the councils were finally held, problems remained. The Minister of the Interior was interpellated over plans for the elections. The ballots were to be written in. In a country where almost eighty per cent of the people are illiterate, this was a blatant violation of the secrecy of the ballot. Further, the committees to monitor the elections were structured in such a way as to be an open invitation to abuse. The central concern was with the conduct of the ASU in attempting to influence the outcome of the elections.

> I have heard that there is talk in the meeting of the political organi-zation for the success of the candidates of this organization . . .
>
> There are leaders of the ASU who are running for membership in the local councils in various parts of the country and I wish that the matter be left to the electorate to choose those who will repre-sent them in the local councils.
>
> I request that the First Secretary of the ASU announce that there are no candidates of the political organization, except those who the people are satisfied with.[7]

In many ways, this election was a preview of the national elections for the People's Assembly held the following year. It was hard fought and rife with charges of abuse. Immediately after the elections, the local councils set to work with some vigour. Some of them seemed intent on testing the meaning of their mandate. One incident, which ultimately found its way into a debate in the Assembly, involved a confrontation with a member of the Assembly. By law, members of the Assembly had the right to attend meetings of the council and participate in debate (though not to vote). The local council seems to have wanted none of this. A number of other incidents found the councils battling with governors, ministers and various other offices of the state.[8]

The conflict carried over into the legislative elections of 1976. In considering the conditions for candidacy for the People's Assembly, a proposal was put forward to require members of the local councils to resign before standing as candidates in the legislative elections. At least in committee, the proposal seems to have had considerable sup-port. However, the local government council for Cairo (a not incon-siderable body) threatened to resign *en masse* in protest. The Assembly backed down, though not without criticizing the 'undemo-cratic' behaviour of the Cairo council.

Thus, the political actors seemed to treat local government in much the way Dahl suggests that it should be treated — as a training ground for political activists, a springboard for national politics and an additional layer of 'responsive institutions'. Unfortunately, the political conflict over local government was so intense and so much of it involved national political figures and national institutions acting out their own battles at a subnational level, that there was not much chance for it to serve its proper function of building political institutions up from below.

The Press

A second area in which the legislature became involved repeatedly was the behaviour of the press. The importance of the press in the liberal conception of democracy hardly needs emphasis. As a vehicle for the expression of opinions, a free press is a cornerstone of political freedom. This had been acknowledged all the way back to the Open Society Debates of 1967. As the polity liberalized, the press did become more active. One way to see this activity in a systematic fashion is to examine those incidents in which the members of the People's Assembly entered comments about the press in the legislative record. These represent issues that were sufficiently important or instances in which the members felt sufficiently harassed to mention it in the record. These incidents suggest the kinds of issues that provoked comment, the principles invoked by the parties to the dispute and the general nature of interaction between political actors and institutions. They are not limited to direct confrontations between the Assembly and the press. It seems that when the press became involved with other institutions in society, except the Presidency, the dispute frequently found its way into the Assembly as a forum to discuss the issue. In other cases, the Assembly inserted itself into the issue. It seems that both the press and the Assembly were trying to establish a role as an 'organ of public opinion' and to police the other institutions.

In Table 10.4 I have classified these comments according to the general principle involved, the institutions that are party to the dispute, the substantive content of the issue and the general direction of the response. The general principles of press responsibility involved are not categories that I have created. In almost all cases, the member who entered the comment on the record also stated the aspect of behaviour to which he objected or upon which he was commenting. In fact, a number of parliamentary debates had occurred in which these principles had been formulated, although they never were formally expressed in a law.[9]

Table 10.4: Legislative Comment on the Press

Cause	Institutions	Substance	Direction of impact
Improper behaviour toward the press	Executive-Press	Executive abuse	Defence of the press
	Legislature-Press	Press leak	Call for Press responsibility Exercise of Legislative responsibility
Incorrect reporting	Executive-Press	Sensationalism in the press	Call for Press responsibility
	Legislature-Local government	Intermediation, slowness	Clarification
	Legislature	Sensationalism in the press	Clarification
	Legislature	Slowness	Call for action
Right of response	Legislature-Executive	Abuse of powers	Clarification
	Legislature-ASU	Intermediation, slowness	Call for press responsibility
	Legislature-Executive	Intermediation	Clarification
	Legislature	Corruption	Clarification
	Legislature	Intermediation	Clarification
Unfair reporting	Legislature-Press	Corruption, slowness, rules (quorum)	Call for press responsibility Call for action
	Legislature-ASU	Corruption	Call for press responsibility
	Public sector	Corruption	Call for press responsibility
	Legislature-Executive	Multiple appointments	Clarification
	Legislature-Executive	Corruption, slowness	Call for action
	Legislature-Judiciary	Rules (debate)	Clarification
	Legislature-Executive	Rules (debate)	Clarification
Morality	Press	Nudity in the press	Call for press responsibility Call for action
Statement of information	Agriculture	Corruption	
		Treatment of Egyptians in Libya	
	Executive	Excess profits in housing	
	Legislature-Executive	Intermediation	Clarification
	Public sector	Intermediation	

Only two of the incidents actually involve the issue of press freedom. Both of the cases in which the executive abused the press occurred in late 1974. Perhaps the most celebrated of all the incidents was a case in which the Socialist Prosecutor General/Minister of Justice tried to intimidate a member of the press by threatening to prosecute for libel.[10] The Socialist Prosecutor General had argued that the attack on him in the press (in the form of a cartoon) impaired his ability to investigate, and hence constituted an attack on a state institution. The important point in the incident is that once it began, a host of critical ambiguities about the Socialist Prosecutor General were raised in both the press and the Assembly. The press had successfully turned it into a debate over the office. Ultimately, the Office of Minister of Justice and the Office of Socialist Prosecutor General were separated.

Immediately on the heels of the flap over the Socialist Prosecutor General the second incident of executive abuse arose.[11] It seems that after a series of requests to the administrative apparatus, considerable administrative manoeuvring and a number of missed publication dates, a new journal had been put out under a name (*al-Hurriya*) to which someone else had a prior claim. Therefore, it was shut down after one issue. Whatever the details of the infighting, a number of the members of the Assembly perceived that the issue was one of whether or not administrative details could be permitted to define the right to publish. They asked that the magazine be allowed to appear under 'any name'. The Minister of Justice refused, arguing that he had no recourse under the law, except to shut it down.

The other incidents that caused comment by members of the Assembly dealt with presumed abuses by the press and several comments about substantive issues that the press had raised. In most of these cases, the press had accused someone in one of the branches of government of bungling, inefficiency, improper use of office, or illegal behaviour. For example, one of the most frequent charges made was that a member of the legislature had abused his office by 'intervening' in some matter before the government. The member of the legislature responded by accusing the press of unfair reporting or irresponsible behaviour and demanded a clarification, retraction or the right to publish a response.

While we should not make too much of these incidents, they are part of an important pattern.

First, they were fought over issues and with institutions that are at the centre of a liberal polity in providing the function of mutual checking and supervision. If victories could be won at this point and at these levels, there were few that could be won at any point or any level and, consequently, the interconnected responsibility of institutions could never be created.

Second, it was clear that the press needed a defender. It was outmatched in a confrontation with the executive and the state apparatus. A number of the members of the Assembly understood this and wanted to make the People's Assembly a primary defender of press freedom. The Assembly did not respond to this challenge with any great vigour for a number of reasons: (a) it had trouble winning its own battles with the executive and the state apparatus; (b) it had to approach the issue through the ASU, which had legal control over the press; (c) the Speaker, who was strategically placed to direct the legislature's activity, was dead set against this battle; (d) the Assembly was not exempt from the criticism of the press so that there may have been a certain sentiment not to fight this battle; (e) the members were divided as to how the press should be operated.

Third, the frequency with which the members of the Assembly complained about reporting of legislative activity reflects the fact that the press became increasingly systematic in reporting that activity. It followed laws and reported debates, often reprinting whole sections of the debate.

Fourth, the press did much the same for local government. It rarely missed a dispute that arose between the members of the local government councils and other political institutions. It was, in fact, watching the political activity of others.

Fifth, the fact that one quarter of the incidents do not directly involve the Assembly suggests that the press was, in turn, being watched.

Sixth, substantively, the press came to focus on one of the weak points in the political structure – the interface between institutions. About one half of the incidents deal with this problem and very often in the form of abuse of power or corruption.

The full significance of the incidents lies in the nature of the activity that they depict. If we scrutinize the incidents we find repeated confrontations between members of the various institutions. A member of parliament, occasionally accompanied by citizens from his district, took an issue to a minister or governor. After the confrontation, one party went to the press, accusing the other of using undue influence. It was then that the issue found its way into the legislative record as a form of self-defence. That this type of interaction took place is not unusual; that it became a point of public and national debate is noteworthy. The political actors were defending their political power and struggling to define their roles as members of political institutions. No doubt they were pursuing their individual interests, but they were also consistently able to mobilize their institutions in their support. None wanted to admit that it did not have the right to deal with certain issues or give up the right to represent various popular interests.

Presidentiality and Representative Democracy

The pattern of political activity in the executive, legislature and other institutions does suggest that there was an attempt to establish a clear set of powers, interconnected roles and mutually checking responsibilities. The legislature, press, and local government seemed to fare well when they challenged each other. They were able to force a stand-off which recognized their respective powers and elicited the appropriate responses. When they challenged the executive, however, they did not do as well. The legislature never quite called the executive to account; the press was unable to push criticism to an effective conclusion; local governments never quite forced governors to respond to them in a regular fashion.

Within the pattern of behaviours we can find ample reasons for the failure to call the executive to account. On the one hand, there may never have been a majority willing to put up the necessary fight – i.e. a failure of will on the part of the politicians. However, the failure may equally have stemmed from the ambiguity and the imbalance of political forces within the political structure. The individuals may have perceived that the executive held the bulk of the political resources and they seemed genuinely uncertain about what the other institutions could do about it. While the Assembly and the press had played important parts in the confrontation of May 1971, there is no gainsaying the fact that the President had played the largest part. The political structure which he had subsequently defined made it extremely difficult to challenge the executive.

Under these circumstances, the inability to mobilize against the executive may seem inevitable, yet such an interpretation misses the actual unfolding of the process. Formal Presidentiality still had to be demonstrated in fact. There was a moment in 1972 when the contending institutions were in balance. Sadat was not the imposing figure that Nasser was or that he would later become. The President was hard pressed on the issues of war, civil unrest and the economy. The government had difficulty formulating and executing policy and the Assembly seriously questioned whether a coherent policy existed. The Assembly challenged the government on the handling of the budget and criticized it for its dealings with the students. The Assembly was at the peak of its activity; proposal laws had expanded; response to complaints was at its peak; even the action of committees on complaints was at its peak. The content of legislative activity was also the most substantial. It had proposed and was in the process of passing the whole body of laws completing the Constitution and defining political rights.

At that moment, one could easily have envisioned a resolution to the confrontation that would have negotiated a larger role for the Assembly. On the streets the students asked, Where is the war? And in the Assembly the members asked, Where is the budget? If the government could not produce a foreign policy that made sense, a budget that was real, or an economic policy that worked, the legislators seemed to say that they would.

Could the President give the Assembly (not to mention the demonstrators) their victory? Could he share power at this moment?[12] To do so he would have given up a large part of his claim to power. It would have meant allowing the legislature to claim to represent the same interests that the President claimed to represent. Ultimately, rendering the government even partially responsible to the parliament meant shifting the whole focus of the executive branch. The strong personal loyalty of the administrative staff and the paternalistic conception of the Presidency would have to have been reduced. Such a resolution would probably have required a considerable period of turmoil. More ministers would have had to come under attack and some would have had to fall. A procedure for prior consultation, advice and consent would have had to emerge.

At this particular moment, the pressures on the executive branch and especially the Presidency did not predispose them to tolerating either a compromise or a long period of turmoil. As pointed out in chapter 6, the political chaos constituted a serious threat. The military might not stand still for much more of it. To the political scientist, it might appear to be the ideal opportunity to move toward a parliamentary system. To those in power, it looked dangerously close to a precipitous loss of power, if not a complete breakdown of social order and an eventual expulsion from power.

The President took the Prime Minister's portfolio, moved against the left and set upon a path towards war. Having done so, he radically altered the domestic political situation. It was one thing to criticize the government; it was quite another to criticize the President (could one interpellate him?) and the President was intent on using all of his powers — President, Prime Minister, Military Governor General, Head of the Arab Socialist Union. Where things would have gone without the President in the Prime Ministry is difficult to say; with him there they could go nowhere. Perhaps all the concentrated power was necessary to execute the October war, but the President lingered in the Prime Ministry for half a year after the war had ended. In that year legislative activity atrophied; questions dropped off; committee actions on questions all but disappeared; no requests for debate were made; no interpellations of ministers were advanced; the response to complaints dropped off; decree laws resurged. The President had demonstrated that effective power was his and that the Assembly could not go too far.

The parliament was not allowed to have its victory in early 1973, nor did it have the capacity to impose one. October 1973 was to be the final solution to the pressures on the Presidency. When that victory began to be doubted, when the claim was again questioned, the President resorted to a plebiscite. It combined a glorious recounting of the victory with an elaborate statement of an economic policy that would ensure the interests that were bound up with the Presidency. It also called for the completion of the political transformation which had always been biased in favour of the Presidency. In President Sadat's mind the claim to leadership had been decisively demonstrated and the *October Working Paper* merely formalized it. The supremacy of the Presidency had been affirmed.

An account of the Presidential impulse can easily over-represent the systematic nature of behaviour. Each discrete act may be an improvisation to meet immediate circumstances. The personality of the President must be adequate to the task. Still, the structure creates a tendency to choose certain types of action. Improvisation takes the direction of the powers that the President has and the pressures that build up on him. The pressures — the stakes — are massive, not only in terms of political survival, but also in terms of the interests which surround and emanate from the office. The powers, too, are massive, and the President, whoever he is and whatever his personal preferences happen to be, is inclined to use them in defence of both himself and the interests with which he is associated.

11 POLITICAL PARTIES

Interests and Institutions in the Debate to Reorganize the ASU

There is no better area of the polity to observe the interweaving of interests and institutions, as well as the chaotic nature of developments, than in the reorganization of the Arab Socialist Union. In early July 1976, Boutros Ghali, Director of the Institute of Strategic and Political Studies of *al-Ahram* and later to be Foreign Minister during the crucial months of November and December 1977, posed what he considered a vital question:

> What is the desired relationship between the Arab Socialist Union, as the framework for political activity, and the three platforms, as independent organizations, to work within this framework? These relations, in spite of hundreds of speeches and hundreds of reports, have not been clearly defined and there is no agreement on their contours. The true importance of these relations will appear in the coming elections.[1]

In the middle of August — after a much publicized disagreement between Khalid Muhyi-al-Din, leader of the left organization, and Mustafa Khalil, first Secretary of the Arab Socialist Union — the head of the National Teachers' Union offered a different opinion of the 'hundreds of speeches and hundreds of reports':

> The form of the relationship between the Mother Organization and the three political organizations is as clear as day and I do not think that it requires a dispute or debate. It suffices to return to the *Paper for the Development of the Arab Socialist Union*, to the report of the Committee to gather points of view about it, to the limits which the General National Conference set down for the substance of the idea of platforms, and to the *Report of the Committee on the Future of Political Activity*, to realize that the matter is not in need of such exertion. All these documents agree that these organizations are platforms within the Alliance — they are platforms, not parties.[2]

Less than three months later President Sadat declared that the political platforms/organizations would henceforth be considered parties.

Given the fact that these are active, high-level political figures, the uncertainty is striking and it indicates that political institutions were in a thoroughly chaotic state. In fact, there was more than chaos. Two years of open political debate about how to conduct organized political activity had created strong feelings and sharp conflicts. The fundamental left/right division which we have observed throughout the period had been given free reign in the discussion and debate. As a result, some intense feelings had been stirred up.

The regime had put out a *Paper for the Development of the Arab Socialist Union,*[3] which was liberal in tone, but lacked specifics and did not go very far in its liberalization.[4] The regime then attempted to conduct a series of discussions within the ASU about the *Paper.* However, the debate immediately went far beyond anything that had been envisioned. On the right, sentiments were expressed to do away with many of the 'accomplishments' of the socialist revolution[5] — agrarian reform, worker participation in management, redistribution of landholdings, the public sector, and so on.[6] Associated with these attacks was a demand for free political parties. In this fashion, parties came to be associated with the counter-revolution.

> Some voices repeatedly demand parties and I consider this an out-growth of reactionary thought. It is aimed at a step by step attack on the revolution. If we allow parties today, we will allow the end of the fifty percent (worker and peasant representation) tomorrow. Then we will allow the end of agrarian reform and the socialist laws and that under the guise of free debate and democracy.
>
> Ninety percent of the ills of the people throughout the length of the revolution were caused by an absence of democracy . . . but democracy — like all medicine — has dangers and the danger with the spread of democratic sentiment is represented in providing the reactionary camp with the opportunity to come to life and be established.[7]

The left, in addition to responding to the counter-revolution, took a very different view of matters. It argued that the ASU had failed because it had never been given a chance to succeed.[8] The ASU had been used by the central authorities as a tool for dominating and suppressing the masses, rather than as a mechanism through which the masses would become politicized and express themselves.[9] Assuming that Egyptian society was still a class society in which one had to struggle to prevent the domination of one class over the others,[10] the left called for an approach which would make the ASU a powerful, political organization, independent of the state. It would be completely separated from state power (separate the ASU and the People's Assembly, the Presidency and the leadership of the party, prohibit holding of posts in the ASU and the bureaucracy at the same time, and so on.)[11] Its decisions would be binding on state power.[12] Needless to say, this was a radically different vision of the polity from that held by the right.

The content of the debate clearly pitted the left against the right.[13] So, too, did the underlying structure of the debate. The reactionary proposals came from the meetings of the technocrats and professionals. The response came from the meetings of workers, peasants and 'popular' meetings in the provinces. The leaders of the various corporate organizations within the ASU or the representatives of various departments of the state apparatus came forward to make very aggressive statements defending and advancing the interests of their constituencies. There was no doubt that they were in conflict.

Of equal note was the dynamic way in which proposals unfolded. The workers and peasants had been as aggressive as any others, but the turning point seems to have come with the meeting of the professionals in mid-September 1974.[14] It was at these meetings (under Muhammad Abu Wafia, brother-in-law of the President and Chairman of the Complaints and Proposals Committee in the People's Assembly) that the 'counter-revolution' seemed to be released. The meeting of professionals called forth a series of 'popular' meetings in the provinces[15] and meetings of traditionally radical groups at which the counter-revolution was vigorously denounced.[16] Momentum built up until the workers meetings on 20 and 21 September. On 22 September there was an attempt to moderate the tone of the debate. A front page editorial of *al-Ahram* tried to be reassuring about the sanctity of the socialist gains.[17] The General Secretariat of the ASU came out with an official statement to the same effect.[18] The heat could not be so easily reduced. As one worker put it at the next meeting:

I ask the speakers; we read in the papers the statement of the General Secretariat of the Arab Socialist Union supporting all the words which the workers spoke in the previous meeting, but where was the Secretariat before the meeting of the workers and before we raised our voices?[19]

The leftist press was also up in arms:

Therefore, every progressive, nationalist, democratic, socialist element, in all of their inclinations, should be wary of the awaiting
trap set, with all dexterity and intelligence, by the counter-revolution in the name of the defense of freedom. These counter-revolutionary forces use the issue of freedom to defend their existence and
their autocracy.[20]

After the flurry of activity stimulated by the *Paper for the Development of the Arab Socialist Union*, a general debate simmered on and off
in the press for almost a year. It was not until July 1975 that any sort
of decision was made. The National Conference of the ASU met and
sanctioned a change in the structure of the ASU that followed the
outline of the *Paper* closely. Arguing that the majority had rejected
both parties and a single party, it opted for platforms within the
ASU.

Freedom of opinion within the alliance is the only alternative to
the expression of opinion outside of it and it is the rational means
for endeavoring to discover the reasonable solutions for realizing
shared interests and the true obligations of conflicting interests.[21]

It then set down the nature of platforms. They were to be *in* the
alliance on the basis of shared interests. They were not to be along
corporate lines or lines of ideology, since this might divide the national
unity. They would express opinions and be bound by democratic means
and mutual respect. They would not be created by administrative
decision but result from practice and political agreement on specific
issues. The ASU would create the proper conditions for them. Above
all, the expression of opinions would not be considered a violation of
the obligations of membership, in the ASU, while the minority would
have to respect the opinion of the majority.

Diversity had been sanctioned, but not too much, and the details
were left unspecified. To many, this suggested that change would not
come easily. In fact, some of the steps that the *Paper* had called for
were implemented, others were not. Elections remained partly pyramidal, and as many as 20 per cent of the 'basic' units did not hold any
elections.[22] The President ended up appointing roughly one-fourth of
the members of the conference.[23] These appointments included the
entire upper level of the executive branch, thus continuing the overlap
between the political organization and 'state power'. As per the *Paper*,
the Parliament was automatically included in the National Conference.[24]

Thus, the overlap between the legislature and the political organization had been maintained. At the conference itself, not only was Sadat elected President of the ASU but the conference passed a resolution endorsing him for a second term as President of the Republic (thus endorsing the continued union of the two offices).[25]

In mid-August the first meeting of the Secretaries of the ASU stipulated a strategy of 'open days' of debate to form the basis of platforms.[26] In September, the President appointed a temporary General Secretariat, presumably so that things could get moving.[27] In October, the First Secretary announced that platforms already existed but the natural way to create them was still through 'open days'.[28] In fact, very little was actually happening and even moderates within the ASU were becoming impatient. For example, a long editorial in *al-Ahram* on 21 October 1975 argued:

> As for the future of the platforms, I believe this is premature, for the most vital issue today is to create them as a starting point and not to worry about their future after they are created. Here it can be said that the creation of platforms and their permanence, in thought and organization, will open the door to more than one political form for the shape of our political organization.[29]

The next day, Muhammad Abu Wafia declared his intention of setting up a social democratic platform. On the same day, an article expressing the opinion of *al-Ahram* strongly applauded the move:

> The debate about the means of creating platforms had swirled for a long time, but in the long run, the process of the debate threatened to be a primary obstacle, blocking the foundation of platforms.
>
> The enterprise of Muhammad Abu Wafia deserves the credit for transforming the facade of platforms into reality and creating them in fact. No doubt, it breaks the procedural obstacles. Practice will lead to the discovery of the most suitable form for completing their construction and carrying out their tasks.[30]

The Autonomous Expression of Political Tendencies

Abu Wafia and his platform were just about the farthest thing from a threat to the regime or the ASU that one could imagine. Given his credentials, one cannot help but suspect that the top of the political elite had been given plenty of notice. His platform would later become 'the centre organization'. Perhaps the top level of leadership was unable to stop him or was unconcerned about his action. In either case, they seemed genuinely unprepared for what ensued.[31] The log jam had broken. Within a month, twenty-nine platforms had been declared (see Table 11.1).

Table 11.1: The Announced Platforms

Name of platform	Political position of founder as given in the press	Date of announcement in press
Social Democratic	People's Assembly; Central Committee	22 October
Liberal Socialist	People's Assembly	26 October
Progressivist Revolutionary	People's Assembly; National Conference	29 October
Free Moslem	Council of United Nations	2 November
Socialist Youth of Egypt	People's Assembly; National Conference	2 November
National Progressive	Central Committee	6 November
Nasserist Socialist	Central Committee; National Conference	6 November
Democratic Council	People's Assembly	6 November
Liberal Nationalist	People's Assembly; Central Committee	6 November
Nationalist Socialist	None	7 November
Voice of Faith	Central Committee	(by 18 November)
Ikhnatun[a]	None	
al-Khayriyun, al-Amun, al-Nahun[a]	None	
Islamic Democratic Socialist Republican	None	(by 22 November)
Socialist Thinkers	Assistant ASU Secretary	
Egyptian Justice	None	
Egypt of the Revolution	Assistant ASU Secretary	
Scouts	None	
Islamic Worker	Former National Assembly	
Allah	None	
Science of Faith	Assistant ASU Secretary	
Liberated Thought	None	
Women's Union	Assistant ASU Secretary	
Nationalist Consciousness	None	(by 19 November)
Liberal Nationalist	None	
Socialist Egyptian	None	
Conservative	None	
Science and Faith	People's Assembly; National Conference	
Progressive Nationalist	Former minister	

a. These seem to be religious references.

There are a number of characteristics of those platforms and the activity surrounding them that are of importance in understanding the flurry of political activity that followed.

1. In the first two weeks each individual platform received separate attention in the press. Later they received less attention. This must be partly attributed to the political characteristics of the founders of the first ten or so platforms. Of these, eight have very substantial political credentials. Included in the group in addition to Abu Wafia, were Khalid Muhyi-al-Din (Nationalist Progressive) and Kemal Ahmad (Nasserist Socialist), both original Free Officers, members of the ASU Central Committee, and major leftists. On the right was Mustafa Kemal Murad, Chairman of the Economic Committee in the People's Assembly. This was a group of politicians which could not easily be ignored.

2. After the first two weeks, not only did the credentials of the founders change, but the symbolic identifications of the platforms shifted markedly. Only one of the first ten had a religious referent, while seven of the next nineteen did. While five of the first ten used the word 'socialist' and two used the word 'progressive', only four of the next nineteen used either. Thus, there were some active politicians and some aspiring politicians who thought they saw an opportunity to represent a more religious and more conservative section of the population.

3. Within the limits of the often stipulated principles to which the platforms would have to adhere, some of the names were very threatening. They raised either the spectre of an unacceptable ideology (Nasserist, conservative), or an appeal to particular groups (youth, women, workers).

4. Some of the platforms started acting as though they were real. The more substantial of the founders kept issuing statements about their immediate plans.[32] Abu Wafia made claims about membership and addressed a meeting of students in Alexandria.[33] The students issued an invitation to the founders of other platforms to address them as well.[34] Within a couple of weeks, at least a dozen of the platforms had issued programmatic statements of one form or another. In less than a month, *al-Jumhurriyya* was involved in a systematic survey of the programmes of the platforms (see Table 11.2). There was clearly a policy basis for the distinction between platforms. The three economic issues (economic liberalization, sale of land to foreigners and freedom of capital) which *al-Jumhurriyya* asked about show a clear division over economic policy. The one social issue chosen (relations between the sexes) shows a secular/religious division. Though there are

only shades of difference between 'neighbouring platforms', there is a full spectrum of opinions represented. That spectrum is best described as a left/right spectrum.

Table 11.2: The Programmes of Selected Platforms

Platform	Economic liberalization	Sale of land to foreigners	Freedom of capital	Relations between the sexes
Liberal Socialist	1 Make it effective 2 World market for capital 3 Free the pound	Yes, for tourism, luxury housing, administrative offices and desert	All fields except heavy and strategic indus- try; tax exemp- tions; commerce open to all	Equal rights within Islam
Egypt Nationalist	Open to all nations	Yes to Arabs	Yes, as long as non-exploitative and properly taxed	Koranic teaching
Socialist Youth of Egypt	Necessary after years of closure and a tie to one block created backward industry	Renting only	Participation within a plan	*Shari'a*
Democratic Council	Commercial capital and industrial in new fields is OK	No absolute sale	As long as it doesn't conflict with national interest	*Shari'a*
Voice of Islam	Liberalization is the only way to revive the economy	Joint owner- ship	Yes, but no obstacles to the public sector; no agents or parasi- tic incomes	Islam creates equality
Islamic Democratic Socialist	Islam supports it on the basis of profit not interest	For production and not permanent	Non-exploitative and properly taxed	*Shari'a*
Republican				
Nasserist Socialist	1 Foreign invest- ment within limits 2 Non-conditional government loans 3 No special privileges and no return to foreign domination	Perhaps, but only in name and for a limited time	Planning takes precedence; no parasitic incomes	Complete equality; Koran decrees it
Islamic Worker	Self-reliance; then Arabs	No sale	Yes, but Islam says based on work not exploitation	*Shari'a*
Progressive Nationalist	1 Self-reliance 2 Non-conditional government loans 3 Private only in plan and high technology 4 Importing con- sumer goods only makes BOP problems	No sale	Increase role of the state; set fields for private; no market operations	Equal rights

R I G H T

L E F T

5. Whether or not the platforms were substantial, they did represent a new kind of political activity. Politicians at a variety of levels had made claims to policy positions and declared their intentions to begin focusing political activity around those positions. The sheer number of platforms threatened to make political debate tumultuous. If they went beyond debate and gave rise to broader political activity, they would be difficult to monitor. One could expect some of the platforms to attract a following. The unknown and former politicians were 'outsiders' and their criticism of the political system threatened to be especially pointed. Their activity, in general, was most unusual. Some of the slogans could be divisive, if they were allowed to develop into political identifications backed by political organizations.

The ASU seems to have had a great deal of difficulty keeping up with the rapid pace of developments. After Abu Wafia announced the existence of his platform, the First Secretary of the ASU insisted that the Central Committee had the right to discuss and debate the proposed platform.[35] After a second platform was declared, he insisted that no national front could be formed (the ASU represented national unity).[36] After a youth platform was declared, he insisted that no platform could be formed within the youth organization itself.[37] On 2 November a meeting of the Central Committee was announced for 10 November. On 6 November the meeting was pushed back to 20 November. On 16 November the threads of the First Secretary's remarks were finally put together into a working paper to be presented to the meeting of the Central Committee.[38] He took a very narrow view of platforms[39] which was immediately attacked in the press.[40] Finally, at the Central Committee meeting on 20 November, the President intervened personally and forcefully.[41]

After a long account of the history of politics in Egypt, he lashed out at the Nasserist Socialists and the Social Democrats because 'these will never achieve what we want at this stage'. He insisted:

> I want the base, the foundation, the people, and the nation as a whole to give its complete opinion. I know what is necessary and what is in the minds of the people or what they want from me because I can make the evaluation. I can come and share my opinion with you after I have formed it and after you have formed your opinions.[42]

If he would not say exactly what he wanted, he would say what he did not want:

The people approved the system of the alliance of the popular working forces as the limit for its political life because we are in a battle of construction and progress to bring the most to this society.

Therefore, I refuse the call to fragment the national unity in an artificial form by means of creating parties. However, I also do not accept the theory of the single party which imposes its tutelage on the populace, oppresses the freedom of opinion, and effectively prevents the people from practicing their political freedom. Therefore, I desire the alliance to be the true limits for the national unity.[43]

By calling for another round of debate and criticizing two of the most substantial platforms, the President had shifted the initiative back to the top level of the ASU.[44] However, it continued to plod along. On 29 December a decision was made to convene a committee to study the issue.[45] On 3 February the committee finally met. It proved to be another lively round of debate. Roughly ninety speakers (thirty members of the Central Committee, twenty-two members of the People's Assembly, nineteen experts and twelve founders of platforms) dragged out all of the issues that had been discussed over the previous eighteen months.[46] In the end, four positions were pounded out and put to a vote – fixed platforms within the ASU (66 votes), moving platforms within the ASU (33 votes), fixed platforms inside and outside of the ASU (2 votes) and parties (8 votes).[47] The publication of the vote totals is itself unusual, since one rarely sees such breakdowns. Presumably they dispel the illusion of unity which the ASU is intended to maintain and represent.

In the final report of the committee each of the positions claims some superior characteristic for itself and criticizes the others for failing to maximize that characteristic (see Figure 11.1). Each of the positions stipulated the operational steps that it believed were necessary to carry out the change within the ASU that it advocated. The importance of this exercise lies in the fact that it points out just how much had not been resolved. Almost two years of debate had failed to decide any of these issues. The moving platform position would leave all real power within the ASU (see Table 11.3). The fixed platform position gave less power to the ASU and less discretion to the leadership by stipulating procedures and mechanisms to be implemented. The primary difference between the two is that the fixed platforms were expected to run candidates in elections and form permanent blocks in the various political bodies. For the party position and the in/out position, the

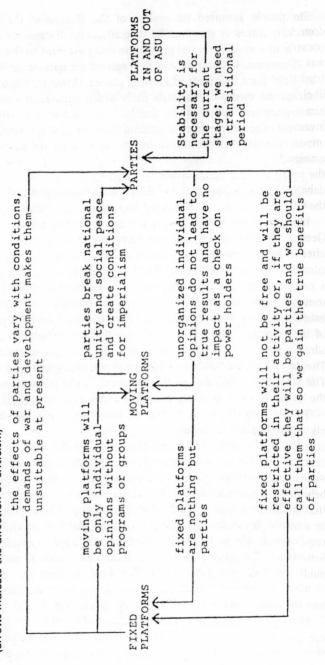

Figure 11.1: The Critical Structure of the Final Report of the Committee on the Future of Political Activity (arrows indicate the direction of criticism)

ASU would become a separate organization with little power over the other independent organizations.

Table 11.3 Proposals for Operationalizing Platforms/Parties

Issue	Moving platforms	Positions Fixed platforms	Platforms in and out of ASU	Parties
Creation of platforms	1 Legal scholars to study requests 2 President to resolve disputed requests	1 Request from 20 members of Joint-Central Committee and Parliamentary Organization 2 Full Joint Central Committee and Parliamentary Organization to study programme and internal organization 3 No class or corporate group platforms	ASU to set specific geographical and mass membership requirements	Free
Means of operation	1 Elected leadership with 50% worker and peasant 2 ASU sets conditions for membership and operations on *each* specific issue	1 Election campaigns on the basis of platforms 2 Formation of permanent blocks in the Central Committee, National Conference, and People's Assembly 3 Mutual trust and open debate 4 No contact with foreign parties or organizations	1 Any to join 2 After a transition run two candidates for People's Assembly and local government	1 Candidates run on the basis of platforms 2 Free joining
Relations to ASU	ASU will establish these, especially a leadership b founders c finance	1 ASU controls finance 2 Bound by duties of ASU members 3 Bound by decisions of General Secretariat 4 Basic units will reflect the weight of the platforms 5 Higher levels of ASU must have representation on each platform	Keep it as a platform	Make it a party

Issue	Moving platforms	Fixed platforms	Platforms in and out of ASU	Parties
Relations to the government	ASU will set these	1 *Not* bound to form a majority government		1 Majori
Role of the President	President is arbitrator	1 President is arbitrator	1 Arbitrator and guarantor of stability	
The press	Equal access	1 Equal access 2 Possible separate press under direction of the Higher Council for the Press	1 Separate	1 Separa

Both called for a separate press and a government formed by the party/platform which received the majority of the seats in the Assembly.

In a speech on 15 March in the Assembly President Sadat endorsed the fixed platform position. Parties were rejected and three platforms were endorsed within the limits of the alliance of the working forces (i.e. the 50 per cent rule, national unity, socialism, etc.). The statement that the President made was hardly neutral, however:

> The committee suggested that it is reasonable and acceptable to begin the experiment with three platforms: a platform representing the right in a general way, a platform representing the center, which is always the basic tendency in our country, and a platform representing the various tendencies of the left.[48]

Political Platforms

With platforms endorsed by Sadat on 15 March, they were 'officially' born as 'organizations' on 29 March.[49] A minor semantic difference, it reflects the continuing uncertainty about what exactly they were. In fact, immediately after the President's speech, the Parliamentary Organization of the ASU (i.e. the People's Assembly as a whole) met and seemed to change the conception of the platforms/organizations in vital ways.[50] The key decision was to make them effective electoral vehicles by declaring that the elected majority in the Assembly would form the next government and a parliamentary opposition would be recognized.[51] In effect, the alliance had been broken and the polity would now recognize 'ins' and 'outs'. As a result, the platforms were certain to attract considerable attention.

The regime certainly acted as though the platforms would matter by moving forcefully to capture all the available political resources for the centre. Indeed, it moved so forcefully to ensure that the centre would prevail that it cast considerable doubt on the 'openness' and 'fairness' of the election. The President had presumed that the centre would be the majority and he kept intervening to ensure that outcome. Most notably, on 28 March Sadat personally confronted the spokesman of the left platform — Khalid Muhyi-al-Din — over the issue of Nasserism.[52] Sadat insisted that he was the true Nasserist, not Muhyi-al-Din. An intense campaign against the left had already begun and Sadat seemed to be endorsing it.[53]

At the meeting of the Central Committee on 29 March, Mamduh Salem, the Prime Minister, represented the centre platform as its spokesman.[54] Thus, it became the incumbent organization and the issue of governmental involvement in the election was injected into the campaign. It would prove impossible to keep the governmental apparatus out of the campaign (if that was ever the intention). While Salem said that other ministers would not join platforms, a number did.[55] While Salem asked governors not to join platforms, a number did and the Minister of Local Government kept insisting that the current local governments were considered centrist.[56]

Similarly, it proved difficult to keep the ASU neutral (if that ever was the intention). ASU secretaries joined the centre, or refused to give the other platforms access to the resources of the ASU.[57] Further, immediately upon the announcement of the existence of platforms, mass joinings by ASU groups began, i.e. whole organizations within the ASU declared their enrolment in a platform.[58] These violated the principles under which the platforms/organizations had been created (individual membership was their basis). However, the mass joinings were overwhelmingly in favour of the centre and little was done to stop them.

The advantages that the centre enjoyed became immediately apparent in the internal organization of the platforms. The centre platform, calling itself Arab Socialist Egypt, created huge committees of well-known political leaders at every level (see Figure 11.2). It claimed 293 members of the People's Assembly as members of the centre platform and a total membership of several hundred thousand.[59] The structure of the platform, and its very name, suggest what had happened. The centre had appropriated the key referents — Arab Socialist — from the Arab Socialist Union. In many ways its structure mirrored that of the ASU. It placed a great emphasis on corporate groups. It maintained a distinction between corporate and political leadership. At the national level its political office included an alliance section. All of this was quite convenient if one was going to absorb not only the symbols but also the resources of the ASU. The expertise existing in the ASU could be immediately translated into the structure of the centre organization. In fact, the centre created a bit of a crisis of overabundance for itself. So many people wanted to join that it had difficulty accommodating them all and some feelings were hurt. Still, the centre kept expanding its organization along the lines of the ASU to try to keep up with the demands.

The crisis of abundance that the centre faced was nowhere near as

Figure 11.2: The Structure of the Arab Socialist Egypt Platform

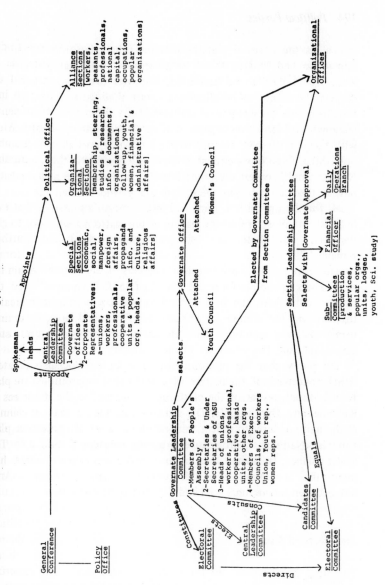

critical as the crisis of scarcity that the other platforms faced. The opposition had insisted that a long period of organizational ground-work would have to be permitted. For over two years it had been desperately asking to be allowed to start that work. Now, just six months before the election, it confronted the difficulty of basic organ-izational work and the exigencies of an election campaign. Moreover, with the number of platforms whittled down from well over forty to only three, there was a critical problem of leadership in the opposition. No one would contest the Prime Minister for leadership in the centre, but on the left and right there were many who claimed the right to speak for the opposition. Long and intense negotiations were conduc-ted with the most prominent leaders of the platforms which had been dissolved, but these were not entirely successful and conflicts remained.[60]

The right claimed only fourteen members of the People's Assembly as members of the platform and a total of 35,000 members.[61] The left claimed only three members of the People's Assembly as members of the platform and at most 10,000 members.[62] By and large, these plat-forms had small structures that were partly unfilled (see Figure 11.3). The names and the structures of the platforms reflect the conception of the polity that the platform held. The Liberal Socialists (on the right) conceived of themselves as a traditional opposition (Mustafa Kemal Murad, leader of the platform, campaigned as the 'Founder of Parliamentary Opposition'). The structure included a shadow cabinet at the national level to reflect this traditional form of opposition. The Unionist, Nationalist, Progressive Grouping considered itself a sort of leftist alliance. Its highest level national office was called a secretariat, rather than a committee, and it contained 'Liaison' officers as the link between the national level and the geographic districts.

The Electoral Structure

The stage had been set for a real electoral struggle, yet an electoral structure appropriate to conduct it had not been defined. The task of making sense of the mixture of the socialist past and the liberal future now fell to the legislature. Unfortunately, this was not a particularly good moment to be undertaking such an endeavour. The final decisions were not made until mid-July. The political organizations had existed for two and one-half months. They were already involved in widespread organizational activity. The lines of conflict and contestation had

Figure 11.3: The Structure of the Liberal Socialist Platform

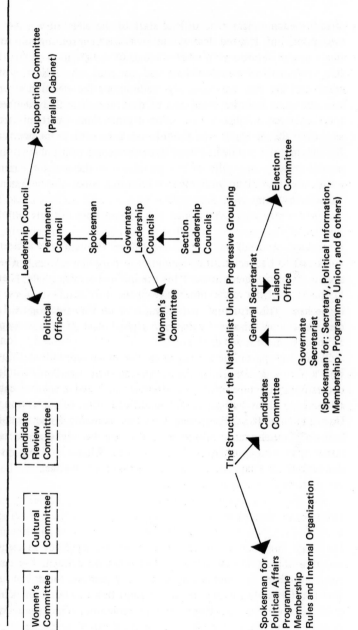

already become clear. The official start of the election was less than two months off and the election itself was less than four months off. In this atmosphere, no matter what the logic of the situation dictated, and two years of interminable debate had not made the logic very clear, every decision that the Assembly made about the electoral structure was bound to be interpreted as a partisan one. With 293 members of the Parliament enrolled in the centre organization, it certainly looked as though the Assembly was about to stack the cards in its own favour. By dallying, the regime had run a two-year debate over the most fundamental issues — the rules of the game — into the election campaign where they linked up with other substantive issues and became campaign issues themselves.

The country was divided into 175 two-member districts with election by an absolute majority. That is, each citizen cast a ballot for two candidates. A candidate had to receive an absolute majority of the votes cast to be elected. If no candidate or only one candidate received such a majority, then a run-off for the unfilled seat(s) is held. Further, at least one of the representatives from the district had to be a worker or peasant. This structure, which was brought forward from the past, can yield some bizarre results and a good deal of it was debated, although none of it was changed.[63]

What the opposition wanted from the Assembly, but did not get, was a thorough reorganization of the electoral structure to ensure neutrality and fairness. The proposals it put forward were extremely far-reaching and may have gone beyond what the Assembly could do. Unfortunately, it was not clear what the Assembly could and could not do. Consequently, whatever it did not do was assumed to be (implicitly) biased in favour of the centre. Whatever it did do was denounced as (explicitly) biased in favour of the centre. Let us briefly review some of the most important points.

The issue of a free press, one of the most bitterly contested in the political debate and the election campaign, falls in the area of ambiguity.[64] Each platform repeatedly demanded a divided and free press. Each kept threatening to open its own newspaper. None actually did and it would have been illegal to do so. The press was tied up in the ASU and there was not much that the Assembly could have done about it. Certainly the Assembly could not have redistributed it to the political organizations. However, the Assembly could have forced journalists to resign their posts or go on vacation from the moment that they became involved in the campaign.

A second area of concern was the involvement of a number of other institutions in the elections — universities,[65] the religious establish-ment,[66] the legislature itself.[67] The opposition wanted them neutral-ized. The Assembly might have done something about these, but did not.

There were other areas where the Assembly clearly had the power to act but did not. These can be divided into two general sets of issues. First was the execution of the election. The opposition was particularly wary of having the Ministry of the Interior run the election.[68] It pro-posed to shift the primary responsibility from the Ministry of Interior to the Judiciary. The second area might be called the structure of representation. The left, in particular, asked for reapportionment, a lowering of the voting age, a lowering of the age for candidacy and a shift to proportional representation.[69] Needless to say, it believed that its constituencies would be expanded by these changes. The urban and industrial areas do seem to have been under-represented in the distribu-tion of seats. The young could be expected to vote on the left and younger candidates could be expected to attract that vote.

Most interesting, perhaps, is the call for proportional representa-tion.[70] This would have diminished the ability of candidates to use personal influence and credentials. It would have short-circuited the tie between powerful individuals or families and electoral districts.[71] The thrust of the proposal would have been to undercut the advantage that the centre was sure to have in terms of powerful personalities. The absolute majority rule had the possibility of freezing out significant minorities from representation in each district.

> The consequence will be that the other organizations will have no representation whatsoever, or will have a representation which does not accord with their effectiveness or importance. Therefore, to guarantee the representation of all opinions and tendencies, so that the other political organizations will not feel frustrated, so that a bloc can be formed in the Assembly that achieves a political balance, and so that a representative opposition can be formed in the Assembly, it is absolutely necessary that we apply the system of proportional representation.[72]

The opposition knew it was going to be outpolled and it wanted every vote to count.

It is difficult to measure the impact of these kinds of technical issues on the election itself. Most of them did come into play in one form or another. Perhaps the most important point about the technicalities was that they were in dispute and the candidates cared about them. Simply running an election was not enough. One had to run it fairly and well. With the regime making great claims for its new political experiment, with the structure itself in doubt, having been unable to gain any concessions in this regard, the opposition paid careful attention to technical questions and their impact. It entered the campaign with every intention of winning a large share of the seats and as various factors reduced that share, its frustration mounted.

Conclusion: The Dynamics of Debate and Reform from Within

Thus, a change had occurred in the political organization, but the process of bringing that change about had not been particularly auspicious from the point of view of creating a liberal polity. Before we move on to the most direct expression of the liberalizing polity — the elections for the People's Assembly — it is helpful to reflect on why the effort to reform the political organization took the form that it did and how that contributed to or detracted from the long-term prospects of the liberalization.

Why Liberalize?

In spite of the tendency to discount political debates such as these as mere sophistry, a brief reflection on the circumstance of the debate suggests that they were more than that. The aim of conducting the protracted debate over political reform does not seem to have been to secure control for the existing political leadership. They were already in power and their ability to control political organization and political expression was certain to diminish to some extent as a result of the changes they suggested, not to mention the changes that actually were introduced or demanded by the opposition. Nor does it seem that the regime was seriously threatened, not until long after the liberalizing experiment had been undertaken. That is, one does not get the impression that it could not survive without some immediate restructuring. It also does not seem that the objective was to give a veneer of democratic legitimacy to a rigidly controlled structure. The structure was, in fact, not very rigidly controlled. The direction of debate and the scope of changes entertained seemed to go beyond mere window-dressing. Yet, the regime certainly did not throw the entire political structure open and it tried to maintain a firm grasp on the changes that were introduced. I believe that the reality was a blend of three factors: 1) the pressures of what the elite felt it had to do; 2) the objectives that it hoped to achieve; and 3) the means it had for negotiating between the two.

We should not dismiss the desire of the regime to democratize too easily. It is easy to deprecate the belief in democracy but the President and his closest associates would have liked nothing better than to produce a stable, social democracy, albeit one in which they played a large role. The conception of democracy that they held — open debate in organized circumstances and nothing more, with the President and others to arbitrate — was certainly self-serving and may have been inadequate to the political reality that they faced, but it was, nonetheless, genuine.

There were a number of factors, in addition to the more general social forces that were pushing for liberalization, that made a political restructuring necessary.

First, there was a great deal of discontent with the ASU as it was. The right had long been opposed to it. The left had become thoroughly disillusioned with it. A significant section of the supporters of the regime — particularly the elements pushing for and benefiting from economic liberalization — was not comfortable with it.

Second, there was a tremendous potential for explosive division in society and fragmentation in the polity. Social peace was fragile and the regime needed an alternative organization that would contain the social forces churning near the surface, while enabling it to organize its bases of support.

Third, the regime, portraying itself as liberalizing in a general sense, needed a new form of organization to validate its claim to being democratic.

Why Try to Create Diversity Within Existing Organizations?

We should not be too quick to dismiss the genuineness of the belief in certain values. The problems that Egypt faced were massive. The logical connection between those conditions and the need to stress national unity and the alliance of the working forces is clear. Even if the alliance had not worked effectively, there was still some basis for believing in and insisting upon it.

Much more than belief went into making the starting point an effort to develop the ASU. There was a tremendous amount of rhetoric surrounding the ASU. It was no easy matter to delegitimize the ASU without delegitimizing the other concepts which the regime had put forward. Indeed, the regime was faced with the ASU in its own Constitution as '*the* political organization'.

Ideology and rhetoric aside, there was a great deal of practical benefit that the regime reaped by proposing change from within. By staying within the ASU there was a tremendous amount of discretion for the top leadership. There was absolutely no reason that a decision should be made prior to the National Conference, which the leadership could easily control. Thereafter, there was no reason that any concrete action should be taken, except by the Central Committee.

Centring the debate on the development of the ASU, rather than some more 'radical' step, placed the participants in a configuration that served the interests of the regime. For ideological reasons of conducting an 'open debate', the regime had to let the ideas of the right into the polity. Yet, in this form, the regime could maintain some distance from them. Further, the left, which was deeply opposed to parties at the outset, particularly in their association with the other counter-revolutionary proposals, was placed in the position of staunchly defending an organization (the ASU) which, in fact, had been used against it.

This brings us to the most directly practical benefit of keeping the ASU. It had long since ceased to be a real threat. It had been subject to an intense attack in the aftermath of the 1967 defeat. It was divided and weakened in the electoral reform of 1968 and had been shaken up in May 1971. In September 1971, it had been pre-empted in the elections and had begun to operate as a support to the regime through patronage. Throughout 1972 and 1973 its leadership was constantly shuffled. In 1973 it had been used to block journalists from writing. It was not completely passive and it had its 'own interests', but by 1974 it was less of a threat than a tool.

The Failure of Organizational Change

Given these basic choices, I believe that the regime seriously mismanaged the movement toward a new polity. To begin with, the line between debate and immobility was not very clear. Reform from within is always vulnerable on this point, but the concept of 'democracy as debate' made it particularly so. The President kept saying that there had not been enough debate, but even some of the staunchest supporters of the regime said otherwise. There were key moments when they felt that a final resolution was vital and they urged decisive action, yet the regime plodded along. Sadat and those around him, who apparently had a tremendous sense of timing when undertaking bold executive actions, proved to have a poor sense of timing in satisfying the demands of diverse interests and political activists. The qualities of arbitrator, negotiator, compromiser, of coalition and consensus builder are quite different from those of forceful President and leader. Sadat, who repeatedly showed his flair as the latter, seemed to lack the former entirely.

The action that could be taken within the regime's concept of democracy was rather restrictive. Not only would those in power not recognize freedom of organization, but they held back on freedom of publication and ruled out all forms of intermediary political activity — petitions, demonstrations, resignations on matters of principle, and so on, were all defined as undemocratic, if not antidemocratic. One was expected to speak one's piece at a specific time in a 'controlled' context and nothing more. This was extremely meagre fare for anyone with much of a political appetite. The narrow conception was going to be resisted. Someone was going to try to speed the regime along and test the limits of the conception. This did not necessarily have to pose a threat to the regime or the 'democratic experiment'. It could have provided an opportunity for strategic and well-timed compromise that might have won support, but the regime was not in a compromising position. It had not been prepared for the kind of response it got and it had underestimated the intensity of the feelings that had been released. Left and right had serious, even desperate, demands which the regime had not anticipated and had no idea how to satisfy.

Each time the regime delayed a decision, tensions built up. The debates did not dissipate the tensions (as it seemed the regime hoped they would) and the long periods between 'official' debates made matters even worse. The final decision was certainly no solution to the problem of the intensity of conflict. Once defiance had occurred, once the depth of social division and the potential for political fragmentation had been manifest, the regime went into an angry and defensive posture. It acted as though its primary concern was to maintain control. In the resulting atmosphere, the regime and the opposition entered into a series of escalating interactions that was self-propelled and counterproductive.

It is difficult, perhaps impossible, to conduct debates and execute changes such as these to the satisfaction of all the participants. Some are going to feel that they have not been fairly dealt with — because their representatives have not been properly chosen, because they have not had an equal opportunity to speak, or because their proposals have not been accepted. The embattled atmosphere increased the number of people who felt that they had been mistreated. Here, concessions are of utmost importance. As the regime altered its concept towards something that even moderate opposition would accept, it compensated, even over-compensated, in seizing the operational sources of power and escalating its rhetoric. There was no sense that concessions were being made. As the limits of fairness were shown, the gap between the justification for the 'experiment' and its reality grew.

The regime also acted forcefully to prevent fragmentation. Though the fear of fragmentation was legitimate, it is not clear that fragmentation was more dangerous than polarization. This was the effect of the effort to limit the opposition to two positions. A few central issues came to have mutually exclusive answers which obliterated subtle distinctions and cross-cutting categories. The result was rigid and virulent distinctions. The regime may have wanted a form of parliamentary opposition that it could manage; it created two charged ideological camps.

The polarization served to alarm the 'moderate' middle that was genuinely interested in a semi-liberal polity. The threat to stability that they saw coming from the right and left came to outweigh their feeble commitment to democracy. The approach that the regime took served to weaken the position of a 'loyal' opposition and thus diminish the support for the experiment. Having let the right into the debate, it refused to let other elements enter — the religious right and the more extreme left. The former it tried to co-opt, the latter it simply excluded. Even within the regime there were many who believed that it was better to let these groups into the polity and deal with them from within than to drive them underground.

There was a crucial point at which the embattled leadership came to define support for the regime as support for the liberalizing experiment. From that point on it began to lose those who were ready to support the latter, but not the former. If there had been a manipulative strategy at work, it was at that point that it broke down, for it ceased to generate support and began to generate active opposition.

I have argued that a key moment in the process of creating a balance between political institutions occurred in early 1973 when the government was hard pressed on all fronts. The matter misfired when the President took personal control of the government and put a firm hand on the domestic situation in order to prepare for war. A moment of similar importance to the process of creating free political organizations occurred in late 1975. Once again, the leadership was hard pressed by political developments. Perhaps, this was the moment to let the political positions sort themselves out — to give them a free rein and see what would happen. In the end, there probably would have been considerable consolidation of positions, especially as the elections approached. The leadership refused to risk it. The President intervened forcefully, stifling the expression of opposition and the formation of groups in an attempt to redirect them within the narrow limits which the leadership felt were more acceptable.

In sum, the debate and partial reform had established a very tense political configuration and an awkward structure from which to conduct a free election. Yet those elections were rapidly approaching and the liberalizing polity would have its opportunity, ready or not, to demonstrate in the most direct manner possible whether or not it had successfully negotiated the transformation.

12 THE ELECTIONS

The Importance of the Elections

In a nation whose electoral tradition is patchy at best, where there has not been a competitive election for more than a quarter of a century, where the return to competition is under considerable restrictions, and where the outcome is never in doubt, it is easy to dismiss the first semi-free election as merely a show. I believe that this would be a serious mistake. Not only was a tremendous amount of effort put into the campaign, but the results clearly reflect the underlying political dynamics of the Egyptian political economy. Even cursory analysis shows a pattern of support and opposition that should have sent a clear message to the government. Either the government could not hear the message or did not believe it. Soon after the elections it made a critical mistake in judging its opposition. The mistake led to the most violent riots Egypt had witnessed in a quarter of a century. The political analyst only repeats that mistake if he does not pay very careful attention to the election and its results.

Table 12.1 shows the election results broken down by political position and corporate category. On reviewing the table one must certainly be struck by the overwhelming victory that the centre achieved. With 80 per cent of the seats, it had crushed the opposition. However, for the moment, let us concentrate on some of the 'quirks' in the data. For example, the centre's share of the popular vote on the first round, where competition was 'unrestricted' in the number of candidates, is considerably lower (63 per cent) than the number of seats which it held in the Assembly (82 per cent). There may be reason to question the impact of the electoral structure in these figures. Further, the performance of the centre varies considerably between the corporate categories. The centre completely dominated the peasant category (97 per cent). It gained 'only' 81 per cent of the professional seats and 'only' 75 per cent of the worker seats. While the majority in every category is large, a 22 per cent difference between worker and peasant seats can reasonably lead to questions about the class or 'interest' basis of the support for the regime.

In this chapter, I analyse the 'overwhelming victory' for the centre along three lines: the dynamics of competition, the corporate categories and the geographic distributions. I argue that all three elements suggest

Table 12.1: The Election Results[a]

	Total[b]	Centre		Right		Left		Independent	
	No.	No.	%	No.	%	No.	%	No.	%
Number of candidates	1,660	527	32	171	10	65	4	897	54
Vote (000)	7,608	4,773	63	619	8	123	2	2,093	28
1st round victors	125	101	80	3	2	1	1	20	16
2nd round victors	217	174	80	9	4	1	0	29	13
Total	342	275	80	12	4	2	1	49	14
Corporate distribution									
Professional	161	130	81	4	2	1	1	27	17
Peasant	58	56	97	0	0	0	0	2	3
Worker	122	93	76	8	7	1	1	20	16

a.Political affiliations are taken from press accounts and may differ from official figures.

b.Several seats were decided in special elections after the general election and they are excluded.

a weakness in support for the regime, a weakness which can help to explain the massive riots which followed soon after the elections. What unifies the elements is a socio-economic pattern. Simply put, the industrial areas — hence the worker category — represented a relatively large negative vote for the regime, one which could have been predicted from the years of debate. I have discussed at great length in earlier chapters the interest structure that was behind the policy of economic liberalization, stressing that the industrial areas and especially the public-sector working class were disadvantaged by that policy. I have argued that a pattern of conflicting interests stretched all the way back to the very first debates about political and economic reform in 1967-8. I have shown that these interests became more and more pronounced over time. I will now argue that people 'voted' for their interests, first in the elections and then in the riots.

Candidates

One good indication of the nature of the campaign is the distribution of candidates and their backgrounds (see Table 12.2). The most striking thing about this distribution is the flood of independent candidates. Independents had been attacked, before the fact, as an exhibition of lack of faith in the political experiment.[1] The centre kept arguing that the proper manner of expressing political opposition was to choose either a left or a right position, not to be independent. Obviously, many individuals were not convinced. Independents constituted the largest single group of candidates (54 per cent) and ultimately the largest group of opposition members of the Assembly (14 per cent). While it can be argued that many of these candidates were 'inconsequential' because they possessed few political resources and polled a small number of votes, it is notable that so many people were willing to incur personal expense to test the political waters. This was a natural and predictable extension of the flood of platforms in November 1975 and an indication of continuing active political interest — political interest which was decidedly independent of the regime's notion of politics.

Independents aside, the distribution of candidates among the political organizations is about what we would expect, given the distribution of political resources among them. The centre fielded roughly three times the number of candidates that the right did and eight times the number that the left did. It is notable that the centre fielded 175 candidates in excess of the total number of seats being contested. This

Table 12.2: The Distribution of Candidates

	Number of Dist.	Centre	Political Position Right	Left	Indep.
Aggregate					
Number		527	171	65	897
Per cent		31.7	10.3	3.9	54.0
Number of seats		280	12	2	48
Per cent		81.8	3.6	.6	14
Governates					
Industrial Delta					
Cairo	19	55	24	9	141
Alexandria	9	24	15	8	95
Kelyubia	7	19	3	6	43
Menufiya	10	26	4	3	57
Gharbiya	11	30	15	4	62
Behaira	11	28	7	4	51
Agricultural Delta					
Sharkiya	12	37	15	2	41
Dakahliya	13	40	18	7	53
Kafr as Shaykh	6	14	7	0	13
Damayata	3	9	4	1	15
Upper Egypt					
Giza	8	25	5	3	53
Feyum	6	30	7	2	45
Beni Suaif	6	17	3	1	31
Minya	9	27	10	3	47
Sohag[a]	11	39	5	1	39
Asyut[a]	9	23	3	2	25
Qena[a]	10	38	7	4	47
Aswan	3	12	2	5	20
Small fringe					
Port Said	2	7	2	1	18
Ismailiya[b]	2	4	1	0	0
Suez	1	3	2	0	8
Bahr al Ahmar[a]	1	2	0	0	4
Matruh	1	2	2	0	1
Waadi al Gadeed[b]	1	1	1	0	1

a. These figures are taken from press releases rather than official announcements of the Ministry of Interior. As a result, the columns do not sum to the totals shown at the top of each column.
b. In these governates, there were late withdrawals from the elections.

reflects an important weakness in the organization. From the beginning, the leadership had insisted that there would be one and only one candidate per seat, but it could not hold the line.

Having tried to attract as many public personages as possible, selectivity was difficult to impose and discipline was hard to maintain.

Attachment to the organization was weak. It was not clear that membership in the political organizations would matter a great deal in the elections (especially with the flood of independent candidates) and the centre had to move very slowly in rejecting candidates.[2] Where it could not 'decide' between candidates, it chose to keep its hands off, giving no help to any of its candidates. This was hardly the strategy for building a political organization.

From another point of view, the opposition was concentrated in the urban governates and in the industrial governates of the delta. This uneven distribution of opposition candidates suggests several basic features of the polity. The centre, with its massive resources and its strategy of mirroring the ASU, was able to blanket the country with a fairly even number of candidates. This was achieved because the centre was able to penetrate the rural areas; the opposition could not. It was feeding on the intense politics of the cities and the industrial areas. Cairo and Alexandria, the two great metropolises, alone account for one-fourth of all the opposition candidates. If we add a few of the industrial governates of the delta, we quickly come to almost half of all the opposition candidates. In this light, the call for reapportionment of the legislative districts takes on its importance, for these districts, which represent more than half of the population of Egypt and in which the opposition fielded half of its candidates, had less than 40 per cent of all seats.

One set of data that is directly related to the distribution of candidates and suggests a similar interpretation is the background characteristics of the candidates. While I do not have a complete breakdown of these characteristics, there are a number of partial sources available. A sample survey of members of the parliament carried out in the summer of 1976 included a question on political affiliation.[3] Of the 55 members surveyed, 90 per cent said they had joined the centre. Abu Wafia had claimed that 293 of the members had joined the centre (84 per cent), so this would seem to be a fairly representative sample. In the sample survey the distribution of the members is fairly even across the corporate categories, but there is a striking difference in the distribution between geographic areas. In the large cities only 66 per cent of the members belonged to the centre, compared to at least 92 per cent in all of the other geographic sections of the country. Thus, if incumbency represents a political resource, then the centre had an overwhelming advantage, but the advantage was smallest by far in the cities.

As a second source for the background characteristics of the candidates, I have examined the newspaper articles which reported on the races in individual districts. The survey produced more than four hundred biographies which cover a considerable number of candidates from each of the political positions.[4] I have divided the background of candidates into twelve categories and examined their distribution among the political positions. The twelve categories are: (1) incumbents; (2) ASU officials (secretaries and undersecretaries); (3) local government members, elected or appointed; (4) senior administrators (directors, assistant directors or trustees of administrative bodies or public-sector companies); (5) former elected representatives, elected to a national representative body; (6) ministers; (7) former ministers; (8) union leaders; (9) judges; (10) retired military officers; (11) representatives to the Federal Arab Republic; (12) no political credentials.

As Table 12.3 shows, the centre had a tremendous advantage in incumbents, accounting for 80 per cent of all the incumbents in the sample. Incumbents represented 42 per cent of all the centre

Table 12.3: The Distribution of Political Backgrounds between Political Positions

| | Centre | | Right | | Left | | Independent | |
	No.	%	No.	%	No.	%	No.	%
Incumbent	71	42	2	6	1	5	14	8
ASU official	30	18	3	9	2	11	14	8
Local government	16	9	2	6	1	5	20	10
Administrative	14	8	8	22	3	16	41	21
Former representative	13	8	5	14	1	5	16	9
Minister	8	5	0	0	0	0	0	0
Union	6	4	0	0	1	5	8	4
Judge	2	1	1	3	0	0	10	5
Officer	2	1	1	3	1	5	8	4
Federal Arab Republic	2	1	0	0	0	0	1	1
Former minister	1	1	1	3	1	5	2	1
None	6	4	13	36	8	42	58	30

dates in the sample. This is consistent with the earlier estimates. In contrast, only 8 per cent of the independent candidates, 6 per cent of the right candidates and 5 per cent of the left candidates were incumbents.

A second category which seems to have flowed to the centre is the ASU officials. The centre accounts for 61 per cent of all the ASU officials in the sample and these constitute 18 per cent of all centre candidates. In comparison, they constitute 8 per cent of the independents, 9 per cent of the rightists and 11 per cent of the leftists. These two categories, incumbents and ASU officials, account for 60 per cent of all centre candidates. In these terms we can say that the centre incorporated the existing political elite.

With the exception of the category of ministers, which the centre completely monopolized, the other categories are more evenly spread among the political positions. Most notable is the high percentage of administrators in the independent, right and left positions. They account for 21 per cent, 22 per cent and 16 per cent of the candidates in these positions. This would suggest an effort by non-political personages with important administrative credentials to turn those non-political resources into political power.

There seems to be an intermediate category between the political elite, monopolized by the centre, and the non-political elite seeking a political expression through the opposition. This category, which we might call lesser politicians, is made up of local government representatives, former representatives, unionists and former ministers. These divide evenly among the political positions.

Finally, there is a category of apoliticals, judges and former officers, which shows a tendency to be in the opposition, but this is not a very large category.

As for the category of no credentials, the independents, rightists and leftists had many more of these. One would suspect that independents should have been more likely to have no political credentials than the right and left organizations. On the whole, however, I think the figures reflect the important difference between the political positions: many powerful politicans in the centre, few in the opposition.

The Content of the Campaign

The nature of the people who ran for office is one indication of the nature of the campaign. The content and style of the campaign are other important indicators of its nature. There are a variety of other sources available with which to gauge that content and style. For example, analysis of newspaper articles about the campaign was conducted by the Institute for Political and Strategic Studies of *al-Ahram*.[5] In these articles, we observe many of the basic features of the polity which have been identified in the previous chapters. Independents, for example, were quite ready to offer their reasons for running

Table 12.4: Content Analysis of Newspaper Articles Dealing with the Campaign (per cent)

Reasons for choosing independence	
Reject working in the ASU	38
Doubts about the enterprise due to stipulations on it	23
Desire to be independent	19
Rejected as a centre candidate	12
Refuse to choose a faction because of criticism it entails	7

Critical articles	
Distribution	
Left	84
Right	7.8
Centre	7.8
Content of Criticism	
Marxist	37.5
Society rejects the left	37.5
Left is anti-religious	31.8
Left runs an inciteful campaign	3.1

Substantive campaign issues	Centre	Right	Independent
Solve problems of the masses	57	18	40
Call for parties	14	–	–
More freedom	–	27	19
Balance individual and society	28	–	–
Apply Islamic law	–	54	25
More supervision of government	–	–	16

Source: Yassin, p. 92.

as independents and they were precisely what one would have predicted (see Table 12.4). By far the most frequent reason for independency (61 per cent) is some form of criticism of the political structure: refusal to work within the ASU (38 per cent) or doubts about the political organizations (23 per cent). Another 19 per cent said that they simply wanted to be independent. A considerable number of the independents (12 per cent) admitted that they had run as independents because they had been rejected by the centre organization. Finally, 7 per cent of the candidates said they had run as independents because of the criticism that running in one of the organizations would entail. Here, I think the left is expressing itself. In fact, rightist journals kept claiming that many of the independents were leftists and the left organization openly admitted that it was actively supporting thirty independents.[6] With the intense attack on the left in full swing long before the election got under way, membership in the left platform was a label that was not worth bearing.

We can get an idea of the nature of the attack from the same survey of newspaper articles. Of the articles which were critical of the political organizations, 84 per cent were directed against the left while only 8 per cent each were directed against the right and centre. The content of the articles critical of the left involves charges that it is Marxist (37.5 per cent), charges that the society rejects the left (37.5 per cent), and charges that the left is anti-religious (31.8 per cent). This was fairly standard fare. The substantive content of the articles − the campaign issues, so to speak − is quite revealing with respect to the nature of the platforms. Solving the problems of the masses was the most frequent campaign issue among the centrists and the independents, but the least frequent among the rightists. If the right represents the bourgeoisie to a significant degree − Mustafa Kemal Murad, spokesman for the right, did claim in his campaign literature to be the 'first to call for economic liberalization' − then its somewhat reduced concern for the problems of the masses could be easily understandable.

On the right and among the independents there is a call for more freedom, which is considerably more pointed than the call for parties among the centrists. Few doubted that parties would soon be formed: the issue was the conditions and constraints under which they would be formed. More freedom had come to mean not only the free formation of parties, but other things as well, such as freedom of the press.

Even more prominent among the rightists and independents was a call for the application of Islamic law. This is the most frequent campaign issue among the rightists and the second most frequent among the independents. I believe that it reflects the same religious sentiment which had pushed its way into the political debate in November 1975 in the second round of platform formation.

Finally, we note that some of the independents seem to have turned their political opposition into a substantive issue in the form of a call for better supervision of the government.

We can suggest a left/right division in society on the basis of these campaign issues. The division is explicit on the issue of religion and implicit on the issue of the problems of the masses. We might also identify two groups of independents, one on the left and one primarily religious group on the right.

A second type of data which sheds light on the nature of the campaign and the issues involved are the campaign posters which were used. Campaign posters have become a ubiquitous feature of Egyptian politics. Throughout the country, but especially in urban areas, posters and placards cover the walls and dangle from every available space. They seem to have become the primary and freest form of political expression. In a few words the candidate identifies himself and makes his claim to votes. The posters give a thumbnail sketch of what the candidates think the electorate will vote for. *Al-Ahram* found in a survey of posters in Cairo that they were notably non-political (see Table 12.5). The posters stressed personal and community service above specific political issues. Only 17 per cent of the posters were political in any sense, which is barely more than the number that involved religious slogans. Of the political posters just one-half contained specific political programmes, which is 9 per cent of the total number of posters.

I conducted a similar survey in both Cairo and Alexandria. Though I covered roughly the same number of candidates, I covered three times the number of posters and many more districts. My categories are not exactly equivalent to those of the *al-Ahram* survey, but, in general terms, the results are similar. Non-political categories ('name only' and 'occupation') would be roughly equivalent to their categories of 'personal' and 'community service'. In their sample these account for 63.6 per cent of the posters, in mine they account for 63.8 per cent. Though no systematic sampling strategy was used, the sample seems to have been fairly representative in terms of the distribution of the candidates. The point of my survey was to test the effectiveness of the political organizations as symbols and to examine the difference between the various political positions in their use of symbols.

What we find is that the centre did not use the centrist identification

Table 12.5: (a) Content Analysis of Campaign Posters[a] (Cairo, per cent)

Personal characteristics	*42*
Support of community	*21.6*
Commerce, youth, workers	(50)
Sports, religious, pensioners	(50)
Political	*17.4*
General	(25)
Personal political activity in the Assembly	(22)
Political programmes	(24.5)
Social programmes	(18.6)
Economic programmes	(9)
Religious	*16.1*
General	(68)
Islamic law	(32)
Other	*2.5*

(b) Content Analysis of Campaign Posters (Cairo, Giza, Alexandria)

	Centre	Right	Left	Independent
Cairo/Giza				
No. of candidates	18	4	4	28
% distribution	33	7	7	53
% in governate	24	10	4	62
Content				
Name only	119	16	1	104
Occupation	25	—	—	15
Political history	27	—	—	—
Party identification	17	16	1	45
Political slogan	30	36	3	53
Alexandria				
No. of candidates	16	7	1	51
% distribution	21	9	1	66
% in governate	17	11	6	67
Content				
Name only	72	6	2	185
Occupation	36	9	—	61
Political history	—	—	—	2
Party identification	0	12	—	85
Political slogan	17	5	2	86

a. *Al-Ahram*, 15 October 1976.

a great deal. Only 8 per cent of the posters in Cairo used the centrist identification and none in Alexandria did. In contrast, the right and left were much more likely to use their organizational identifications in both cities. On the other hand, the centrists were much more

likely to use occupational or personal political credentials as an identification. The other political positions were much more likely to use
some sort of political slogan. The centre was relying on its credentials;
the opposition was more political in its approach.

In carrying out the survey, a number of qualitative aspects of the
campaign became apparent to me. For one thing, it seemed clear that
the campaign was an emergent and learning process. As it proceeded it
seemed that individuals became more and more convinced of its reality
and openness. Slowly over the weeks, they escalated their political
rhetoric. Second, when the posters were political, they were by no
means simplistic. While they did not contain specific policy proposals,
they tended to attack the key political ideas which had been debated —
'no freedom without parties', 'the right to strike for the masses', and
so on. Third, and this is only partially reflected in the figures in Table
12.5, one got an overwhelming sense of the distribution of resources
being brought to bear on the campaign. Some candidates, especially in
the centre, covered their districts with posters while many others had
only a few.

Campaign Practices and Campaign Violence

The evidence until this point suggests that the official political platforms and symbols of the political organizations were not terribly relevant to the individual campaigns. Still, we should not disregard them altogether. The right and left did use the available symbols with considerable frequency. Further, the debate between the leadership of the
organizations and some of the more powerful and famous independents
did contribute to increasing the intensity of the campaign.[7] Over time,
the exchanges became more heated and a clear map of the polity began
to emerge. Key symbolic referents, such as the claim to being a
Nasserist, and key issues, such as the right to strike or freedom of the
press, began to define identifiable positions. The left/right division,
which had emerged in the long years of debate over political change,
re-emerged and solidified in the election campaign.

It is difficult to say exactly how deeply this debate penetrated or
how much it mattered in the campaign. However, whether or not the
people were listening to the debate, the regime did not ignore it. Two
weeks after the campaign began, a two-day bus strike occurred in
Cairo over rumours that the annual bonuses would be withheld. The
President, who claimed to be maintaining a neutral stance, lashed out

at the 'extreme left and the extreme right'. There was no doubt, however, that the primary target was the left.

> It is regrettable indeed that some have taken the opportunity of freedom in the country and started a campaign aimed at stirring discontent. This is a crime against the homeland. It is so simple to talk about existing difficulties or problems ignoring that we are all for solving them by all possible means and that we are dealing with them by means of up-to-date scientific and technological resources.
>
> One organization attempts to exploit the strike of bus drivers and issues a leaflet demanding the right to strike. I have said before that the right to strike exists only in capitalist states in which the owner of an enterprise cares only for his profits, even if they are at the expense of workers. How should I accept this in a socialist society in which fifty percent at least, of the membership of any elected council must be workers and farmers?[8]

What the regime called exploitation of the economic difficulties of the country, the opposition saw as the legitimate discussion of issues. In either case, the people were subject to constant reminders of the problems that the country faced. One suspects that they were agitated by the debate, regardless of whether or not they believed that the politicians actually had a solution for them.

The campaign was not all rhetoric and debate. On the streets individuals put a great deal of energy into getting elected. The political organizations did not play a large role in this in terms of finance, administration or coordination, but that in no way diminished the intensity of the campaign. In some areas, especially rural districts, the contest was between powerful families and clans. This meant the traditional politics of the countryside.[9] In these areas the campaign was carried out in visits to the local notables. In the cities, campaigning was more impersonal in some respects — 'by placards and posters' — but also more direct with a good deal of house-to-house canvassing, appearances at popular gatherings and political meetings.[10] Both in the country and the city the campaign proved to be more intense than many had expected.

Measures of this intensity can be found in the large number of candidates and the large sums of money spent on the campaign. The members of the parliament, who were interviewed in the survey cited above, said that they could not see how 'in the smallest district publicity and efforts in the election campaign would cost less than 1,000 L.E.'[11] It seems that, in fact, considerably larger sums were spent, with figures well in excess of 5000 LE frequently cited and numbers as high as 20,000 LE given on occasion. By international standards, these may not seem large, but recalling that the GNP per capita in Egypt was only 150 LE at the time, they are very considerable. To spend twenty or thirty times the GNP per capita is in line with international standards.

A more systematic indication of the intensity and nature of the campaign can be gained through a study of the extent and distribution of violence that it called forth. In roughly four weeks there were 70 incidents involving 216 injuries, 222 arrests and 11 deaths (see Table 12.6). There were some spectacular incidents − such as the shooting of an ASU governate secretary,[12] or a gun battle involving several dozen people that lasted for several hours − and these received a lot of attention, but there was also a pattern of persistent, minor incidents. By election day the violence had become so intense that the Ministry of the Interior was placed on a state of emergency, special Underministers were dispatched to specific districts to try to keep them under control and special regulations concerning assembly and the use of microphones were issued.

Table 12.6: Campaign Violence

	Shootings	Fights	Wounded	Arrests	Killed
1st Round					
9-27 October	14	16	135	138	3
28 October (election day)	1	6	2	15	3
2nd Round					
29 October-4 November	4	4	35	44	2
5 November (election day)	5	21	44	35	3
Total	24	47	216	222	11

The campaign had been lively, hard fought, expensive and, in the end, somewhat bloody. As expected, the centre won an overwhelming victory. However, as the next section shows, the efforts put into the campaign reflected some very real and fundamental political processes, processes which ultimately had a major impact on political developments.

Political Credentials and Electoral Success

There are a number of features of the outcome of the election to which
the supporters of the 'democratic experiment' point as an indication of
its soundness.[13] First, they point to a large turnover in the members of
the Assembly. Overall, only 43.6 per cent of the incumbents were
returned to the parliament, a rather low percentage. When we consider
that this low rate of successful incumbency came on top of large turn-
overs that had occurred in 1969 and 1971, it constitutes an upheaval.
New faces were seen as an indication of renewal and fairness.

Second, there were a number of ministers who ran for election.
This was seen as an indication of the politicization of the cabinet. Of
the eight ministers who ran, six were elected on the first round and two
were forced into the second round. That two ministers were severely
tested and could not win outright was also seen as a positive indication.

Third, there were a number of rather significant opposition members
elected to the parliament. The spokesmen for the left and right were
elected (though the spokesman for the right, Mustafa Kemal Murad,
was forced into the second round before he won his seat). Two former
Free Officers were elected as independents (in addition to Khalid
Muhyi-al-Din, spokesman for the left). A number of leaders of the old
Wafd party were elected, as were a number of leaders of opposition
during the Nasserist period (e.g. Hilmy Murad).

Fourth, there were a large number of rather important public personages who did not win. Sadat's brother-in-law was defeated, as were
a number of former ministers and former ASU secretaries. Even among
those who were currently active at high levels, there were some surprises.
The heads of a number of major administrative apparatuses were
defeated — the High Council for Islamic Affairs, the Telecommunica-
tions Authority, the High Sports Council, the Cairo Water Authority.
Among political figures who were defeated were two ASU secretaries at
the governate level, all those in the ASU general secretariat who ran
(Youth, Organizations, Workers), and four of the five chairmen of
the permanent committees of the People's Assembly (Education, Youth,
Housing, Health, Foreign Affairs).

While the fates of particular, well-known individuals are important,
they do not stand for all the races and we must look more carefully at
the results in order to discover systematic patterns. If we examine
the political biographies in my sample, I think we find that the general
qualitative impressions are sound (see Table 12.7).

Table 12.7: Political Background and Electoral Success (per cent)

	Overall			Centre			Right			Left			Independents		
	Win	2nd Rnd	Lost	Win	2nd Rnd	Lost	Win	2nd Rnd	Lost	Win	2nd Rnd	Lost	Win	2nd Rnd	Lost
Incumbents	52	17	31	55	20	25	50	0	50	100	0	0	33	7	60
ASU Officers	24	27	49	27	30	43	0	33	67	0	0	100	29	21	50
Local Government	23	13	65	50	13	37	0	50	50	0	0	100	5	15	80
Administrative	11	18	71	36	29	36	13	0	18	0	0	100	2	20	78
Former Representatives	20	26	54	15	38	47	40	0	60	0	100	0	18	18	64
Ministers	100	0	0	100	0	0	–	–	–	–	–	–	–	–	–
Union	33	0	67	50	0	50	–	–	–	0	0	100	25	0	75
Judges	23	8	69	50	50	0	0	0	100	–	–	–	20	0	80
Officers	50	0	50	50	0	50	0	0	100	0	0	100	63	0	37
Federal Arab Republic	33	33	33	50	50	0	–	–	–	–	–	–	0	0	100
Former minister	60	0	40	100	0	0	0	0	100	0	0	100	100	0	0
None	11	7	82	17	0	83	0	0	100	0	0	100	14	9	77

1. Incumbency. The overall rate of successful incumbency in the sample of candidates is slightly higher than in the election as a whole (52 per cent). However, there are important differences between the political positions. In all of the political organizations incumbents did well. However, among independents they did not do as well. It was primarily the incumbents who had gone into opposition via the independent route who did poorly.

2. Ministers. One is certainly struck by the strength of ministers and former ministers in the election. Overall these constitute the two most successful categories of candidates. The centre had monopolized all of the ministers who ran, but even among the former ministers, the three who ran as centrists or independents were victorious, while the two who ran as rightists or leftists were not. One can interpret this strength as a continuation of the 'executive' nature of the political system.

3. Officers. One is also struck by the strength of the officer category. It has a pattern similar to that of the ministerial categories. Overall, it is the fourth strongest category, coming just after incumbents, and it is the centrists and independents who were successful. Again, this suggests the continuation of certain patterns of traditional politics.

4. The return of old politicians. Former representatives constituted roughly 10 per cent of the candidates, evenly spread among the political positions, but highest in the right organization (14 per cent). Overall, they were not very successful. However, they were most successful when representing the right (40 per cent of them being elected). Thus, the sense that the old politicians were returning seems to have a basis in the election. Of the 29 combinations of opposition/background characteristics, the former representatives on the right had the fifth highest rate of success, coming after incumbents (right and left), former ministers and officers (independent).

5. ASU Secretaries and Undersecretaries. Major ASU figures did poorly in the election. Overall, less than one-fourth were elected. The poor performance was spread throughout the political positions. The ASU was definitely on the decline and these figures seem to bear this out.

6. Administrators. Overall, administrators did very poorly – no better than those without any political credentials. The opposition ran a large number of administrators and these figures suggest that the effort to turn administrative position into political power was not very successful. Even in the centre they did not do very well.

7. Other categories. The group of categories which I have called

minor political positions, especially unionists and local government, did not do well overall. However, they fared well in the centre. Thus, these political credentials, in themselves, were not sufficient to break through to the national legislature. They had to be coupled with membership in the centre party. Here, the local government category would be most important since it accounted for 9 per cent of all centre candidates (third after incumbents and the ASU). With 50 per cent of them successful, one can understand the long, political struggle over local government. In the centre, at least, local government was a stepping-stone to national politics.

In general, the patterns of success and failure in this analysis fit with the impressionistic view given above. With caution, we can estimate the composition of the centre in the Assembly. The centre was made up of a core of incumbents (50 per cent), surrounded by a variety of others recruited from the existing political institutions – local government (10 per cent), ASU (10 per cent), unions (4 per cent) – and a few administrators/ministers (3 per cent) and others (6 per cent). It is an expected pattern and certainly not an upheaval in political leadership. In a sense, the regime had run a lively election, but had guaranteed its outcome, not by rigging the election, but by monopolizing tangible and intangible resources in its support. The opposition had been severely outmatched. If there was turnover and change, it was within the centre, not between the centre and opposition. New centrists in the Assembly outnumber the opposition two to one.

Having examined the impact of political credentials on the election, I next examine the impact of the electoral structure on the outcome of the elections.

The Effects of the Electoral Structure

Table 12.8 depicts each of the types of second round races in terms of their competitiveness and the average change in turnout and votes for each of the political positions. Figures for the rate of participation in the election are not available but it seems to have been rather low, less than 50 per cent. It was even lower in the urban areas. However, by comparing the turnout for the first and second rounds, we gain some insight into the dynamics of competition. What we observe is that the more competitive the second round, the higher the rate of turnout. This suggests that competition was an effective political phenomenon. It aroused interest and brought people to the polls.

Table 12.8: Change in the Vote; First and Second Rounds

Type of race	Average change in turnout (%)	Average change in vote (%)			
		Centre	Right	Left	Independent
2-seat, 3-party (6)	+3.8	+32	+15	+41	−27
2-seat, 2-party equal (5)	+2.0	+26	−	−	−11
2-seat, 2-party unequal (4)	+1.6	+67	+36	+27	−41
2-seat, 1-party (3)	+0.8	−	−	−	−
1-seat, 2-party (2)	−7	−	−	−	−
1-seat, 1-party (1)	−7	−	−	−	−

When we examine the pattern of the change in vote between the rounds, we find that the independents could not hold their vote. In every type of two-seat competitive race their average vote declined. On the other hand, each of the political organizations was able to increase its vote. Further, since the increase in their vote is larger than the increase in the turnout, there must have been considerable migration of votes from the independent category. On average, there is not much difference between the political organizations in their ability to pick up votes in the second round (the large figure for the centre in the two-seat, unequal category would be a function of having twice the number of candidates in those races). Thus, there is a basis to ask whether the overwhelming number of seats which the centre held in the Assembly is a true representation of the electorate. Even with the great number of minor candidates removed from the second round, the independent vote did not collapse completely and the other political organizations showed an ability to attract votes in the second round which was almost as great as that of the centre.

A second way to examine the impact of the electoral structure is to examine the distribution of the centre's share of the first round vote, total seats, and its performance in winning seats on the first and second round. These figures are presented in Table 12.9. From one point of view we find that there is a widespread over-representation of the centre in the Assembly. In every governate the centre ended up with a higher percentage of seats than its vote on the first round. Here, a

Table 12.9: Centre Success

Governate	% of vote	% of seats	% of seats won on 1st round	% of seats won in competitive 2nd round	Net Diff. Seats minus Vote	Net. Diff. 2nd minus 1st round
Alexandria	38	50	22	46	12	24
Suez	41	50	50	100	9	50
Aswan	45	83	66	50	33	−16
Gharbiya	46	59	18	46	13	28
Kelyubia	47	64	30	46	17	4
Cairo	49	71	26	55	22	29
Dakhaliya	50	75	17	75	25	58
Beni Suaif	50	83	50	67	33	17
Menufiya	51	79	35	73	18	38
Behaira	52	50	50	100	− 2	50
Bahr al-Ahmar	52	76	82	70	26	47
Sharkiya	52	88	44	91	18	27
Feyum	55	83	40	67	20	3
Kafr as-Shaykh	56	75	47	50	23	19
Asyut	56	88	56	75	15	62
Giza	60	75	13	75	39	25
Port Said	61	100	75	100	39	25
Matruh	62	100	100	—	38	—
Minya	67	91	64	80	24	16
Qena	68	91	80	100	23	20
Damayata	70	100	83	100	30	17
Sohag	71	91	59	85	20	26
Ismailiya	100	100	100	—	0	—
Waadi al-Gadeed	100	100	100	—	0	—

number of observations are in order.

Once the centre received roughly 60 per cent of the vote on the first round, it tended to claim all of the seats. In contrast, in districts where the opposition was most intense, i.e. where the centre received less than 50 per cent of the first round vote, the opposition held up on the second round. It would seem that it is in the middle of the vote distribution (50 to 60 per cent) that the impact of the electoral structure was greatest. Here, opposition seems to have collapsed on the second round. In these governates, the centre did a great deal better in gaining seats in the restricted competition of the second round.

Next, let us examine the manner in which the centre won seats in

Table 12.10: The Effectiveness of the Centre in Corporate Categories

	% of seats decided on 1st round taken by centre	% of candidates on 2nd round	Won on 1st round	% of centre seats No Comp. 2nd round	Comp. 2nd round	% of all seats won by centre on 1st round
Professional	80	62	45	20	35	52
Peasant	81	65	43	29	28	70
Worker	64	53	32	20	48	48

each corporate category (see Table 12.10). The centre won 80 per cent of all the peasant and professional seats decided on the first round, but only 64 per cent of the worker seats. Further, it had 62 per cent of the professional and 65 per cent of the peasants who entered the second round, but only 53 per cent of the workers. Thus, in the worker category it had fewer seats won on the first round and fewer candidates in the second round (in relative terms). More importantly, we find that the centre won 35 per cent of its professional seats in competitive second round races and 28 per cent of its peasant seats, but 48 per cent of its worker seats. Thus, if there was a 'bias' operating it was operating in the category in which the centre was the weakest. That is, the absolute majority rule eliminated competition first; then the centre won its worker seats. To put the matter most pointedly, the centre won 70 per cent of the peasant seats in the unrestricted competition of the first round, 52 per cent of the professional seats, but only 40 per cent of the worker seats.

We can put these figures together to create estimates of the impact of the electoral structure on the outcome. The estimates are necessarily rough but I think they are of some importance (see Table 12.11).

Table 12.11: Actual and Hypothetical Distributions of the Outcome (per cent)

	Centre	Right	Left	Independent
Actual				
Votes	63	8	2	14
Total seats	83	4	1	14
Vote/Candidate	54	21	11	14
Hypothetical				
Vote adjusted for 2nd round migration	66	11	4	20
Geographic				
Avg. vote & seats	67			
Avg. vote & 2nd	72			
Avg. 1st & 2nd	57			
Corporate	71			
Actual number of Seats				
Professional	130			
Peasant	56			
Worker	122			
Hypothetical number of seats				
Professional	113			
Peasant	49			
Worker	80			

We can hypothesize a number of ways of apportioning the vote to reflect the electorate in the absence of the absolute majority rule: 1) apportion seats by first round popular vote; 2) apportion seats by votes per candidate; 3) adjust first round vote for second round vote migration. It should be noted that these estimates do not include any effort to re-apportion the seats between districts. Given the under-representation of the industrial/urban areas, re-apportionment would reduce the centre total. On the basis of these estimates a figure of roughly 60 per cent of the seats in the Assembly for the centre seems reasonable. Re-apportionment would ensure that it would not be more than 60 per cent. While there is no doubt that the centre held a solid majority, one can argue that there is a qualitative difference between an Assembly with an opposition of 17 per cent and one of 40 per cent. A proportional representation rule would have made a big difference.

Geographic Groups, Corporate Categories and Socio-Economic Patterns

The underlying pattern of the geographic and the corporate distribution of the vote has begun to emerge in the discussion of the electoral structure. In Table 12.12 I have divided the governates into four categories and reported the results in each governate. As one moves from the industrial delta to the agricultural delta to Upper Egypt to the small fringe governates the percentage of votes for the centre increases steadily. There are slight variations in the different measures of the centre's strength but this basic pattern holds throughout.

In the total vote, the centre did considerably worse in the industrial delta and considerably better in the fringe. The difference between the industrial delta and the other groupings is most clearly reflected in the worker category. In the industrial delta the centre held only 53 per cent of the worker seats, while in the other groupings it held at least 75 per cent of the seats. In none of the individual governates of the industrial delta did it hold more than 66 per cent of the seats, while in 14 of the 17 governates outside of the industrial delta in which there were worker representatives it held at least 83 per cent of those seats.

In the professional category the centre starts with 68 per cent in the industrial delta and rises to 86 per cent in Upper Egypt, before declining slightly in the fringe. Here, we might draw the line between the delta as a whole and the rest of the country. While the centre generally did well in the professional category, we note that in the delta in only one of ten governates did it hold more than 90 per cent of the seats, while outside of the delta it held 90 per cent of the seats in 10 of 14 governates.

Table 12.12: Geographic and Corporate Distributions of the Centre Vote

Governates	% of vote 1st Round	Total	% of Seats Professional	Peasants	Worker
Cairo	49	71	61	—	66
Alexandria	38	50	78	—	33
Behaira	52	50	80	73	60
Kelyubia	47	64	71	—	57
Gharbia	46	59	50	83	50
Industrial delta average	46	59	68	78	53
Menufiya	51	51	89	100	50
Dakahliya	50	75	75	50	88
Sharkiya	52	88	83	100	86
Damayata	70	100	100	100	100
Kafr as-Shaykh	55	75	50	100	100
Agricultural delta average	56	78	79	90	85
Feyum	55	83	100	100	50
Beni Suaif	50	83	100	50	100
Minya	67	91	90	100	89
Aswan	45	83	100	0	100
Giza	60	75	50	100	100
Qena	68	91	80	100	100
Asyut	56	88	78	100	100
Sohag	71	91	90	100	83
Upper Egypt average	59	86	86	81	90
Matruh	62	100	100	100	—
Suez	41	50	0	—	100
Bahr al-Ahmar	52	50	100	—	0
Port Said	61	100	100	—	100
Ismailiya	100	100	100	—	100
Waadi al-Gadeed	100	100	100	100	—
Small fringe average	69	83	83	100	75

In the peasant category the centre did extremely well and the variation between groupings is smaller still. It held at least 73 per cent of the peasant seats in 13 of the 16 governates in which there were peasant representatives.

The geographic and corporate group patterns suggest an underlying socio-economic pattern. The level of industrialization is the key variable. The more industrial the area, the lower the centre vote. In four of the five governates of the industrial delta, it did not even receive a majority on the first round. This pattern can best be studied by correlation and regression analysis. At the same time, the earlier analysis can be quantified and studied in a more streamlined fashion in that statistical mode of analysis. Thus, let us turn to a quantitative analysis of the elections.

A Quantitative Analysis of the Election Results: Data and Method

As a matter of convenience I shall describe all of the variables to be used in the analysis at one time (see Table 12.13). The unit of analysis is the governate. This is the primary administrative unit in Egypt, though not the primary electoral unit, which is the district. Though this obscures some differences between districts, it is the unit of analysis for which data can best be reconstructed and it also tends to be the unit of identification and press reporting.

The first four variables are simply the percentage of the vote obtained by each of the political positions on the first round (counting independents as a political position). The second four variables are the number of candidates per district fielded by each of the political positions. The next eight variables are measures of the success of the centre organization.

The geographic groupings I use as dummy variables are the industrial delta, the agricultural delta, Upper Egypt, and the small fringe governates which are defined in Table 12.12.

The final four variables are measures of the economic characteristics of the governates. Public-sector size is public-sector employment as a percentage of total employment. Agriculture is the ratio of agricultural employment to industrial employment. Capitalist industry is a rank order variable based on the ratio of private-sector industrial employment to public-sector industrial employment, with the highest score assigned to the highest ratio. Similarly, capitalist agriculture is a rank order variable based on the ratio of orchard crop area to cotton crop area, with the highest score assigned to the highest ratio.

In Table 12.14 I have presented the correlations between the vote on the first round and the economic variables. First, I think we should note the set of relationships between the vote for each of the political positions. There is a very high negative correlation between the centre vote and the independent vote. Mathematically, this was to be expected because of the large vote which the independents got on the first round. However, the other relationships are somewhat surprising. The right vote shows a small negative correlation with the centre vote, whereas The left vote shows a much larger negative correlation. Since the right

Table 12.13: Definition of the Variables

Variable	Construction
Vote	
Centre	% of vote on the first round
Right	" "
Left	" "
Independent	" "
Number of Candidates	
Centre	Candidates per district
Right	" "
Left	" "
Independent	" "
Centre Success	
Professional	% of candidates who won on first round or
Peasant	entered second round who were from the
Worker	centre, in each category
Seats, first	% of all seats decided on first round (won or no competition in second round) which were taken by the centre
Seats, second	% of seats decided in competitive second round races (races with more than one position) which were taken by centre candidates
Seats	
Professional	% of seats in category held by centre
Peasant	" " "
Worker	" " "
Geographic	
Industrial delta	Dummy variable
Agricultural delta	"
Upper Egypt	"
Fringe	"
Economic	
Public sector	Public sector employment/total work force
Agriculture	Agricultural employment/industrial employment
Capitalist industry	Rank order of private industrial employment/ public industrial employment
Capitalist agriculture	Rank order of orchard crop area/cotton crop area

fielded three times the number of candidates and got five times the number of votes that the left did, we might expect the opposite to be the case on mathematical grounds. Since both left and right received such a small share of the vote, we can interpret this as a basic pattern of opposition. Further, note that the independent vote is negatively correlated with the right vote, but positively correlated with the left

vote. We observe an easily identifiable independent/left versus a centre/
right pattern.

Table 12.14: Economic Variables and Vote Totals (correlation
coefficients)

		Vote		
	Centre	Right	Left	Independent
Centre	—	-.10	-.42	-.93
Right		—	.03	-.23
Left			—	.26
Independent				—
Public sector	-.51	-.19	.18	.56
Agriculture	.48	.30	-.36	-.54
Capitalist agriculture	-.14	.08	-.29	.07
Capitalist industry	.38	.39	-.16	-.50

The economic variables make the pattern of opposition even clearer.
Centre and right voting are both negatively correlated with the size of
the public sector, while independent and left voting are positively
correlated with it. Both agriculture and capitalist industry are positively correlated with centre and right voting, while they are negatively correlated with independent and left voting. It is only for capitalist agriculture, which has generally smaller correlations, that the
pattern does not hold. The centre/right versus independent/left pattern
which is defined by a public-sector versus agriculture/capitalist industry
dimension in the economy has been the central argument presented
throughout this work.

I have examined this assertion by subjecting the groups of variables
to a factor analysis (see Table 12.15). The economic variables yield one
factor which accounts for 58 per cent of the variance between them. It
shows the basic dimension in the economy. The variables load in such a
way as to suggest a public-sector (-.76) versus agriculture (.84) and
capitalist industry (.76) dimension. The voting variables yielded two
factors. The first which accounted for 54 per cent of the variance in
the data, suggests a centre (-.66) versus independent (.64) and left
(.39) dimension. The second factor, which accounts for 27 per cent of
the variance, might be called an organized opposition factor, primarily
defined by the right (.92).

Table 12.15: Factor Analysis of Economic Variables and Vote Totals

Economic variables	Factor loadings	
Public sector	-.76	
Agriculture	.84	
Capitalist agriculture	.23	
Capitalist industry	.76	
Variance explained	58%	

Political variables	Factor loadings	
	1st factor	2nd factor
Centre	-.66	-.12
Right	-.06	.92
Left	.39	.30
Independent	.64	-.23
Variance explained	54%	27%

Economic and Political	1st factor	2nd factor
Public sector	.51	-.54
Agriculture	-.54	.59
Capitalist agriculture	.20	.40
Capitalist industry	-.35	.74
Centre	-1.00	0
Right	.01	.49
Left	.45	.05
Independent	.84	-.27
Variance explained	44%	20%

When we include all of the political and economic variables in one factor analysis, these two factors recur and the economic variables load in the expected pattern. The first factor, which accounts for 44 per cent of the variance, is defined by a large negative loading for the centre (-1.0) and positive loadings for the independent vote (.84) and the left (.45). The economic variables load positive for public sector size (.51) and negative for the other three economic variables. The basic argument being made is that the left and independents represented an opposition which was drawing its support from the industrial and public-sector areas and this is clearly reflected in the first factor. The second factor, which accounts for 20 per cent of the variance, appears quite clearly in this analysis as a right factor —right vote (.49), capitalist industry (.74), agriculture (.59) and capitalist agriculture (.40) load positive, while independent vote (-.27) and public-sector (-.84) load negative.

The final step in the analysis is statistically to explain the outcome of the election using the economic and geographic variables in regression analysis. In Table 12.16 I have presented the results of separate

Table 12.16: (a) Economic and Geographic Variables as Predictors of the Vote

	R^2	Economic Beta's				R^2	Geographic Beta's			
		Public sector	Agric.	Capit. indust.	Capit. agric.		Indust. Delta	Agric. Delta	Fringe	Upper Egypt
Vote										
Centre	.37	-.38	.13	.18	-.28	.26	-.32		.31	
Right	.15			.38	.31	.18	-.17		-.43ᵃ	
Left	.22		-.38			.15			-.39ᵃ	
Independent	.44	.37	-.11	-.30	.24	.19	.40	—	-.10	
Seats										
Total	.44	-.68ᵃ			-.11	.38	-.55		.15	
Professional	.11	-.29			-.23	.37			.70ᵃ	
Peasant	.69ᵃ		.37	.36	.33	.26		.11	-.48ᵃ	.40ᵃ
Worker	.19	-.43ᵃ	-.28	-.09	.27	.35	.39ᵃ	.46ᵃ		.54ᵃ

(b) Best Explanations of the Vote

	R^2 (Sig.)	Beta's			
		Public Sector	Agric.	Capit. indust.	Fringe
Vote					
Centre	.52 (002)	-.21	—	.46ᵃ	.55ᵃ
Right	.15 (061)		—	.38	-.48ᵃ
Left	.29 (029)		-.46ᵃ	—	-.39ᵃ
Independent	.49 (003)	.26	—	-.50ᵃ	.19
Seats					
Total	.50 (002)	-.63ᵃ	—	—	.27
Professional	.32 (049)	-.11	—	.17	.56ᵃ
Peasant	.59 (001)	-.21	.26	.32	-.25ᵃ
Worker	.33 (043)	-.54ᵃ	—	-.46ᵃ	-.58ᵃ

a. Significant at .05 level.

regression analyses for these two sets of variables. I have started with the strongest predictor and included variables as long as they explain an additional one per cent of the variance. In both cases we find that we explain a considerable amount of the variance, with the economic variables explaining somewhat more. The pattern of the signs of the Beta weights is exactly that which would be predicted by a socio-economic argument.

The pattern also suggests a simple way to combine the two analyses. Two geographic variables enter into the vote analysis consistently — the industrial delta and the small fringe. However, the industrial delta was highly positively correlated with the public sector, while the fringe was highly negatively correlated with capitalist agriculture. In a sense, we can use the fringe to stand in for the questionable economic variable (capitalist agriculture), while we do not need any of the other geographic variables. The fact that the fringe recurs so consistently in all of the equations also suggests this approach. One can also make a good substantive argument for the uniqueness of the fringe governates. They are all small, with no more than two districts in any governate. Four have been on the front line of confrontation with Israel for over a decade, remaining under rather strict military control. A fifth, Waadi al-Gadeed, was, to a certain extent, a creation of the government.

Using the three economic variables and the fringe dummy variable, we explain roughly 50 per cent of the variance in centre and independent voting, 30 per cent of the left vote, but only 15 per cent of the right vote. In the seat categories, we explain between 32 per cent of the variance (professional) and 59 per cent (peasant). It will also be noted that the multiple R's and a large number of the individual Beta weights are significant at the .05 level. Finally, the signs of the Beta weights are all in the expected direction.

This argument was tested in a group of 18 governates which excluded the fringe, and the results were much the same. It was also tested in a group of districts representing the largest urban areas and the argument holds as well. In fact, it is even stronger.

The Implications of the Election for the Polity

I think three characteristics of the election — a systematic socio-economic weakness in support, an artificially large majority, and a difference of opinion about the fairness of the election — interacted to produce an explosive turn of events soon after the elections. The centre had clearly gained control over the traditional political structures of the agricultural areas and in the fringe, but it could not dominate the politics of the cities and the industrial areas. It may be that it was there that the real constituency for a policy of political liberalization lay and that it was in these politically active areas that one had to win support. I would also argue, though I do not have the data to test it directly, that the negative effects of the policy of economic liberalization were also most deeply felt in the urban and industrial areas. As one moves away from these areas their impact, especially the impact of inflation, lessened. The electoral structure may have masked the true extent of the weakness in the support of the government. The evidence clearly suggests that there was some substance to the opposition's assertion that the structure was not entirely fair.[14]

In the overwhelming majority that the centre got, it was easy to miss the message of considerable weakness in the urban and industrial areas. Ultimately, the net effect of a frustrated opposition and an overly confident regime was to reduce the chances for a successful liberalization. Given the tension between the authoritarian tendencies in the regime and the liberalization process, an opposition of 40 per cent, with a left/independent bloc of 25 per cent (both reasonable estimates), might have been a positive restraining force on both the regime and the opposition. The regime would have been more inclined to treat the opposition seriously, properly and carefully, while the opposition would have been less frustrated. 'Loyal opposition' would have looked like a much more respectable occupation. As I have suggested in the discussion of the creation of semi-pluralism, the regime did not value a loyal opposition highly and under the circumstances the opposition was not inclined to behave in a very responsible fashion. The election campaign and the outcome did not induce any of the parties to change their attitudes and behaviours. It may have made matters worse.

It is difficult to measure the extent of the frustration felt by the opposition and the various factors that went into creating it. It is equally difficult to measure how much the regime's behaviour was based on overestimating its support. It is also difficult to know precisely how behaviours would have been altered given a different outcome. However, I think frustration and misjudgement were important factors contributing to the breakdown of the liberalizing polity. That breakdown did not take very long to occur.

13 THE JANUARY RIOTS

Between Elections and Riots

With the centre organization having gained 83 per cent of the seats in the Assembly, I think it is safe to say that the regime could have produced a legislature of approximately the same composition at any point in time that it chose. In fact, it may be that the previous Assembly had almost as much opposition. It seemed that one could regularly muster twenty or thirty votes to call for a debate which the leadership wanted to avoid. While the regime could have produced the Assembly in any way it had wanted to, it had actually been created in a long, contentious political debate and a heated, violent election campaign. The regime had affirmed its commitment to a certain degree of liberalization and, having gone through the effort, it wanted to reap the rewards. Pointing to the debate and the campaign, it declared the political experiment a success and expected to have things its own way.

No act better symbolizes this attitude than President Sadat's speech to the first meeting of the new Assembly in which he declared that the political organization would thereafter be considered parties.[1] He probably did not have the legal right to do so.[2] He was more sensitive to a potentially grand gesture than to the legality of the situation.

This attitude permeated the new political structure. The cabinet was not effectively politicized. When new governors were appointed, half were military or police officers.[3] When the newly-elected Prime Minister presented his programme, it was the same hours-long litany of facts and figures that bore no greater relationship to reality than they had in the past. In the Assembly the centre party took every leadership position and totally crushed any opposition member who had the temerity to run for any leadership position.[4] It even tried to gag its own party members.[5]

There is little wonder that the opposition was wary of the centre party. All the claims about the beginning of a new political system to the contrary, the behaviour of the centre party suggested otherwise. Still, the opposition pressed its efforts. More than 180 challenges were lodged against the validity of the election of specific members of the Assembly and 150 of these were passed on to the courts.[6] The right immediately declared its intention to work for the abolition of the Socialist Prosecutor General Office.[7] The left called for an independent authority to oversee future elections.[8] The major independents immediately went into negotiations about how to form a coalition.[9] Hilmy Murad, one of those major independents, challenged the right of Sayyid Marei, whose seat was the only one for which the centre did not run a candidate, to be Speaker of the Assembly.[10] Within the Assembly, there was constant bickering over procedural matters and an aggressive pursuit of substantive issues.[11] Within two months, more questions were posed to ministers than entire years had produced in the previous Assembly.

Things were certainly lively, perhaps too lively, for the parliament to handle. One might have expected as much. The opposition had consistently shown that it was prepared to put up a fight. At the same time, the behaviour of the centre did not enhance the credibility of the political experiment. Perhaps, with time, the structure would have worked its way into a manageable, functioning semi-parliamentary government. By mid-December there seemed to be a realization that tensions had to be reduced, but in mid-January everything came to a halt.

On the night of 17 January official prices were increased by administrative decision without consultation, debate or vote of the Assembly. On the morning of 18 January the man in the street awoke to officially established prices on basic commodities such as sugar, tea and bottled gas that meant an increase in the cost of living of roughly 15 per cent for someone with an average income.[12] The increases had, in fact, gone into effect the day before they were announced. This was politics as usual *par excellence*.

By the morning of 20 January, when the military finally restored order, Egypt had been shaken to its very core. For two full days, from Aswan to Alexandria, Egypt witnessed its worst riots in a quarter of a century. It was twenty-five years, almost to the day, since the 'Burning of Cairo' riots which were a landmark on the road to the overthrow of the Faruk monarchy. Some talked of a second burning of Cairo. Although that was an exaggeration, the riots were intense. Police stations and policemen were a primary target. Property was frequently attacked, especially symbols of the state and foreign presence. Looting was widespread. By the official count, which most observers agree was a gross underestimate, 80 deaths occurred, 560 people were wounded and 1,200 were arrested. For two days, political order had broken down completely.[13]

Political developments came to a standstill. The government dragged out the usual scapegoats — Libya, the Soviet Union, the left. It charged the left party with having been the vehicle for, if not the author of, an organized attempt to overthrow the government.[14] Within three weeks the regime had put together a rather harsh response in the form of a plebiscite which received the support of 99 per cent of the electorate which the government typically claimed in such plebiscites. However, observers were convinced that almost no one voted. The plebiscite had contained an eight-point programme:[15]

1. The conditions for forming parties would be governed by a new law from the legislative Assembly.
2. Membership in clandestine or hostile organizations would be punishable by up to life in prison.
3. Demonstrations with the intent of sabotage or attacks on property would carry the same penalty.
4. Payment of taxes 'is a duty' with the limit for exemption from taxes raised to a level of LE500.
5. Registration of all personal wealth would be required and failure to do so or false statements would carry a penalty of loss of political rights.
6. Rioters or instigators of public disruptions, or those who disrupted government, the public or private sector, or education, or who threatened to use violence, would be liable to penal servitude.
7. Workers whose strikes might harm the national economy would be subject to penal servitude as well.
8. Demonstrations which threatened public security would be punishable by penal servitude.

It was a classic blend of harsh penalties for rioters and implicit recognition that some of their grievances had merit. Most of what it declared illegal was already illegal anyway; penalties had merely been increased. It was politics as usual, but with a nasty, harsher tone.

As always, there was another interpretation of the riots. Many said they were a mass protest against economic hard times and the government. These competing explanations always cropped up in the aftermath of disturbances in Egypt. What distinguished this round of assertions and counter-assertions was the fact that there was a legitimate opposition which was willing to state the alternative officially and which believed that it had the right to do so. For example, Khalid Muhyi-al-Din, spokesman for the left, responded to the charges against the left before the Assembly and in the international press, pointing out that the Prime Minister had violated the principle of presumed innocence.[16]

Kemal al-Din Hussein, one of the original core of Free Officers, who had been elected to the parliament as an independent, had the temerity to denounce the plebiscite as unconstitutional in an open letter to the President. He blamed the riots on government policy, stupidity and bungling. The language was strong, but the argument was not uncommon. He was charged with casting aspersions on the Presidency and the Constitution and damaging the legitimacy of the new political institutions. In spite of the fact that he had impeccable anti-left credentials, gave a contrite and apologetic statement in his own defence, and had an arguable legal point (that the plebiscite was illegal because it legislated taxes), he was expelled from the Assembly.[17] Still, he had publicly made his argument.

Al-Tali'ah gave an unblushing interpretation and was closed down for it.[18]

Even *al-Iqtisadi* hinted at the alternative explanation. Since it is such an 'establishment' publication, it is worth noting the analysis:

> For the sake of Egypt and the interest of the Egyptian people, we must face the facts of the moment, which we have pointed out numerous times in the pages of this magazine, when we said that Egyptian society was bulging with a time bomb and it is in a frightful conflict with time to stop its explosion. What we expected has, in fact, occurred. We wish that it not be repeated. Regrettably, the majority of the Egyptian people has come to feel no confidence in Egypt in light of the new consumer society, but they believe — and this feeling was expressed in numerous debates with the observers of the operations of sabotage — that they live in the shadow of a system of economic apartheid, that is, economic discrimination that prevents the majority from the fundamentals of life and gives fabulous gains and fabulous advantages to groups newly added to the society, whether this new group is that of parasitic incomes, or members of a new class in Egyptian society, or the Arab tourists who come to Egypt with dreadful buying power, dismembering and destroying Egyptian society with it.[19]

They were describing nothing short of open class warfare.

Within six weeks after the riots the stiff penalties had been passed; the left had been bitterly attacked and was under legal investigation in a variety of forms; Hussein had been expelled from the legislature; and the cabinet had been re-organized, making the Prime Minister the

Minister of the Interior as well, while adding two deputy Ministers of Interior at cabinet level. The regime had definitely gone on to a hostile footing.

The harsh reaction, to what many believed was as much a general social protest as a plot, was too much for some to bear. Rumour has it that some of the long-term parliamentarians, even those who might be inclined to disagree with Hussein's argument, refused to take part in the vote to expel him (which was 281 to 28 with 3 abstentions). A similar open secret was the fact that Gamal al-Oteify, architect of the political legislation of 1972-5 and a proponent of political liberalization as far back as 1968, left the cabinet as much because he could not tolerate the plebiscite as for the official reasons of health. Many of the supporters of the regime recognized the causes of the riots and lamented the fact that there was very little tolerance for genuine opposition in any arena — the streets, the press, the cabinet, the parliament — but they were unable to moderate the regime's response.

The Dynamics of the Riots

In reviewing the harsh reaction to the riots, we should not overlook the fact that the regime felt very threatened. The riots were severe and the regime seemed unprepared for them. It took a long time to get the military on to the streets (some said it refused to clean up the mess which the government had created). The police absorbed a great deal of abuse before the military came to the rescue.[20] There were signs of organization in the riots. Identical anti-regime literature appeared simultaneously across the length of the country. There were systematic attempts to cut internal communications. There seemed to be co-ordinated attacks on neighbouring police stations so that they could not support one another. There was a selectivity of targets, concentrating on state property. It seemed that the rioters were working in relays to tire the police out. However, even if we take all of these indications of organization as real, the evidence of a 'plot' is not very persuasive and it is hard to imagine that this set of rioters was directly capable of overthrowing the regime.

What the regime may have been truly threatened by was a genuine lack of support. The economic policy was clearly at the root of the problem, but the political experiment certainly had not been a great success. Whether the regime honestly believed that the rioters presented a direct threat to its existence, or that the military was wavering in support, or that its support was slipping away, its inclination was to take a hard line.

In this interpretation I have blended economic and political factors. I think that the economic argument is clear, both in the general terms of the earlier analysis and in the very close connection between the rise in prices and the outbreak of rioting. There is no doubt that these were fundamentally urban food riots triggered by a rise in official prices for people who had been severely pushed by years of inflation, but I think they were more than that. They were also political. First, they expressed opposition to the government and its policies. Second, the political structure and the political process had generated them. There is, in fact, a close relationship between elections and riots in Egypt. Both elections for the People's Assembly were followed by riots. In every set of riots, whether they follow elections or not, one of the prime targets is the Assembly. The rioters do not look on it as an object of attack; rather, it seems that they want to use it as a forum in which to be heard.

If this is the case, then this mechanism would have been operating most profoundly in early 1977. These elections in particular aroused and politicized large numbers of people and, with the capricious raising of prices, the demonstrators felt that the elections and the Assembly had failed them. Having gone through an intense election campaign, having elected sixty or so opposition members to the Assembly, the price increases were put through administratively, overnight, in secret, without comment, discussion or debate. All those votes cast had not even brought the opportunity for the chosen representatives, opposition or otherwise, to offer their opinions before the fact. Thus, I attach great importance not only to the price increases as the precipitator of the riots, but also to the manner, the moment and the political context in which the decision was made and executed. Indeed, I believe there were ways in which the decision could have been executed which would have reduced the violent response, although there was certain to have been some reaction to it. The leadership was simply not attuned to such an approach − which would have required bringing in the opposition, allowing it to criticize and then co-opting it in one way or another − thereby allowing the violent reaction to be spread out and dissipated.

Because the situation was so mismanaged, we can pose a series of pointed questions about how the decision was executed.

1. In the first place, why was this particular decision made? Here, there is a simple explanation. Egypt had become totally dependent on

international economic institutions and a conservative government had been put in place in Egypt. International bankers have a particular fondness for reducing subsidies on consumer goods — basic consumer commodities — as a way of improving domestic accounts. The Egyptian regime had little inclination to resist, even though there may well have been alternatives to this approach. For example, the manipulation and abuse of the subsidies programme, if eliminated, probably could have saved as much as the increase in prices. One might have decided to reform taxes and register property before the riots, instead of after. One could have cracked down on luxury consumption. Given its bases of support, the regime was not inclined to take any of these actions. An increase in prices appeared to be the easy decision. The international backers wanted it, the powerful interests supporting the regime would tolerate it and the regime had the administrative resources to execute it.

2. Why spring the decision so suddenly? For motivation we may cite the regime itself. On the morning of 18 January, with the rioters in the streets, but the intensity of the riots as yet uncertain, the Minister of Economics (el Kaisouni) argued that to subject the issue of price increases to a long debate would open a wide field for abuses and manipulation of supplies.[21] He argued that the step was legal and that an increase in prices had been envisioned in the general programme of the government.[22] With strong motivation and some justification, there was little to do but make the decision. The economists were told to do what they had to do and leave the rest to the politicians.

3. How did the regime misjudge the situation so completely? The politicians obviously did not have as firm a grasp on the situation as they had thought. They certainly expected some protest and objection, but the reaction was not what they expected for a number of reasons.

The timing was bad. The dead of winter was not the moment to raise prices. Riots have become a winter phenomenon in Egypt. This is partly because life is hard in the winter — which is certainly not the moment to raise the price of bottled gas — and partly because school is in session and there are large bodies of students who are easily mobilized in protest.

The regime simply misjudged the level of economic discontent. It had repeatedly faced protests over standard of living issues in the past. It had frequently refused to interpret them as such. Many times the issues had been isolated and very specific. The regime failed to realize the power of so generalized and visible an issue as an across-the-board price increase in basic commodities.

The regime misjudged the level of energy in the polity. From one point of view, it believed its own argument that simply casting a ballot was enough. It had campaigned on a platform of solving the problem of the masses, but this solution was certainly not one which the masses had voted for — it cut too deeply. If the regime thought that by casting ballots the electorate had lost its intense political interest, it was mistaken. The electorate did not quickly lose its sense of involvement and the heated activity in the Assembly after the elections maintained the interest. Literally and figuratively, the electorate was still engaged in the debate up to and during the riots.

From another point of view, the regime seems to have misjudged the nature of the clandestine organizations. The problem was not that they were highly organized or powerful, but that there were so many small groups — right and left — that were willing to take action. The regime knew they were out there and tried to keep tabs on them, but it had not realized that they were so spread around and that so many would take to the streets.

Most importantly, the regime had run all the various sources of discontent together. Those who wanted to overthrow the regime, and there were some, had a perfect opportunity. Those who thought that the semi-liberal experiment had been a sham, or felt cheated by the political process in one form or another, had their proof positive. Those who could no longer stand the crushing economic burden gave at least their tacit approval. Some of these discontents had not been expressed in violent protest in the past, nor need they have been in the future; but concentrated at a moment in time, and once the violence began, they tended to feed on one another.

The observations of the editor of *al-Iqtisadi* suggest a striking aspect. While some rioted, burned and looted, the members of the middle class stood by watching and debating the economic policy. Other press accounts suggest that different groups engaged in different behaviours. Some lit fires or engaged in armed attacks on police stations. Hordes of the urban underclass looted. Others took to protest marches, aiming at specific targets — the People's Assembly, the American University, the night clubs. I do not have the data to prove the point but it seemed to me that different people were on the streets expressing different discontents in different ways. Some would have taken to the streets for almost any reason. Others would have done so only under the most unique of circumstances. In all likelihood, the latter groups would have hesitated to engage in the kinds of activities that the former did. In a sense, each was out on the streets because the others were and all saw an opportunity to register their objections.

Conclusion: Understanding the Intensity of the Riots

The impact of the politicization of grievances is so important and, I believe, so deeply imbedded in the process of liberalization, that it warrants a more general formulation. The difficulty with liberalizing debate and the first free political activity is that they tend to intensify political struggle around major political issues and isolate certain groups, predisposing them to extreme action.[23] The mechanism by which this occurs can be understood in terms of Weber's conception of class action, here applied to political action. Weber suggests a hierarchy of action consisting of five levels:

1. No action.
2. Mass action, defined as a multitude of 'essentially similar reactions'.
3. Amorphous communal action, defined as 'a vague sense of a feeling of community'.
4. Communal action, defined as action that is 'oriented to the feeling of the actors that they belong together'.
5. Societal action, defined as action that is oriented 'to a rationally motivated adjustment of interests'.

The first free election and debate raises the level of action of many individuals in society, draws political actors into sharply-defined categories, and juxtaposes those categories. As the intensity of the political struggle builds, certain groups come to feel a sense of isolation and frustration which they link to their political situation. Thus, they may become prone to extreme action.

For a large number of individuals, the first free election represents a movement from the first to the second level of action. Those who only vote move from no action to mass action. While casting a vote is generally a mass action, in these instances it tends to be much more. Political expression has been inhibited in the past and this act represents a release of political energies. Voting becomes communalized, a valued and intense form of expression which is a shared experience.

For certain segments of the society, this first political activity represents a movement to a higher level of action. Active political organization has been inhibited in the past and the new conditions of organization call forth strenuous efforts. Allowing new political organizations involves many people in action motivated toward pursuit of their interest – creating organizations and getting elected. They move to societal action.

It is not only those who have been invited or permitted to participate in politics who increase their activity at this level. Clandestine or
illegal organizations, seeing the activities around them, also increase
their efforts to build their organizations.

The strenuous efforts that go into the first political campaign
contribute to a sharpening of definitions and the transparency of the
situation as well. Because the campaign is a release from a period in
which political expression was repressed and because political possi-
bilities are unknown, the activists endeavour to create clear symbolic
definitions.

This tendency is reinforced by the nature of the issues that tend
to be raised. This first activity is not simply a process in which the
distribution of power is decided for a short period. It tends to be a
process in which the structure of power itself is at stake — not one
rotation of power, but the opportunity to decide the future distribution of power.

The intensification of politics bears most heavily on minority
positions. In the search for symbolic identifications, minorities are
attacked from two sides. They are caught between the more extreme
positions which endeavour to pull their constituency outside of the
polity and the less extreme positions which endeavour to pull it inside.

This is the point at which the issue of management becomes critical.
The ambivalent groups need not be isolated or lost to the new liberalizing polity. The art of strategic compromise is possible — to give the
feeling that the opposition is participating in defining institutions and
that its prospects are not hopeless. The art of compromise is difficult
to practise, because those in power tend to see every issue as too vital
to compromise on. Above all, they fail to appreciate the importance of
the loyal opposition. In trying to ensure and expand their own constituency, they end up reducing the constituency for the polity which they
have defined. It was exactly this art and these management skills that
were lacking in Egypt. The regime never gave the opposition the feeling
that a compromise had been struck. It immediately set about circum-
venting whatever had been conceded. The opposition could not help
but get the impression that there was not much point in playing the
game. The outcome of the election, so loudly trumpeted and so
quickly contradicted by presumptuous and uncompromising action, up
to and including the decision to increase prices, continually reinforced
this impression.

In defining the dynamics of the first free election in these political terms, I do not intend to suggest that there is no social structural base to politics. Rather, I suggest that there is an interaction between the two (as outlined in chapter 2). The link between the socio-economic and the political lies in the fact that groups are located at various points along the political spectrum for social structural reasons. The politically active seek their constituencies at particular social structural locations. They know the class divisions in society well and they exploit them in mobilizing their bases of support. The intense political struggle can be said to activate and accentuate existing social divisions. The political leadership expends great efforts to raise the level of action of its constituency. This places the socio-economic divisions in society in particularly clear relief (see Figure 13.1).

The process comes to focus on the minority positions because of the uncertainty of the nature of constituencies and because of the ill-defined nature of the political structure. In this way, the social structural base available for extremism is expanded and support for the liberalizing polity is reduced.

We need impute no sinister motives in this, and I think there were none or very few in Egypt. The efforts expended are strictly legal and well-intentioned, being aimed at the elections, but the polity is energized. When the election puts this type of pressure on the 'wings' of the political spectrum, frustration results. In this atmosphere, if the regime acts in such a way as to exacerbate those frustrations, if it provides a precipitator, a major outbreak of violence is possible.

Thus, I believe that the intensity of the riots and the harshness of the response reflected both the crushing failure of economic liberalization and the dynamic, uncontrolled energy of the liberalizing polity.

Figure 13.1: Political Processes in the First Free Election and the Generation of Violence

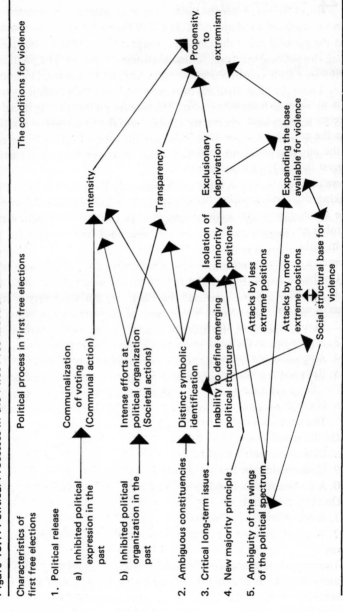

14 JANUARY AND JERUSALEM: THE FINAL TRANSFORMATION

Domestic Turmoil, International Peace

It is at these low points, filled with domestic tension, that Egyptian foreign policy makes its outwardly startling turns. I believe that this was the case in 1967, as Arab Socialism exhausted itself, and in 1973, as the initial promises of the Corrective Revolution went unfulfilled. I suggest that in 1977 it was the foundering of the political and economic liberalizations of the *October Working Paper* that pushed Sadat into making the most startling turn of all, a peace initiative to Jerusalem. The starting point for such an analysis must be in the victory of the October war of 1973, a victory that proved so ephemeral.

In early 1974, the October war looked like a success. The Egyptians claimed a number of results of the October war.

On the home front:

1. A real impetus for the possibility of the Egyptian economy to open to the rest of the world and flourish.

2. A restoration of the self-respect and honour of the Egyptians.

3. An upsurge in the nationalist legitimacy of the regime.

4. A mandate for the political system to reform.

5. Reductions of strains in the military.

On the Arab front:

6. Unity in the Arab world.

7. The true mobilization of the oil weapon for the first time.

On the Israeli front:

8. Diplomatic isolation of Israel.

9. Undermining the Israeli concept of security.

10. A demonstration that Israel had not achieved self-sufficiency.

On the world front:

11. A demonstration of the limits of détente.

12. A more responsive attitude on the part of Western Europe and Japan.

The Egyptians claimed to have accomplished everything they desperately needed to accomplish. Perhaps some progress had been made toward the goals which Egypt claimed to have achieved, but in the intervening four years every accomplishment slipped away. Let us take them in reverse order. In spite of the much-publicized nuclear alert in

1973, détente hardly seemed shaken and the super-powers seemed no more willing to push the underlying problem in the Middle East to a solution. For all the pressures brought to bear on Israel, it seemed no more willing to give ground. The world quickly adjusted to the new conditions in the oil market just as it had adjusted to the closing of the Suez Canal half a decade earlier. Arab unity soon collapsed.

It can be said of these factors that they were beyond the control of Egypt. Egypt could not control the interests of all the various parties that it had, momentarily and miraculously, brought into a favourable configuration. It should also be said, however, that Egypt was not in a position in terms of its own internal interests to do so. Its internal situation was not secure enough to permit it to take a firm stand vis-à-vis the external situation and actors.

For all that had not happened on the international front, it was on the domestic front that the failure of October became critical. Egypt did not have the time or leeway to wait out the process. Within six months the symbolic significance of October began to slip away. *The October Working Paper* was intended to reinvigorate it. Critics and doubters were directly attacked for failing to appreciate what had been done, for doubting that a new day had dawned. It was a rhetoric that the regime had never intended to have to use again and it was a rhetoric that became more and more intense as time went on.

As the symbolic benefits slipped away, so, too, did the economic benefits. I have suggested that under the best of circumstances it is doubtful whether liberalization could have succeeded for Egypt. Be that as it may, Egypt could not wait for the best of circumstances and the policy proved to be a failure. October was claimed as too great a victory and it was invoked too soon. It had not achieved the desired objectives: a belief that peace was just around the corner, which would reassure the foreign investors; a reduction in military expenditure, which would allow the economy to revive; and an outpouring of Arab support to honour the greatest victory of the Arab cause in a millennium.

Liberalization had been promised as far back as 1967 and the promise had become ever more extreme as time went on. The regime now tried to deliver. The result of an ill-thought-out, ill-timed policy was a rampant inflation and an ever-increasing foreign debt. The economic problems of 1972 and 1964-6 looked small when compared to the economic problems of 1975-6. The shift in distribution of welfare in Egyptian society and the show of wealth by Egyptians and foreigners alike might have been acceptable if there had been a generalized improvement in the economy, but there was none.

If October 1973, had not produced the necessary conditions in the economy, much the same can be said of the polity. If we look at how the October victory was achieved on the home front, with the President in the Prime Ministry, the cabinet re-militarized, opposition journalists barred from writing, the parliament subdued, and clandestine organizations under extreme pressure, we must conclude that it was achieved with a very firm hand on the domestic political throttle. That was understandable enough. However, if we look at the efforts to reform the polity after the war, we are struck by foot-dragging, uncertainty and unfairness. The regime seems to have been thoroughly afraid of the polity, unwilling to dismantle the old structures and incapable of creating effective new ones. The fears were not unfounded. The polity was surging with energy. The regime could not overturn the ASU for fear of the upheaval that might result. It could not free political organizational activity for fear that it would be overwhelmed by radical and quasi-radical extremist opposition, both right and left. When the press was partially freed, such a flood of criticism was released that it had to back down, lest all confidence in the government be lost. The regime slipped into the freest elections Egypt had witnessed in a quarter of a century in an unwieldy and self-defeating structure. The semi-pluralist structure was riddled with internal contradictions. It was free and clean in the strict sense of the word — ballot boxes were not stuffed — but every form of influence had been thrown on the side of the regime and the weight was oppressive.

I think it is clear that if the economy had not gone bad so quickly, that if the October war had been a clearer victory to provide the regime with a greater sense of legitimacy, that if the critics and doubters had not so quickly re-emerged, things would have gone much better in the polity. As it was, the two sources of weakness converged in the riots of January 1977. To set the economy right, the regime decided to finally move against price subsidies. This was, perhaps, the most anti-populist of the available alternatives. It struck hard at groups in the society that had been severely pressed by three years of galloping inflation released by economic liberalization. The impact went beyond that. The government readily admitted that it was so totally lacking in control of officially priced goods that it could not open the decision to increase prices to debate. The reality led to a self-debunking act. The decision had to be taken in the most undemocratic manner possible, administratively, over-night, without debate.

Let it suffice to say that in the riots the worst fears of the regime were realized and it took a hard tack. It must also be said that in the harsh response the worst fears of the opposition had been realized. For many, there was no place to go but underground. Repression and opposition now began to feed on one another. The left, legal and illegal, was attacked; then the right, legal and illegal, was. When the first independent party was formed under the new law for political organizations, it called itself the 'new Wafd'. Sadat belittled its leaders, calling them mummies, but they were real enough. One could have predicted this development, if one read the list of platforms of November 1975 carefully enough. The regime did not like this turn of events one bit, and it took the first opportunity to abolish the party. Even serious, legitimate opposition would not be tolerated.

I have not gone into a detailed study of the events after January 1977, for it seems to me that the pattern had been set. The regime escalated its rhetoric and used its repressive means while the opposition turned to illegal activity. The regime tried to revive the economy and insisted that it had not killed the political developments, but it could produce no results in either area. Above all, January 1977 brings us back to a repeated configuration in Egyptian politics, one that mirrors early 1973 in particular, but is also similar to 1965-6. As with the student and worker demonstrations in the winter of 1972-3 and the Last Muslim Brotherhood Conspiracy of 1965, the January riots had set a time bomb ticking. Something would have to be done in short order.

Mid-1977 begins to look a great deal like mid-1973. The economy was under a severe strain and going nowhere. There was nothing left to be tried in the polity. There was a loss of legitimacy in a regime that had let three years slip away since declaring the victory of October. There was continual political upheaval in Egypt in the political institutions and on the streets (with manifestations, this time, of political robbery, kidnapping and terrorism). There were severe strains in the military. The Israelis were acting unilaterally and threatening to render the situation permanent. The super-powers seemed unwilling to break the deadlock. Egypt had lost respect among Arab and other foreign friends.

There could be no more pretence about the economy or the polity. There were no short-term solutions, and time may, indeed, have been growing short. Sometime between the first of November and the last of February this weakened regime could well face riots and there was a growing suspicion that it would not survive. Whether or not we believe that its existence was directly threatened in January, the belated entry of the military on to the streets suggested that it might not come to the rescue the next time.

With no recourse to the interior, there was only the exterior. It was back to the well of foreign affairs; one more effort to pull off the international miracle that will solve the domestic problems and ensure the legitimacy of the regime. This is the key link between the domestic and the foreign situations. There may be deep-seated reasons for this repeated recourse to the exterior. Four generations of Egyptians have defined their political consciences in foreign affairs — first with respect to the British, then with respect to Israel. In many ways Nasser had built his regime on success in foreign affairs. Sadat had always reserved foreign affairs to himself. In February 1971 he had offered to open the Suez Canal and negotiate with the Israelis, a position he maintained throughout. In 1972 he expelled the Soviets. In 1973 he managed the October war. In 1974 and 1975 he disengaged in the Sinai. Each move created some opposition and each move was executed over some opposition, but each move also froze the opposition and seemed to capture the attention of the people. One simply had to wait and see what would come of it.

A serious effort at peace would be the most startling move of all. But why peace this time instead of war? In the broad sweep of Egyptian history we can argue that in the mid-1960s it was the closed, socialist experiment that was going under. It was the self-proclaimed leading edge of progressive forces in the Arab world that was threatened. It was the Soviets and Eastern bloc that had offered support for the socialist experiment and it was they who had to be forced to commit fully to save it. Radicalization at home and hostility to the West, America and Israel abroad seemed the strategy that would attract their interests. By the mid-1970s, the situation had inverted completely. It was the open, semi-liberal experiment that was going under. It was the self-proclaimed leading edge of democracy and moderation in the Arab world that was threatened. It was conservative Arab and Western money which had offered support for the liberalizing political economy and it was they who had to be forced to commit fully to save it. Moderation, not radicalization at home and accommodation, not hostility abroad seemed to be the strategy to attract their interests.

For a more concrete, tactical explanation we can go back to the pressures, accomplishments and failures of 1973 and after.

Egypt had, in fact, pulled itself together for a desperate effort. It was drained. It now had the victory of October to look back on. The psychological weight of the 1967 defeat had been partially lifted. War would be difficult to mobilize for another time, materially and psychologically. War was not what had been promised in the *October Working Paper* nor was there any way to pay for it.

In spite of all the world pressures brought to bear on Israel, through diplomatic and economic means, the impact was greatest where it was least effective. Europe and the Third World are secondary if the Americans are not shaken and the way to move the Americans is not through war on Israel, but peace with Israel.

Arab unity and the oil weapon are not a characteristic of the entire Arab world, they are a characteristic of the moderate Arab world — Saudi Arabia, Kuwait, the oil sheikdoms. (It is worthwhile noting that this is a group of nations headed by royal houses.) With the economy disintegrating and continuing military costs, it was the moderate Arab states that would foot the bill. The Iraqis and the Libyans would never underwrite Sadat's regime. They were the first and loudest to decry the treachery of October 1973. The rest of the radical states — Syria and Algeria — could not underwrite the regime even if they were inclined to do so. These are important, too, as a host of republics claiming socialism of one form or another.

Egypt had, in fact, tried to create a new trump card in the Middle East — the threat of peace. Once you start on this path, it becomes self-reinforcing. Every step away from the Soviets and towards the Americans suited the Egyptian understanding of the problem. It fitted the promise that had been made after the October war, and it satisfied the moderate Arab supporters. Every step towards peace reduces the option for war because the radical Arab states increase their hostile rhetoric and the Soviets reduce their military aid. The international coup would be peace this time, not war.

A strategy that stands on three legs emerged, a strategy that can be summarized in a phrase often repeated in Egypt: 'the Soviets can give you war, only the Americans can give you peace'. And, in Egypt, the observation was always added, 'and the Soviets cannot give you economic development' — they had tried in the 1960s and failed.

All three legs of the strategy are cemented in the domestic situation.

1. A moderate Arab front must come into existence. The radical Arabs had always maintained that America and Israel are an identity, not two nations whose interests can be split. The moderates had to demonstrate that the radicals were wrong, for they had long been tied to the Americans. Furthermore, they had a real interest in stabilizing the situation. They had achieved tremendous material gains with the October war and another war might disrupt them. Thus, Egypt emerges

as the great anti-communist warrior in Africa and the Saudis refuse to raise the price of oil. Egypt would become the sword and oil money the financial source for a new alliance.

2. The Americans must be made to balance their position, if not to create an immediate peace, then at least a non-hostile antagonism in which Egypt can get out from under its war burden — directly through American aid, indirectly through moderate Arab support — a non-hostile antagonism in which the economy can flourish. The Americans had, after all, balanced Greece and Turkey in such a relationship for decades; they could do so with Egypt and Israel.

3. As the economy grew worse it became clear that Arab dollars alone were not enough. Egypt needed material, expertise, whole factories and food in massive quantities, cheaply, at once and with a long-term commitment. This was the kind of task that only the Americans could execute. But they would do so only for trusted allies. As the Americans held back, there was no recourse but to peace — to more and more moderation to try and woo them.

Orchestrating the Final Transformation

The final initiative was no accident or momentary impulse. We know of the letter from Carter to Sadat. A bold initiative was asked for and a bold initiative was produced — in a very careful fashion. In the two weeks before the idea of a trip surfaced, Sadat followed Begin to Rumania, one of the few places in the world where he could get information about the Israelis unfiltered by anyone else's interests. He flew to Iran and stopped in Saudi Arabia on the way home. Soon after, King Hussein came to Cairo. He had already talked to Numeri of Sudan. He need not raise the issue directly, he need only gauge the mood. Hussein had been ready for this for years but could not take the initiative. The Shah could not possibly mind as the prime supplier of Israeli oil. The Saudis would not seriously damage his position, not with chaos in the horn of Africa and Khadafi in Libya idolizing Nasser. Nasser, the arch-enemy of Faisal, remained the symbol most likely to be raised in the absence of Sadat. The Saudis could be placated in other ways. The single most surprising thing about Sadat's speech in the Knesset was the talk of Arab Jerusalem. He mentioned it before the Palestinians and he dwelled long on it. Jerusalem is the heart of the issue for the Saudis who still consider themselves the defenders of the faith.

If the domestic situation demanded it and the international situation would tolerate it, when should it be done? It had to be bold. The Israelis wanted a week's notice to get ready but that was too long to wait. Why let the international pressures build up? Why give the dissidents at home time to regroup? Moreover, there was the Beiram feast. The mood would be light and the universities would be closed. Better to make the trip a *fait accompli*, without any dire consequences, before the opposition, domestic and foreign, had a chance to regain its balance.

We arrive at Jerusalem in a whirl of political management created by one of the survivors of forty years of Egyptian politics, a very rough political game indeed, with its blend of revolution and continuity, democracy and authoritarianism, and constant international pressures. It was a media event of monumental proportions, which may mark the beginning of the age of politics by satellite television. But, again, the accomplishment seemed to slip away. Sadat had not misjudged his fellow Arabs. The radicals did not hold together. Even after a year they were barely unified in their opposition. The moderates did not abandon him. Only after a year did they really threaten to. Why a year? Had he misjudged the Israelis? He could not have expected them to roll over and play dead, not after the resignations of two foreign ministers and the vocal disagreement of Hafez Al Asad of Syria, who Sadat tried to bring along on his trip, at least symbolically.

But we must remember the strategy. It was always primarily aimed at the Americans as the indirect route to the Israelis. If Carter asked for a bold initiative, Sadat gave it to him beyond anything he could reasonably expect, yet it was the Americans who could not deliver. In the long tug-of-war that ensued, the fundamental weakness of the Egyptian position was demonstrated; repression at home, concession abroad. The moderation became so rampant that even the moderates began to object. A little progress had been made on one leg of the strategy. The Americans were coaxed to supply outdated planes to the Egyptians and a few worthwhile ones to the Saudis, but the other two legs of the strategy may have come into conflict. All the Israeli complaints about American pressures to the contrary, Sadat may have discovered that he could not get the Israelis through the Americans. In the end, he had to deal directly with the Israelis. In that confrontation he was caught in a bind, for the Israelis demanded more moderation than the Americans and more than the other moderate Arabs would accept.

Stagnation in the Peace Process and the Demise of Sadat

In this context, Sadat's bold initiative proved to be like every one of his earlier initiatives. Stunning at the outset, it lacked the depth of support and careful planning necessary to achieve its final aim. With its origins in a need to defuse domestic pressures, the failure of the peace initiative to produce rapid and tangible results meant that those pressures would become even more intense. Under these circumstances, the impetus to extremism multiplied. Sadat, as the increasingly visible and isolated symbol of a failing economy, a repressive polity and a radically different foreign policy that had not produced much benefit to Egypt, became a very inviting target for extremism. He had been such a target for quite some time, but as the weeks and months of the peace process turned into years, he became a more and more inviting target. Near the end, his own behaviour in flailing out at his opposition may have emboldened it. Thus, although the assassination was largely a random event, it also had deep structural roots.

The process eroding Sadat's initiative and his domestic position are familiar by now. As tough negotiating positions were taken by the Israelis and the details necessary to complete the process consumed more and more time, the inevitable pull of the domestic situation began to take over. Sadat's need for quick results undermined his ability to make strong demands and to persist in those demands. Rather than insisting on and winning major concessions on all points, Sadat took a few quick results in the areas of Egypt's most immediate interest. As a consequence, the isolation and criticism from the Arab world cut more and more deeply. Freewheeling use of Israeli air power and a total lack of progress on the Palestinian issue made it abundantly clear that Egypt had signed a very separate and very limited peace. The opponents of the initiative, who could easily be dismissed as dwarfs at the outset, looked more and more correct as time went on.

Of greater importance than the erosion of the symbolic benefits of the initiative was the failure to make rapid economic progress. The fundamental weakness of the economy and the liberalization policy remained. The tentative reduction of hostile attitudes between Egypt and Israel was still no substitute for a fully-fledged peace. American aid could only replace the loss of support from wealthy Arab states. Even if peace had been achieved quickly, the military burden would not be greatly reduced. The military is not predisposed to seeing its resources diminished rapidly and many alternative justifications could be found to keep the budget high. In the four years after the peace initiative, Sadat offered, or threatened, to send his troops into half a dozen North African or Middle Eastern nations. A flourishing of the economy was not on the cards, certainly not in the order of magnitude necessary to relieve domestic pressures.

Under these economic and symbolic pressures, the political liberalization died a rapid death. For all intents and purposes the façade of permitting an active, legitimate opposition was abandoned. The thrust toward underground, clandestine and/or explicit anti-regime violence was reinforced. Different political tendencies took different routes of opposition, but many were actively and aggressively opposed to the regime.

The religious right proved particularly virulent. Although the flow of international events in the Middle East may have contributed to the impetus for this movement, the flood of platforms in November 1975, which long pre-dated the international events, showed that a potential constituency existed. The multitude of independent religious rightist candidates in 1976 and the continuous clandestine, as well as open, defiance of the regime by the religious right attested to its strength. The left was active as well, but the right seemed to fare much better.

The ability of the right to persist and grow in strength can be attributed to a number of factors. In part, it flowed from the depth of support for a religious revival. In part, it received an impetus from international events (symbolic encouragement in the Iranian situation and perhaps financial encouragement from elsewhere). Finally, the regime invariably struck out harder at the left than the right. The left, the ghost of Nasser, always appeared to be the more immediate threat. There were still well-known Nasserists around who had a legitimacy that could easily be translated into a claim to rule, should the circumstances arise. The immediate past provided the greatest threat because it entailed a political and institutional heritage that was not deep beneath the surface, a heritage which could sweep the regime away. The repressive resources of the regime were always targeted on that end of the political spectrum.

In the end, it appears that the greater threat — at least the one that was not successfully neutralized — came from the right in the form of an assassination that was stunning in its violence and striking in its fanaticism. Such acts certainly involve a major element of chance. However, when they are blatantly political, involve a large number of individuals and some level of complicity in the military and security forces, they just as certainly have structural causes.

Whether or not we accept the official version, that a long-term movement to overthrow the regime was contemplated, the assassins must have believed that the removal of Sadat and his closest associates would have ultimately toppled his regime and its policies. The more pervasive the underlying domestic problems and the more visible they are, the larger will be the number of individuals in society who believe that such an act will initiate a momentous change. Sadat's behaviour in the weeks before his murder must certainly have reinforced such a belief and encouraged those who held it. The public display of difficulties, the extensive round-up of citizens without a major, direct provocation, the bitter attack on the foreign press for reporting domestic problems, all added to the sense that society was on the brink of exploding. A single act became more and more inviting as a potential spark to ignite the explosion. If one assumes that Egypt had been bristling with plotters for over a decade, and one certainly should, then centring attention on Egypt's domestic troubles raised the probability that one of those plotters would be emboldened sufficiently to take a chance.

The great debate in the weeks before the assassination was over whether or not Sadat was giving his opposition more attention and, therefore, more credibility than it deserved. Given Sadat's tremendous sense of timing in these matters and subsequent events, it may very well be that he knew better than outside observers that his ability to control the situation was being seriously eroded. Perhaps he genuinely needed to act in anticipation of what his opposition was planning. But if he intended to stay in power by taking firm political control over the situation and throwing his opposition in jail, then he did not go far enough, for once war is declared on clandestine organizations, they become extremely dangerous. Egypt in 1981 was not like Iran in 1978. As Sadat confidently argued, no Khomeini-style revolution was in the immediate offing. But, Egypt in 1981 may have been like Iran many years earlier, where the regime could only sustain power for a long period by instituting a thorough and pervasive police state. Sadat, who probably believed in the efficacy of his policies to the end, had not made that realization. He responded as he had on a number of previous occasions, but the situation had become far more desperate than it had been previously and the response was inadequate.

Conclusion

The death of Sadat marks the end of two eras in Egyptian history. Just over a decade of rule by a dominating figure who had presided over some of the most dramatic shifts in Egyptian economics, politics and international affairs had ended. Just under three decades of leadership by members of the Free Officers movement, a movement which had led Egypt to independence and the centre of world politics, had ended. Throughout this work I have stressed the structural factors that affected Egypt's political economy, rather than the personalities of the men who led the nation. These are the deeper, stronger forces which affect the flow of events, both internal and external.

Many have looked to the international sphere first to understand Egypt. In doing so, it is easy to argue that Egypt was always disappointed by her international allies – in the 1960s the Russians and the 1970s the Americans. As the pawn of superpowers, Egypt's interests were subjugated to superpower interests and her plight was always worsened. However, such explanations overlook the fact that Egypt was continually increasing demands placed on her allies. Further, how is it that one changes sides so thoroughly in such a short period of time? Who negotiates the alternatives, makes the choices and in whose interest? If international economic and political relations seem to coerce decisions in an indirect fashion, it also seems that there are domestic relations of economic interest and political power that dictate them in a direct fashion.

At the same time, many have looked to personal factors to account for the dramatic changes in Egypt. The two dynamic, riveting personalities of Nasser and Sadat certainly deserve attention and clearly influenced events. However, both of the personalities grappled desperately with the structural difficulties of their respective political economies. In the mid-1960s, the erosion of the economy and the consequent chaos in the polity drove Nasser to war and his defeat in that war set in motion immense pressures in the Middle East, pressures which may have undermined his health. In the mid-1970s, the erosion of the economy and the consequent chaos in the polity moved Sadat to sue for peace with Israel, but the limited achievement of peace and the failure of his economic and political programme spurred his opposition to try to eliminate him.

Without denying the importance of international and personal factors, I have tried to build an explanation of the transformation of Egypt on the basis of systematic factors in the domestic political economy. This is not a very common approach to the problem, nor do I claim to have created a flawless explanation. However, if it is recognized as plausible, then that will suffice, for it will force a rethinking of the approach to what I believe is a critical intellectual and political problem — the transformation of the political economy of Third World societies, the nature of Egyptian society and the dynamics of war and peace in the Middle East.

NOTES

Chapter 1

1. A good example of this approach, which covers a period similar to the one studied in this work, is Alvin Rubinstein, *Red Star on the Nile* (Princeton: Princeton University Press, 1977).

2. A good example of this approach that is available in English is Mahmoud Hussein, *Class Conflict in Egypt, 1945-1970* (New York: Monthly Review Press, 1973). An interesting example in Arabic is T. Shakir, *The Issue of National Liberalization and the Socialist Revolution in Egypt* (Beirut, 197?).

3. The leading proponents of this school are Robert Springborg, *The Ties That Bind: Political Association and Policy-Making in Egypt* (unpublished PhD dissertation, Stanford University, 1974) and Clement Moore, 'Authoritarian Politics in Unincorporated Society: The Case of Nasser's Egypt', paper prepared for the *Annual Meeting of the American Political Science Association*, 1972; 'The Consolidation and Dissipation of Power in Unincorporated Society: Egypt and Tunisia' (unpublished manuscript).

4. Hrair Dekmejian, *Egypt Under Nasir: A Study in Political Development* (New York: State University Press, 1971).

5. R. Hrair Dekmejian, 'Marx, Weber and the Egyptian Revolution', *Middle East Journal*, 1976, p. 171.

6. Theda Skocpol has recently stated this position in precise terms: 'We must not merely look at the activities of social groups alone, but rather at the points of intersection between international conditions and pressures, on the one hand, and class structured economies and politically organized interests, on the other hand' ('State and Revolution', *Theory and Society*, 7, 1979, p. 15).

7. Arthur L. Stinchcombe, *Constructing Social Theories* (New York: Harcourt, Brace and World, 1968), p. 5.

Chapter 2

1. I find Tom Little particularly insightful with respect to understanding the events immediately preceding and following the Revolution of 1952 – *Egypt* (London: Benn, 1958). Other general works on the history of Egypt that are particularly useful are: Jacques Berque, *Egypt: Imperialism and Revolution* (London: Faber and Faber, 1972); P.J. Vatikiotis, *The History of Egypt* (Baltimore: Johns Hopkins University Press, 1980).

2. The seminal article in what has proved to be an intense debate over state capitalism in the Third World is James Petras, 'State Capitalism and the Third World', *Development and Change*, 8:1, 1977.

3. A number of country-specific studies which seem to accept the basic outline of Petras's argument have been conducted. For very good reasons, a great deal of attention has been focused on Peru (Baltazar Carvedo Molinari, 'The State and the Bourgeoisie in the Peruvian Fishmeal Industry', *Latin American Perspective*, 4:3, 1977; Elizabeth Dore, 'Crisis and Accumulation in the Peruvian Mining Industry', *Latin American Perspectives*, 4:3, 1977), Columbia (Raul Fernandez and Jose Ocampo, 'The Andean Pact and State Capitalism in Colombia', *Latin American Perspectives*, 2:3, 1975; Philip Wright, 'The Role of the State and the Politics of Capital Accumulation in Columbia', *Development*

and Change, 11, 1980); Algeria (Karen Farsoun, 'State Capitalism in Algeria', *Middle East Research and Information Project*, No. 35, 1975), Tanzania (Issa Shivji, *Class Struggles in Tanzania* (London: Heinemann, 1976), and Zambia (Ben Turok, 'Zambia's System of State Capitalism', *Development and Change*, 11, 1980).

Critical articles which argue that the conceptualization of state capitalism is, essentially, too shallow and that state capitalism should not be accorded such a major theoretical status as a form of political/economic organization include Alex Dupuy and Barry Truchil, 'Problems in the Theory of State Capitalism', *Theory and Society*, 7, 1979; J.P. Perez Sainz, 'Toward a Conceptualization of State Capitalism in the Periphery', *Insurgent Sociologist*, 9:4, 1980; and the debates that have followed in the wake of Petras's argument (*New Left Review*, 101-2, 1977; *Development and Change*, 8:4, 1977).

4. A formal theory of interest vesting similar to the one used in this work is contained in Faruk Birtek and Mark Cooper, 'Sociological Theory and Economic History', presented before the *51st Annual Meeting of the Eastern Sociological Society*, New York, March, 1981.

5. Marx has argued that there were four moments in the economic process: 'The conclusion that we reach is not that production, distribution, exchange and consumption are identical, but that they all form the members of a totality, distinctions within a unity (*The Grundrisse*, Martin Nicolaus (trans.) (New York: Vintage, 1973), p. 99). There is a rough correspondence between these four moments and the four dimensions I have chosen for empirical analysis as follows:

Production	Distribution	Exchange	Consumption
Ownership	Control	Income	Access

6. Class maps of Egypt have been worked out by a number of authors. These are typically based on quantitative notions of class (percentage of income, size of landholding) rather than conceptual definitions of class relations – see Mahmoud Hussein, *Class Conflict in Egypt* (New York: Monthly Review Press, 1973); T. Shakir, *The Issue of National Liberalization* (Beirut, 197?); Mahmoud Riad, *L'Egypte Nasserienne* (Paris: Editions de Minuit, 1964); Ceres Wissa Wassef, 'Le Proletariat et le Sous Proletariat Industriel et Agricole en Republic Arab Unie', *Orient*, 1969.

7. P.J. Vatikiotis, *The Egyptian Army in Politics: Pattern for New Nations* (Bloomington: Indiana University Press, 1961); Nazih Ayubi, *Bureaucratic Evolution and Political Development: Egypt 1952-1970* (unpublished PhD dissertation, St Antony's College Oxford, 1976); Anwar Abdel Malek, *Egypt Military Society* (New York: Vintage, 1968).

8. Theda Skocpol, *States and Social Revolutions* (New York: Cambridge University Press, 1979).

9. David Apter, *The Politics of Modernization* (Chicago: University of Chicago Press, 1965).

10. See notes 2 and 3 to Chapter 2.

11. Apter, *The Politics of Modernization*, chapter 7.

12. David Snyder and Charles Tilly ('Hardship and Collective Violence in France, 1830-1960', *American Sociological Review*, 37:1972) utilize a framework that places particular emphasis on shifting political functions in the revolution process.

13. Marx's analysis in *The 18th Brumaire of Louis Bonaparte* (New York: International Publishers, 1962) gives politics its most extensive impact on the political economy, while utilizing a conception of the connection between the polity and the economy that is similar to the one utilized in this work.

14. This is most evident in Marx's discussion of the peasants in *The 18th Brumaire*.

262 *Notes*

15. Max Weber, *From Max Weber*, trans. and ed. by H. H. Gerth and C.W. Mills (New York: Oxford University Press, 1946); *Theory of Social and Economic Organization*, trans. and ed. by A.M. Henderson and Talcott Parsons (New York: The Free Press, 1947).

16. Skocpol, *States*, systematically analyses both the lower-class and upper-class organization for political activity. An essential question in her analysis is the autonomy of the lower class from the upper class in its political activities.

17. Mahfouz el-Koshere, *Socialisme et Pouvoir en Egypte* (Paris: Libraire Général de Driot et Jurisprudence, 1972), gives a good sense of this by tracing the personal connections of the various members of the Free Officers with the various political parties and organizations.

18. Little, *Egypt*, p. 189.

19. Robert Mabro, *The Egyptian Economy, 1952-1972* (Oxford: Clarendon Press, 1974) is particularly sensitive to these gains and the fact that given the raw materials she possesses Egypt did rather well in accomplishing them.

20. Two works give exhaustive analyses of the agrarian situation from a perspective similar to that taken in this work; see Mahmoud Abdel Fadil, *Development, Income Distribution and Social Change in Rural Egypt* (Cambridge, Cambridge University Press, 1975); Samir Radwan, *The Impact of Agrarian Reform on Rural Egypt* (Geneva International Labor Office Working Paper, 1977). Other useful sources on the agrarian sector include: Shams al-Din Hifagy, *Agricultural Cooperation: Thought and Law* (Cairo, 1973) (Arabic); Sayyid Basyuni, *Agricultural Ownership: Between Fact and Law* (Cairo, 1976) (Arabic); Ismael Sabry Abdullah, *The Organization of the Public Sector* (Cairo, 1969) (Arabic); Bent Hansen and K. Nashishibi, *Egypt: Foreign Exchange Regimes and Economic Development* (New York: NBER and Columbia University Press, 1976); Mohammed Mahmud Abdel Ru'uf, 'Principal Agricultural Advancement in the Egyptian Arab Republic for the Period 1952/53-1969/70', *Institute of National Planning* (hereafter INP) memo 1029 (Arabic); Abdul Rahman Zaki Ibrahim, 'Price Incentives in the Development of Egyptian Agriculture', *L'Egypte Contemporaine*, 355: 1971.

21. Quantitative estimates of the expansion of employment and the increase in salaries at various levels of the bureaucracy and public sector are available in Mahmoud Abdel Fadil, *Employment and Income Distribution in Egypt* (Development Studies Discussion Paper No. 4, East Anglia University, 1975); Ahmad Rashid, *Bureaucratic Corruption* Cairo, 1976 (Arabic, p. 136.

22. Malek, *Egypt Military Society*, stresses this upper class objective. See especially pp. 141-68.

23. Joseph Schumpeter, *Imperialism and Social Class* (New York: Meridian, 1951) takes this view of upper-class domination:

> Every class, in other words, had a definite function, which must be fulfilled according to its whole concept and orientation and which it actually does discharge as a class and through the class conduct of its members. Moreover, the position of each class in the total national structure depends, on the one hand, on the significance that is attributed to that function, and, on the other hand, on the degree to which the class successfully performs the function (p. 137).
>
> The ultimate foundation on which the class phenomenon rests consists of individual differences in aptitude. What is meant is not differences in an absolute sense, but differences with respect to those functions which the environment makes 'socially necessary' — in our sense — at any given time (p.160

24. Fadil, *Development*, and Radwan, *The Impact*, stress this point.

25. Gabriel Saab, *The Egyptian Agrarian Reform: 1952-1962* (London: Oxford University Press, 1967), *Motorization et Développement Agricole au Proche Orient* (Paris: Sedes, 1960); Keith Griffith, *The Political Economy of Agrarian Change* (Cambridge: Harvard University Press, 1974), presents a formal economic analysis.

26. E. Eshag and M.A. Kemal, 'Agrarian Reform in the United Arab Republic (Egypt)', and 'A Note on the Reform of the Rural Credit System in the United Arab Republic (Egypt)', *Bulletin of Oxford University Institute of Economics and Statistics*, 29, 30.

27. Mark Cooper, 'State Capitalism and Class Structure in the Third World: The Case of Egypt', a paper presented at the *49th Annual Meeting of the Eastern Sociological Society*, New York, 1979, makes an effort to estimate the size and income of the various classes identified in this analysis.

28. Faruk Gweida, *Egypt's Capital: How Was It Wasted?* (Cairo, 1976) (Arabic); Fuad Mursi, *This is the Economic Liberalization* (Cairo, 1976) (Arabic).

29. Robert Mabro and Samir Radwan, *The Industrialization of Egypt, 1939-1973* (Oxford: Clarendon Press, 1976), chapter 4.

30. Official Gazette, Legislative Section, *Minutes of the National Assembly* (hereafter referred to as *Minutes*), 17 and 18 April 1976.

31. Marx observes that the lumpenproletariat is catered to with bread and circuses (see *The 18th Brumaire*).

32. Leonard Binder, 'Political Recruitment and Participation in Egypt', in *Political Parties and Political Participation*, ed. LaPalombara and Weiner (Princeton: Princeton University Press, 1966).

33. Nissim Rejwan, *Nasserist Ideology* (Tel Aviv: Israeli University Press, 1974).

34. See, for example, Carl Friedrich and Zbigniew Brezinski, *Totalitarian Dictatorship and Autocracy* (New York: Praeger, 1965).

35. Louis Awad suggested this to me in a personal conversation.

36. Dekmejian, *Egypt*, p. 164.

37. Malek, *Egypt Military Society*, pp. 327-8.

Chapter 3

1. Mabro and Radwan, *Industrialization*, have the most complete discussion of time series analyses which show the rapid growth of public consumption and the trade balance.

2. Ibid., pp. 45-6.

3. Hansen and Nashishibi, *Egypt*, pp. 104, 105.

4. Ibid., p. 127.

5. Ibid., p. 127.

6. Dekmejian, *Egypt*, p. 229.

7. Ibid., p. 233.

8. Ibid., p. 235.

9. John Waterbury, *Egypt, Burdens of the Past, Options for the Future* (American University Field Staff, nd), The Opening, Part III: Denasserization, June 1975, p. 7.

10. Neither memoirs, such as Musa Sabri, *Documents of May 15* (Cairo, 1976) (Arabic), nor reportage, such as Fuad Matar, *Nasserist Russia and Egyptian Egypt* (Beirut, 1972) (Arabic), nor semi-official accounts, such as that analysed in P.J. Vatikiotis, 'Egypt's Politics of Conspiracy', *Survey*, 18:1972, seem able to resolve basic uncertainties about the period. Still, the evidence supports broad generalizations that rely on overall trends, rather than precise details.

264 *Notes*

11. *Al-Ahram*, 4 August 1967; *Al-Jumhurriyya*, 8 August 1967.

12. *Al-Ahram*, 11 August 1967.

13. *Al-Ahram*, 4, 16 September, 11 October 1968; *Ruz al-Yusif*, 31 July, 7 August 1967; *Le Monde*, 29 August 1967.

14. *Al-Ahram*, 14 September 1967.

15. *Al-Ahram*, 30 September 1967.

16. *New York Times*, 20 May 1968; *al-Ahram*, 28 June, 29 December 1968.

17. *Ruz-al-Yusif*, 21 August 1968.

18. *Al-Ahram*, 1 July, 21 November 1967.

19. *Middle East Report and Record*, uses these labels in quotation marks, which seems a judicious qualification if one wishes to speak in a comparative framework. In Egypt, itself, however, the parties knew who they were and where they stood, even if left in Egypt was not left in Algeria or right in Egypt was not right in Morocco. See Binder, *In a Moment* for a discussion of the positions of various actors.

20. *Al-Ahram*, 15-17 October 1967.

21. *Al-Ahram*, 2 November 1967.

22. *Al-Ahram* 21 November 1967.

23. *Al-Akhbar*, 1-15 January 1968.

Chapter 4

1. The version used in this work is found in *Documents of Abdul Nasser, January 1967-December 1968* (Cairo: Center for Political and Strategic Studies, *Al-Ahram*, nd) (Arabic) (hereafter, *March 30 Program*).

2. Minister of Economics and External Trade, Hassan Abbas Zaki, *Arab Political Encylopedia, Documents and Notes*, July-December 1968, p. 100 (hereafter, *APE*).

3. *APE*, July-December 1968, p. 201.

4. *Minutes*, 13, 14 July 1969.

5. *APE*, January-June 1968, p. 98.

6. Presidential Decree 46/1969, modifying Presidential Decree 2193/1967, which, itself, represented an increase: see *APE*, Minister of Agriculture, 6 February 1969.

7. *APE*, July-December 1968, p. 51.

8. *APE*, July-December, 1968, pp. 166-7.

9. *Conference of Administrative Leadership*, Session on Administration Problems in Industry, Dr Aziz Sidqi, 27 September 1968 (Cairo, nd) (Arabic) (hereafter, *Conferences*), p. 133.

10. *Conferences*, p. 121; *APE*, January-June 1969, pp. 122-3.

11. *Conferences*, p. 122.

12. Ibid., p. 14.

13. *Al-Ahram, al-Jumhurriyya*, August 1968.

14. *APE*, July-December, 1968, p. 54.

15. *Conferences*, Session on Financial and Economic Reform, Hilmy al-A'yid, p. 37.

16. *Minutes*, 13, 14 July 1969, *passim*.

17. Ibid., 15 February 1971, p. 7.

18. Frank Parkin, *Class Inequality and Political Order* (London: Praeger, 1975), p. 180.

19. Ibid., p. 171.

20. Ibid., p. 170.

21. Ibid., p. 175.

22. Ibid., pp. 175, 176.

23. Ibid., pp. 174, 175.

24. Ibid., p. 176.

25. There was not even agreement that the referendum was necessary, with suggestions that it was a bit of trickery. See, for various viewpoints, *al-Ahram*, 12, 19, 24, 25, 26 April 1968.

26. *Al-Ahram*, 13, 17 September, 18, 25 October, 2, 15 November, 20 December 1968: *al-Akhbar*, 16 November, 2, 23 December 1968; *al-Tali'ah*, July, September 1968, May, September 1969. The less explicit, but no less pointed, line was that the war effort would be hurt. See, *al-Akhbar*, 5 March 1968; *Ruz al-Yusif*, 12 February 1968; *al-Jumhurriyya*, 2, 5 February, 1 March 1968.

27. *Al-Akhbar*, 15 November 1968; *Ruz al-Yusif*, 24 July, 14 August 1968; *al-Ahram*, 13, 14, 15, 17 October, 1 November 1968.

28. *Al-Ahram*, 24 May, 20, 24, 26, 27 June, 2, 13, 16 July 1968; *al-Jumhurriyya*, 27 June, 13 July 1968; *Ruz al-Yusif*, 1 July 1968; *Middle East Record*, 1968; *al-Ahram*, 22 November 1968.

29. *Ruz al-Yusif*, 17, 24 November 1969.

30. Giving Anwar al-Sadat a prominent role in setting them up underlines their role in this regard. It should be recalled that he, as Speaker of the Assembly, had taken a prominent role in the communications between the rioters and the National Assembly in February.

31. *Al-Ahram*, 1 July 1968; *al-Jumhurriyya*, 1 August 1968; *Middle East Record*, 1968.

32. Dekmejian, *Egypt*.

33. *Middle East Record*, 1968; *al-Ahram*, 16 September 1969.

34. *Al-Ahram*, 20 December 1969.

35. Mark Cooper, 'Egyptian State Capitalism in Crisis: Economic Policy and Political Interests, 1967-1971', *International Journal of Middle East Studies*, X:4, 1979, gives a detailed account of the economic changes that took place in this period.

36. Ibid.

Chapter 5

1. In addition to Moore, 'Consolidation', and Dekmejian, 'Marx', see John P. Entelis, 'Nasser's Egypt: The Failure of Charismatic Leadership', *Orbis*, 18:1974.

2. Moore, 'Consolidation', *passim*.

3. Entelis, 'Nasser's Egypt', *passim*.

4. Mahmoud Hussein, 'Nasserism in Perspective', *Monthly Review*, 23:1971, p. 40.

5. Hedrick Smith, 'Where Egypt Stands', *Atlantic*, 227:1970, p. 42; Georgianna Stevens, 'What Nasser Did', *Atlantic*, 227:1970, p. 44.

6. *New York Times*, 29 October 1970.

7. *Al-Ahram*, 1 November 1970; Alvin Rubinstein, *Red Star*.

8. *New York Times*, 27, 29 October 1970; Stevens, 'What Nasser Did'; 'Palestine Without Nasser, Egypt Without Leaders, Israel on the Brink', *New Middle East*, November 1970.

9. *Al-Akhbar*, 4 October 1970.

10. *Al-Ahram*, 1 November 1970; *New York Times*, 22 October 1970; *New Middle East*, January 1971.

11. *Al-Ahram*, 21 December 1970; *New York Times*, 29 December 1970.

12. *Al-Ahram*, 5 February 1971; *New York Times*, 5 February 1971.

13. *Al-Ahram*, 5 March 1971.

14. *Al-Ahram*, 2 May 1971.
15. *New York Times*, 14 May 1971.
16. Ibid., 18 July 1971.
17. Matar, *Nasserist Russia and Egyptian Egypt*, pp. 19-22.
18. *New York Times*, 22 August 1971.
19. Even Haykal may have been vulnerable at this point. See Peter Mansfield, 'Egypt After Nasser', *International Journal*, July 1971.
20. *Minutes*, 29 April 1971, p. 29.
21. Ibid., p. 14.
22. *Speeches and Interviews (September 1970-December 1971)* (Cairo: Information Ministry, nd), p. 297 (hereafter, *Speeches*).
23. Ibid., p. 311. See also, *Minutes*, 20 May 1971.
24. *Minutes*, 14 May 1971, p. 25.
25. *Speeches*, p. 297.
26. Per Aherton, 'President Sadat's New Brand of Egyptian Nationalism', *New Middle East*, January 1972, p. 11; Soliman Lotfallah, 'Jusq'au Sadate Peut-il Aller?', *Politique Aujourd'hui*, May-July 1974; *Jeune Afrique*, January 1972; *New York Times*, 29 October 1971; *Jeune Afrique*, January 1972.
27. *Speeches*, pp. 445-63.
28. *Al-Ahram, Ruz al-Yusif*, 25 October 1971.

Chapter 6

1. Ceres Wissa Wassef, 'Le Pouvoir et Les Etudiants en Egypte', Parts I and II, *Magreb Machrek*, 56, 58:1972, 1973; Mahmoud Hussein, *et al.*, *La Revolte des Etudiants Egyptiens* (Paris:François Maspero, 1972); Wa'il Othman, *Secrets of the Student Movement* (Cairo, 1976) (Arabic). *Discourse et Interviews du President Anour el-Sadate, Janvier-Juin, 1972* (Cairo: Information Ministry, nd) (hereafter, *Speeches II*).
2. *Speeches II*, p. 64.
3. *Speeches II*, 25 January, *passim*; Wissa Wassef, 'Le Pouvoir', Part I, p. 76; Othman, *Secrets*, p. 74; Hussein, *La Revolte*, p. 9.
4. Hussein, *La Revolte*, p. 7.
5. Ibid., p. 44.
6. *Middle East Report and Record*, 1972, pp. 1501-2.
7. Waterbury, *The Crossing*, p. 10.
8. *Minutes*, 20 February 1972, pp. 1447-8, 21 February 1972, p. 1532.
9. Wissa Wassef, 'Le Pouvoir', Part II, p. 69.
10. Haykal, p. 181.
11. Ibid., p. 259.
12. Ibid., pp. 215, 220.
13. Ibid., pp. 238, 241.
14. Waterbury, *The Opening*, p. 8.
15. *The October Working Paper Presented by President Mohammed Anwar el-Sadat* (Cairo: Information Ministry, nd; hereafter referred to as the *October Working Paper*).
16. Ibid., pp. 60-1.
17. Ibid., p. 99.

Chapter 7

1. People's Assembly, Legislative Council, *The Law For Arab and Foreign Investment and Free Zones* (hereafter, *Debates*) (Cairo, nd) (Arabic).

2. Ibid., p. 81.

3. Ibid., p. 80.

4. Ibid., pp. 79-81.

5. Ibid., pp. 137-8.

6. Ibid., pp. 82-3, 140, 462.

7. Fuad Mursi, 'Meeting the Thrust of Big Capital', *al-Tali'ah*, March 1975, p. 18; *Debates*, p. 90.

8. *Debates* p. 87.

9. Ibid, p. 200.

10. National Bank of Egypt, Diamond Jubilee Commemoration Lectures, *Cairo as a Financial Center* (Cairo, 1975).

11. *Debates*, pp. 201-2.

12. Ibid., pp. 287-90.

13. Ibid., p. 252.

14. Ibid., pp. 120-3, 253-9.

15. Ibid., p. 123.

16. Ibid., p. 252.

17. Ibid., p. 253.

18. Abdullah, *The Organization of the Public Sector*.

19. *Debates*, pp. 166-8.

20. Ibid., p. 168.

21. *Minutes*, 28 July 1975, pp. 8804-9.

22. Ibid., pp. 8811, 9021-6.

23. Ibid., p. 8810.

24. *Debates*, pp. 201-2.

25. Ibid., p. 8806.

26. Ibid., p. 8810.

27. *Debates*, p. 178.

28. Ibid., p. 182.

29. *Minutes*, 9 February 1972, pp. 1217, 5696-9, 7299-7331.

30. Ibid., pp. 5697, 7325.

31. *Debates*, p. 179.

32. *Minutes*, 25 March 1973, Appendix.

33. Ibid., 23 June 1975, p. 7297.

34. *Debates*, p. 171.

35. *Minutes*, 28 July 1975, pp. 8517-8.

36. Ibid., p. 8517.

37. Ibid., p. 8514.

38. Ibid., p. 8519.

39. *Debates*, pp. 121-2.

40. Ibid., p. 324.

41. Ibid., p. 171.

42. *Al-Iqtisadi*, 15 November 1976.

43. There is a great deal of uncertainty about the status of projects and a great deal of difficulty in following the statistics. See, for example, Middle East News Agency, *Economic Weekly*, 5 February 1977 (hereafter *MENA*); *Middle East Observer*, 16 August 1976.

44. *Al-Iqtisadi*, 15 October 1977.

45. *Al-Iqtisadi*, 1 January 1977; National Bank of Egypt, *Economic Bulletin*, 2:1977, p. 156; *Middle East Observer*, 5 February 1977.

46. The easiest time series data to follow on production are contained in The Federation of Egyptian Industries, *Yearbook*, and the National Bank of Egypt, *Economic Bulletin*.

47. See note 46.

48. *Al-Iqtisadi*, 15 January 1977.
49. *The Economist, Review of the Middle East*, 1977 (London, 1978), p. 158.
50. National Bank of Egypt, *Economic Bulletin*, various issues.
51. Federation of Egyptian Industries, *Yearbook*, various issues.
52. *Al-Iqtisadi*, 15 January 1977.
53. Business International, *Egypt, Gateway to the Middle East* (Washington, 1976), pp. 59-60.
54. Central Bank of Egypt, *Annual Report*, 1976, p. 23.
55. *Quarterly Economic Review of Egypt, Annual Supplement, 1977, The Economist*, p. 21.
56. Radwan, *The Impact*, p. 83.
57. *Al-Iqtisadi*, 1 February 1975.
58. Central Bank, *Annual Report*, 1976, p. 33.
59. *Economic Bulletin*, 2:1977, p. 13.
60. Waterbury, *The Opening*, p. 4.
61. *Al-Iqtisadi*, 1 November 1977.
62. *Economic Bulletin*, 2:1977, p. 129.
63. Waterbury, *The Opening*, gives 2,000 million LE for 1974.
64. See above, chapter 3.
65. See my PhD dissertation, *The Transformation of Egypt*, Yale University, 1979, Chapter 9 for a theoretical explanation of the failure of economic liberalization.
66. *Minutes*, 20 January 1975, p. 1086.
67. *Al-Iqtisadi*, 15 March 1975.
68. Ibid., 15 February 1975.
69. *Al-Ahram*, 6 June 1976.

Chapter 8

1. Robert A. Dahl, *Polyarchy: Participation and Opposition* (New Haven: Yale University Press, 1971).
2. Ibid., p. 3.
3. Ibid., p. 220.
4. Ibid., p. 226.
5. Ibid., p. 221.
6. Ibid., pp. 217-18.
7. Carl Dietrich Bracher, *The German Dictatorship*, trans. Jean Steinberg (New York: Praeger, 1975), gives a thorough analysis of the concept of a legal revolution as applied to the rise of Hitler and the Nazis in Germany.
8. Weber, *The Theory*, p. 124.
9. *The October Working Paper*, p. 14.
10. Law 34/1971, *Official Gazette*, 17 November 1971, Art. 1. Most of the laws cited in this chapter were collected in one volume, *The Rule of Law and Freedom of Citizens* (Cairo, 1975) (Arabic).
11. *Minutes*, 31 May 1971, p. 3.
12. *Minutes*, 2 July 1974, p. 4783.
13. Ibid., 25 May 1974, p. 3556.

Chapter 9

1. Major studies of the Egyptian cabinet include Dekmejian, *Egypt*, and Shahrough Akhavi, 'Egypt, Neo-Patrimonial Elite', in *Political Elites in the Middle East*, F. Tachau:

2. Haykal, gives a strong impression of this intentionality.
3. The methodology used in counting ministers is such that this individual would not appear in the flow of ministers. This is because ministers of state are not included if there was a minister occupying an office with a similar title or if they had no title. The logic is that if the regular minister is in place, he conducts the business. If the minister of state has no substantive title, he has nothing to do. Thus Mahmoud Riyadh was Minister of State for Foreign Affairs, but Isma'il Fahmy was Minister of Foreign Affairs. Clearly, Fahmy was the responsible minister. Therefore, Riyadh does not appear in the flow of ministers. In contrast, Albert Barsum Salamah held the portfolio of Minister of State for People's Assembly Affairs in 1974 and there was no Minister for People's Assembly Affairs. He enters the flow of ministers because he clearly conducted the business of that ministry.

Chapter 10

1. People's Assembly, Secretariat for External Relations, *Structure and Functions* (Cairo, 1976) (hereafter, *Structure*) (Arabic), *passim*; al-Sayyid Yassin, *New Tendencies in the People's Assembly* (Cairo: Center for Political and Strategic Studies, 1976) (Arabic); Saad el-Charkawi, 'Comparaison des Pouvoirs Presidentiels Prévus par le Constitution de La Republic Arabe d'Egypte et les Autres Constitutions Arabes', *Bulletin du Centre de Documentation d'Etudes Juridiques, Economiques, et Sociales*, October 1974.
2. *The Permanent Constitution of the Arab Republic of Egypt* (Cairo: Information Ministry, nd).
3. People's Assembly, Secretariat for External Affairs, *Accomplishments of the People's Assembly during its First Legislative Term (1971-1976)* (Cairo, nd) (Arabic) (hereafter, *Accomplishments*), pp. 24-5.
4. *Minutes*, 12 February 1972, pp. 1528-9.
5. Ibid., p. 1527.
6. Ibid., 3 June 1975, p. 6053.
7. Ibid., pp. 24-5, 29.
8. See especially, *al-Ahram*, 12 August 1976.
9. *Minutes*, 24 June 1972, *passim*.
10. *Al-Ahram*, 10-26 November 1974; *Minutes*, 11, 26 November 1974.
11. *Minutes*, 25 November 1974, *passim*.
12. Max Weber, *The Theory*, pp. 387-8

Chapter 11

1. *Al-Ahram*, 6 July 1976.
2. Ibid., 17 August 1976.
3. *The Paper for the Development of the Arab Socialist Union, al-Tali'ah*, September 1974 (hereafter, *The Paper*).
4. For basic discussions of the liberalism in *The Paper* and its limitation, see *al-Ahram*, 20, 21, 22, 25 August, 2, 25 September 1974; *al-Tali'ah*, September, October 1974, December 1975, January 1976.
5. *Al-Ahram* entitled its article of 22 September 1974, 'Between Criticism and Counter-Revolution', rather strong language for the moderate journal.
6. *Al-Ahram*, 11, 20, 21, 23, 29, 30 August, 2, 9, 11, 17, 21, 22, 25, 27, 28, 29 September 1974; *Ruz-al-Yusif*, 26 August, 30 September 1974; *al-Tali'ah* October 1974; *al-Jumhurriyya*, 11 September 1974.

7. *Al-Ahram*, 27 September 1974; Salah Hafith, 'The Dignity of the Revolution and the Support of Sadat', *Ruz al-Yusif*, 12 August 1974; Lutfi al-Kholi, 'The Regressive Right', *al-Tali'ah*, November 1974.

8. *Al-Ahram*, 12, 19 August 1974; *al-Tali'ah* September 1974, July 1975, January 1976.

9. *Al-Ahram*, 25 September 1974; *al-Tali'ah*, September 1974, January 1976.

10. Kemal Rifa'at, 'We are the Solid National Front', *al-Tali'ah*, July 1975, p. 9.

11. *Al-Tali'ah* October 1974, March 1976; *al-Ahram*, 14, 21, 30 August, 2, 11, 25 September 1974.

12. Ibid.

13. *Al-Ahram*, 21, 22, 23, 29, 30 August, 2, 11, 15, 16 21, 22, 24, 25 September 1974.

14. *Al-Ahram*, 15, 19, 23 August, 11, 15, 16 September 1974.

15. Ibid., 16, 17, 18 September 1974.

16. Ibid., 20, 21 September 1974.

17. Ibid., 22 September 1974.

18. Ibid.

19. Ibid.

20. Abdul Min'am al-Ghazali, 'Hot Debate and Limited Tendencies', *al-Tali'ah*, October 1974, p. 10.

21. *Al-Ahram*, 26 July 1975.

22. 'Report of the Month', *al-Tali'ah*, August 1975.

23. *Al-Ahram*, 22 July, 9 September 1975; *al-Jumhurriyya*, 12 July 1975.

24. *Al-Ahram*, 22 July 1975.

25. *Al-Tali'ah*, August 1975.

26. *Al-Ahram*, 10 August 1975.

27. Ibid., 9 September 1975.

28. Ibid., 13 October 1975.

29. Ibid., 21 October 1975.

30. Ibid., 23 October 1975.

31. Ibid., 29 October 1975.

32. Ibid., 7, 8, 10, 13 November 1975; *al-Jumhurriyya*, 9, 15 November 1975; also see the set of interviews in *Al-Tali'ah*, December 1975.

33. *Al-Ahram*, 23, 26 October 1975.

34. Ibid., 14 November 1975.

35. Ibid., 24 October 1975.

36. Ibid., 26 October 1975.

37. Ibid., 4 November 1975.

38. Ibid., 17 November 1975.

39. Ibid., 16 November 1975; *al-Jumhurriyya*, 13, 16 November 1975.

40. *Al-Ahram*, 20 November 1975; *al-Jumhurriyya*, 17 November 1975.

41. *Al-Ahram*, 21 November 1975.

42. Ibid.

43. Ibid.

44. Ibid., 22, 23, 24, November, 2, 5 December; *al-Jumhurriyya*, 21, 28 November, 5 December 1975.

45. *Al-Ahram*, 29 December 1975, 22, 27 January 1976.

46. Ibid., 30 January, 21 February, 19, 21 March 1976.

47. *Al-Jumhurriyya*, 16 March 1976.

48. *Al-Ahram*, 15 March 1976.

49. Ibid., 29 March 1976.

50. Ibid., 17 March 1976.

51. Ibid., 18, 20, 23 March 1976; *al-Akhbar*, 20 March 1976.

52. *Al-Ahram*, 28 March 1976.

53. See below, Chapter 12.

54. *Al-Ahram*, 8, 9, 30 April, 22 May 1976; *al-Jumhurriyya*, 17 April 1976.

55. *Al-Jumhurriyya*, 18, 22 April 1976.

56. *Al-Ahram*, 24, 26 April, 27 May 1976; *al-Jumhurriyya*, 30 April 1976.

57. *Al-Ahram*, 13 August, 11 September 1976; *al-Jumhurriyya*, 18 April, 11 May 1976.

58. *Al-Ahram*, 13, 16, 23 April, 31 May 1976; *al-Jumhurriyya*, 30 April 1976.

59. *Al-Ahram*, 9, 10, 24 April 1976; 'Report of the Month', *al-Tali'ah*, September 1976.

60. *Al-Jumhurriyya*, 20, 21 April, 3, 26 May, 9 June 1976; *al-Akhbar*, 31 March, 1 April 1976; 'Report of the Month', *al-Tali'ah*, June 1976.

61. *Al-Ahram*, 19 May 1976; 'Report of the Month', *al-Tali'ah*, September 1976.

62. 'Report of the Month', *al-Tali'ah*, May, June, September 1976.

63. *Minutes*, 12 July 1976, morning session, pp. 22-31, evening session, pp. 9-12.

64. *Al-Ahram*, 24 March, 9 April, 2 July 5, 9, 11, 21, 22 August 1976.

65. *Al-Jumhurriyya*, 3 September 1976; *Al-Ahram*, 27 September 1976.

66. *Al-Jumhurriyya*, 14 September 1976.

67. *Al-Akhbar*, 11 September 1976.

68. *Al-Tali'ah*, September 1976, *passim*.

69. *Al-Ahram*, 27 May, 14 July, 19 August, 5 September 1976.

70. *Al-Ahram*, 17, 20 April, 1 June 1976; Milad Hanna, 'Proportional Representation Supports National Unity', *al-Tali'ah*, June 1976.

71. *Al-Ahram*, 20 April 1976.

72. Ibid.

Chapter 12

1. *Al-Ahram*, 17 March, 21, 25 May 1976; *al-Jumhurriyya*, 18, 20 April, 10 May, 3 October 1976; *al-Akhbar*, 9 October 1976; *al-Siyassa*, 22 September 1976; *al-Tali'ah*, 'Report of the Month', June 1976.

2. *Al-Tali'ah*, 'Report of the Month', October 1976; *al-Ahram*, 15 October 1976.

3. Yassin, *New Tendencies*.

4. While my survey includes 25% of all candidates, it includes 32% of the centre candidates and around 20% for the other positions. It is also somewhat top-heavy, including more of the successful candidates, especially those of the centre organization. In geographic terms, it is also slightly biased, with much better coverate of the large governates of the delta and the small governates of the fringe. In the case of the former there was probably a great deal of interest. In the case of the latter, it was easy to cover the entire governate. None of these biases is very strong and I believe that the survey is a useful piece of information about the elections, especially when combined with the other evidence that I have gathered.

5. *Al-Ahram*, 15 October 1976.

6. *Al-Tali'ah*, 'Report of the Month', October 1976.

7. Best for comparing platforms are those cases in which each spokesman answers the same question. See *al-Ahram*, 30 March, 16 April, 14 May, 11, 20, 22 October 1976; *Egyptian Gazette*, 24 October 1976.

8. *Al-Ahram*, 29 September 1976.

9. Yassin, *New Tendencies*, p. 30.

10. Ibid., p. 30.
11. Ibid., p. 31.
12. *Al-Ahram*, 29 September 1976.
13. Local press, all papers, 30, 31 October, 6, 7, 8 November 1976.

14. Apter, *The Politics of Modernization*, has a lengthy discussion of the function of elections as information generating mechanisms – a function which had not been performed in Egypt because of the various factors which 'garbled' the message.

Chapter 13

1. *Al-Ahram*, 12 November 1976.
2. Ibid., 13, 20, 22, 23 November 1976; *al-Jumhurriyya*, 14, 20, 23 November 1976; *al-Akhbar*, 22 November 1976.
3. *Al-Ahram*, 13 November 1976.
4. Ibid., 11, 12, 20, 23 November 1976.
5. Ibid., 24 November 1976.
6. Ibid., 23 November 1976.
7. Ibid.
8. Ibid., 15, 23 November 1976.
9. *Al-Ahram*, 13-15 November 1976; *al-Jumhurriyya*, 14 November 1976; *al-Akhbar*, 16 November 1976.
10. All local press, 10 November 1976.
11. *Al-Ahram*, 13, 14, 19, 21, 24 November 1976; *al-Akhbar*, 14, 15, 16, 19, 20, 22, 23, 24 November 1976; *al-Jumhurriyya*, 12 November 1976.
12. *Al-Ahram*, 18 January 1976.
13. Ibid., 22 January 1976.
14. Ibid., 30 January 1976.
15. Ibid., 4, 11 February 1976.
16. Ibid., 1 February 1976.
17. Ibid., 15 February 1976.
18. *Al-Tali'ah*, February 1976.
19. *Al-Iqtisadi*, 1 February 1976. In crossing downtown Cairo roughly an hour earlier, I had much the same impression.
20. The Egyptian military is an inscrutable entity. My observation was that extreme care was taken in putting the military on to the streets. Not only was a great deal of force displayed, but there seems to have been a good deal of selectivity about which troops were put in which districts. Later rumours circulated to the effect that before the military would go on to the streets, it insisted upon 1) the rescinding of the price increases, 2) an understanding that it was not going to do battle with the citizenry, 3) keeping the special Presidential forces (in essence, a palace guard) off the streets since they apparently were willing to do battle, and 4) a reintegration of the palace guard back into the regular military after things had quietened down. The behaviour of the military in waiting to get on to the streets and during its time in action does nothing to discredit these rumours.
21. *Al-Ahram*, 18 January 1976.
22. Ibid.
23. Weber describes the relationship between class and levels of action as follows (*From Max Weber*, p. 184):

The degree to which 'communal action' and possibly 'societal action' emerges from the mass action of members of a class is . . . linked to the extent of contrasts that have already evolved and is especially linked to the *transparency* of the connections between the causes and the consequences of the 'class situation.' The fact of being conditioned and the results of the class situation must be distinctly recognizable . . .

The communal action that brings forth class situations, however, is not basically action between members of the identical class; it is an action between members of different classes . . . Each kind of class situation . . . will become more clearly efficacious when all other determinants of reciprocal relations are, as far as possible, eliminated in their significance.

Seymour Martin Lipset describes the relationship between a feeling of isolation (essentially, the transparency of relations) and extremist political action as follows (*Political Man*, (New York: Anchor, 1963), p. 76):

Inherent in all democratic systems is the constant threat that the group conflicts which are democracy's life blood may solidify to the point where they threaten to disintegrate society. Hence, conditions which serve to moderate the intensity of partisan battle are among the key requisites of democratic government . . . Wherever the social structure operates so as to isolate naturally individuals or groups with the same outlook from contact with those who hold different views, the isolated individuals or groups tend to back political extremists . . . Where a man belongs to a variety of groups that all predispose him toward the same political choice, he is in the situation of the isolated worker and is much less likely to be tolerant of other opinions.

The essence of the argument is that the first free political debate and election serves to make the situation 'transparent' and to 'isolate' the far ends of the political spectrum ideologically. This renders them more prone to extremist actions.

INDEX

Abu Wafia, Muhammad 180, 182-4, 186

Agriculture: activity 111, 113; capitalists in state capitalism 24; co-operativization 23-4; cotton stocks 45; credit 24; exports 60; fruits 24, 45, 60, 101; inputs 24-5; investment 101, 108-11; landholding 45; land markets 101-2; orchards 45; production 57; role in semi-legal revolution 137; state control of 23-5; terms of trade 61; vegetable crops 24, 45, 60, 101; *see also* economic liberalization, economic structure of state capitalism, economy

Ahmed, Kemal 158

Al-Infitah al-Iqtisadi see economic liberalization

Al-Iqtisadi (also *Al-Ahram al-Iqtisadi*) 107, 115, 118, 124, 238

Al-Sawy, abd al-Munam 153

Al-Sibai, Yusef 153

Amer, Field-Marshal: Committee to Liquidate Feudalism 38; opposition to Arab Socialist Union 41; suicide 41, 63

Arab capital: efforts to attract 91-4; investment patterns 106-11, 248, 251, 253; investment preferences 40, 101, 104, 106; loans 120-1; patterns and profits 94; *see also* economic liberalization, foreign investment

Arab Socialist Union (ASU): and the legislature 32, 56, 166, 181; and the President 181; as a political vehicle 30; breakdown 38; candidates in elections (1976) 209; coup d'état (1967) 41-2, 81; elections to (1968) 56; in the May 1971 crisis 80, 200; in the polity 249; June War (1967) 200; leftist criticism of 179-80; local government 168-9; opposition to economic reform 53; opposition to political reform 56; political liberalization 128, 181, 199-200; political platforms in 186-7, 192, 208, 210; political parties and 179-81; post-war activity (1967-8) 43; rebuilding 50; role in economy 46, 52; role in semi-legal revolution 136; role in succession of Sadat 67; structure and function 31-2; weaknesses 32; *see also* political platforms, political structure of state capitalism, polity, Sadat

Automobiles: imports 57-8, 115; *see also* consumer durables

Balance of payments 35, 107, 122-7

Camp David Summit 158

Carter, President 253

Centres of power 54, 70, 72

Civil disturbances, 1967-8; interpretation 40-2; Nasser resignation 11; regime response 42-3

Civil disturbances, 1971-3; impact on cabinet 160; other groups 84; religious strife 84; students 83-4; workers 74, 84

Civil disturbances, January 1977 *see* January 1977 riots

Civil disturbances, Last Muslim Brotherhood Conspiracy 38

Class: and equity 61-2; and political parties 179; divisions 18; in state capitalism 17-18, 25; labour: employment policy 28-9, interest in reform 53, public sector 25, share in income 61; lower: consumption subsidies 28-9, in state capitalism 25, peasants 25; middle: bureaucracy 25, consumption relations 27-8, in state capitalism 19, mobility 29; upper: capitalists 26-7, elite 23, 27, in state capitalism 19, technocracy 25, 46, 50, 55; *see also* election results, Sadat

Communist Party: Egypt 135; Sudan 74